THE GEORGE GUND FOUNDATION
IMPRINT IN AFRICAN AMERICAN STUDIES

The George Gund Foundation has endowed
this imprint to advance understanding of
the history, culture, and current issues
of African Americans.

The publisher gratefully acknowledges the generous support of the African American Studies Endowment Fund of the University of California Press Foundation, which was established by a major gift from the George Gund Foundation.

New Philadelphia

New Philadelphia

An Archaeology of Race in the Heartland

Paul A. Shackel

UNIVERSITY OF CALIFORNIA PRESS
Berkeley · Los Angeles · London

University of California Press, one of the most
distinguished university presses in the United States,
enriches lives around the world by advancing
scholarship in the humanities, social sciences, and
natural sciences. Its activities are supported by the UC
Press Foundation and by philanthropic contributions
from individuals and institutions. For more
information, visit www.ucpress.edu.

University of California Press
Berkeley and Los Angeles, California

University of California Press, Ltd.
London, England

Library of Congress Cataloging-in-Publication Data

Shackel, Paul A.
   New Philadelphia : an archaeology of race in the
heartland / Paul A. Shackel.
      p.   cm.
   Includes bibliographical references and index.
   ISBN 978-0-520-26629-2 (cloth : alk. paper)
   ISBN 978-0-520-26630-8 (pbk. : alk. paper)
   1. New Philadelphia (Ill.)—History.
2. New Philadelphia (Ill.)—Antiquities.
3. Excavations (Archaeology)—Illinois—New
Philadelphia.   4. Community life—Illinois—New
Philadelphia—History.   5. Cultural pluralism—
Illinois—New Philadelphia—History.   6. Frank, Free,
1777–1854.   I. Title.
   F549.N49S53   2011
   977.3'453—dc22
                                        2010020057

Manufactured in the United States of America

20 19 18 17 16 15 14 13 12 11
10 9 8 7 6 5 4 3 2 1

This book is printed on Cascades Enviro 100, a 100%
post consumer waste, recycled, de-inked fiber. FSC
recycled certified and processed chlorine free. It is acid
free, Ecologo certified, and manufactured by BioGas
energy.

This book is dedicated to the McWorter family and the many other townspeople and community members who carry on the vision of freedom and justice inspired by the town's founders.

WE SAW A VISION
BY LIAM MAC UISTIN (1976)

In the darkness of despair we saw a vision
We lit the light of hope and it was not extinguished
In the Desert of Discouragement we saw a vision
We planted the tree of valor and it blossomed

In the winter of bondage we saw a vision
We melted the snow of lethargy and the river
   of resurrection flowed from it

We sent our vision a-swim like a swan on the river
The vision became a reality
Winter became summer
Bondage became freedom

And this we left to you as your inheritance
O Generations of freedom, remember us,
   the generations of the vision

(A poem etched on the wall in the Garden
of Remembrance in Dublin)

Contents

Illustrations

TABLES

Preface

The town of New Philadelphia in Pike County, Illinois, was situated between the Illinois and Mississippi rivers, about one hundred miles north of St. Louis, Missouri. It was the first known town established, platted, and registered by an African American. The account of the town's founder, Frank McWorter, and the McWorter family is a compelling American story that is well documented by Juliet Walker (1983a), Frank's great-great-granddaughter. Enslaved in South Carolina and later in Kentucky, Frank McWorter purchased his wife Lucy's freedom as well as his own. In 1830 he acquired land in Illinois, and the following year he and his family settled in Pike County. In 1836 he subdivided forty-two of the acres he owned into lots, streets, and alleys to form New Philadelphia. Throughout his lifetime, with his entrepreneurial activities and revenue from the sale of the 144 town lots, he was able to purchase his freedom and the freedom of fifteen family members (Walker 1983a:162). African American people as well as people of European descent moved to New Philadelphia and created a multiracial community (King 2006).

Immediately after the American Civil War the town's population peaked at about 160 people, a size comparable to many Pike County communities today (King 2006). By the end of the nineteenth century, however, the racial and corporate politics of America's gilded age resulted in the death of the settlement. The new Hannibal & Naples Railroad bypassed the town in 1869, and many of New Philadelphia's residents began to move away. By the early twentieth century only about six families remained in the town proper.

In 2002 I became involved in an extensive cooperative program to explore the development and demise of New Philadelphia. For me this project serves as an important vehicle to explore issues of race and racism on the western frontier as well as in contemporary America. The research program also developed methods to create a transparent and democratized research program that is accessible to the local and descendant communities as well as scholars.

When I began to help develop the archaeology research program with a cohort of dedicated professionals from the University of Illinois, the Illinois State Museum, and the New Philadelphia Association, I became acquainted with many local residents and descendants. The Association consisted of local white community members who had a concern for preserving the memory of Free Frank McWorter. Within several years the Association became racially integrated, as several African American descendants from the region joined their efforts and became board members. One concerned community member told me that she originally found it "difficult to support the project": "There are many black children hungry and undereducated in the slums of Chicago. I think I can do more good by helping in Chicago than in Pike County." She questioned why she should support an archaeology project that is looking for buildings and artifacts.

I responded by telling her that I thought the project potentially had greater meaning than finding architectural features and other relicts of the past. With the assistance of the local and descendant communities, the archaeology project could help make this place part of America's public memory, with a powerful message of freedom and the accomplishments of African Americans in the growth of the American frontier. Because African American feats and messages associated with their struggle for freedom and success are rarely recorded (Shackel 2003), research and public education can contribute to making this much underreported story part of the official memory. I thought we could use the archaeology to tell the story of race and racism in the past and to make connections to inequalities in the present.

Scholars often discuss some of the great events that changed the world. The development of agriculture, the development of a state society, the invention of the printing press, and the Industrial Revolution are all frequently acknowledged as having the greatest impact on humankind.

Probably the worst legacy of the modern world is the creation of race and the implementation of racism. Even though the concept of race has been shown to have no biological validity and after the end of World War II was denounced by major institutions, including the United Nations and the American Anthropological Association, its legacy survives today. In the United States racism continues to contribute to the impoverishment of minority communities at a far greater rate than found among non-minorities. Malnutrition and substandard education are disproportionately higher in inner-city slums, where people's skin color tends to be brown or black.

Some Americans are willing to acknowledge that inequalities existed in the past but fail to see the impact and long-lasting effects of these inequalities in contemporary society. Some government officials are more inclined to prop up consensus histories—those that support only patriotic stories—rather than incorporating difficult histories. I believe that making people more aware of the injustices that existed in the past and developing their connections to the present can make them more aware that they are part of communities and societies that are racialized and unequal. Perhaps these connections will provide the necessary tools to help us create change in communities by encouraging multivocality and inclusion.

The New Philadelphia archaeology project is a lesson about working with local and descendant communities, each with their own views of the past. While our goal is to be multivocal and inclusive, the diverse views sometimes left us in a dilemma about how to respond to the conflicting memories of the place. The project also serves as an example of how a historic site can be an instrument of civic engagement on many different levels. We share with the local and descendant communities how we are researching and helping to develop a past for New Philadelphia. Our findings are presented to the public in local discussions and public lectures. All of our data and conclusions are posted on websites (those of the University of Maryland and the University of Illinois). Our goal is to be as democratic and transparent as possible. By presenting our findings in a public forum we allow others to use our data and develop their own conclusion about the past. We also pay considerable attention to the way our interpretations of the archaeological record are created. The excavators' views, feelings, and perspectives on the archaeological record are always taken into account; however, the expertise of decades of field experience of the excavation supervisors weighs heavily in our interpretations.

Although written by a single author, this book is the product of a collaborative undertaking. As a faculty member at the University of Maryland, I worked cooperatively on the archaeology project with Terrance Martin, the curator of the Department of Anthropology at the Illinois State Museum; Christopher Fennell, an associate professor of anthropology at the University of Illinois; and Vibert White, an associate professor of history at the University of Central Florida. All of the members of the New Philadelphia Association were also instrumental in making this project happen. Together we shared our passion for archaeology and provided a service for the public good. The following is my perspective on my involvement in helping to shape the memory of a midwestern multiracial frontier town that existed before and after the American Civil War. This book is not the last word on the history of the town. Our efforts at New Philadelphia, with input from the larger community, will build a better understanding of the town and how its history is remembered.

I hope our work will help make New Philadelphia part of the American story and the national public memory. We have had some success building on a long tradition of remembering the place. Juliet Walker's (1983a) book provides significant information about Free Frank McWorter and his experience related to the founding and early development of New Philadelphia until his death in 1854. Her work helps to bring the story of the McWorters and New Philadelphia to a wider audience. Other monographs also provide overviews of the McWorter family and the community's past. These include Grace Matteson's (1964) *"Free Frank" McWorter and the "Ghost Town" of New Philadelphia, Pike County, Illinois,* Helen McWorter Simpson's (1981) *Makers of History,* and Larry Burdick's (1992) "New Philadelphia: Where I Lived." In 1988, because of the effort of the founder's great-great-granddaughter, Juliet Walker, the gravesite of the town's founder joined those of Stephen Douglas and Abraham Lincoln as the only gravesites in the state of Illinois listed on the National Register of Historic Places. In 2005 Michelle Huttes, a graduate student at the University of Illinois, successfully nominated and placed the entire town site on the National Register of Historic Places because of the potential of the archaeology to yield significant information about the place. In 2006 Charlotte King developed a lesson plan for high school children on New Philadelphia (www.nps.gov/history/nr/twhp/wwwlps/lessons/130newphila/). The plan is part of the Teaching with Historic Places program administered by the National Park Service, which uses properties listed on the National Register of Historic Places to help teachers bring historic places into the classroom. In 2008 King developed a National Historic Landmark application for the site, one of the highest designations awarded by the U.S. government. The NHL committee reviewed the nomination in October 2008 and recommended it for designation. The secretary of the interior agreed and approved the nomination in 2009.

Most of the original forty-two acres of New Philadelphia have been returned to agricultural use, planted in prairie grass, or lie fallow. A few scattered foundations are visible in the field, although they are out of sight in the summer, hidden by the tall midwestern prairie grasses. The current landowners of part of the town site, Larry and Natalie Armistead, want to give visitors a sense of the built landscape in an otherwise agricultural setting. Therefore in 1998 they moved a mid-nineteenth-century cabin and two early twentieth-century sheds onto existing foundations.

In the spring of 2002 Vibert White (then from the University of Illinois–Springfield and now with University of Central Florida) was contacted by the New Philadelphia Association to initiate a long-term research project to study and celebrate the history of the town. White's initiative lives on in various forms, including a collaborative project in 2002 and 2003 between the University of Maryland, the Illinois State Museum, the University of Illinois, and the New Philadelphia Association to develop an archaeological pedestrian survey (Gwaltney 2004; also see www.heritage.umd.edu and follow the links to New Philadelphia), followed by three summers of archaeological excavations with support from the National Science Foundation—Research Experiences for Undergraduates (NSF-REU) program.

Our initial archaeological survey work, along with overlays from Geographic Information Systems (GIS), identified several areas with discrete archaeological deposits associated with known house lots (Gwaltney 2004). This information, along with the collection of census, deed, and tax information, provided the research team with valuable information about the general settlement of the site.

During the summers of 2004 through 2006 the University of Maryland served as the host institution for the NSF-REU grant, collaborating with the University of Illinois, the Illinois State Museum, and the New Philadelphia Association. During the 2008–12 field seasons the University of Illinois served as the host institution. Undergraduate students from around the United States participated in this ten-week project each summer, and in 2005 the University of Illinois, under the direction of Christopher Fennell, held part of their summer field school at New Philadelphia. Prior to each season's excavations Michael Hargrave of the U.S. Army Engineer Research and Development Center, Construction Engineering Research Laboratory, conducted a geophysical survey using a magnetometer and electrical resistivity with the aid of NSF-REU students. The geophysical survey work, coupled with the archaeological survey data and the historical records, provided additional information that helped us develop an excavation strategy.

Students worked for five weeks conducting excavations and then an additional five weeks performing laboratory analyses at the Illinois State Museum. In the lab they learned to catalogue artifacts, supervised by Charlotte King (of the University of Maryland), identify macrofloral remains, overseen by Marjorie Schroeder (of the museum), and perform faunal analysis, taught by Terrance Martin (of the museum). By the end of the summer program students had completed the cataloging and artifact analyses and identified macrofloral and faunal remains from several key features. They also participated in weekly discussions about the creation of race and the effects of racism in the United States. Gerald McWorter (also known as Professor Abdul Alkalimat), the great-great-grandson of Frank McWorter, led one of these discussions. We also had guest lecturers come in from all over the country to discuss topics related to the frontier, colonialism, and race.

In this book I describe some of our significant findings and detail our interaction with the community. Working with the various communities and stakeholders has been one of the most rewarding parts of the project. Nevertheless at times this work has made the project more complicated and at other times it has made us rethink our relationship with these groups. I also show how archaeology changed some of our perceptions of the past. The archaeological work has identified several house lots belonging to different families in this multiracial town. We have interpreted our findings to a larger audience through public discussions, lectures, the media, the Internet, and publications. Our goal is to share with professionals and the public our interpretations rather than claim ownership of data or interpretations of the past.

Throughout the book the issue of who owns the past becomes very important to this story, and many of the situations I discuss can be applicable to other places where local and descendant communities are stakeholders. From the very beginning of the project we wanted to make transparent how we developed our questions and interpretations concerning New Philadelphia. All of our data, reports, and interpretations were immediately placed on our website for all to see how we developed our interpretations. However, along the way we were sometimes confronted about our interpretations, and one member in the descendant community has accused us of stealing their heritage. These accusations have strengthened our resolve to democratize our data and make our conclusions more transparent. Understanding New Philadelphia's history and its many stakeholders has broadened our perspective on the place and has added to our goals of illuminating its history and issues of race and racism in society today. Our archaeology is not creating the final history of New Philadelphia; rather, it is opening a dialogue with the local and descendant communities about the possibilities of using archaeology to teach us about uplifting and difficult histories.

Our archaeology is also stimulating discussions on listservs and blogs about whether white archaeologists should investigate the archaeology of a place that once included African Americans. Although the subject is about ownership of the past, for me the issue is also about being a white person involved in antiracism work. Throughout the book I explain how our archaeological efforts have confronted racism in this small rural community, and I hope others see it as a useful model where race is central or even peripheral in a project.

The National Science Foundation's Research Experiences for Undergraduates program (Grant No. 0353550 for 2004–6 and Grant No. 0752834 for 2008–12) sponsored the New Philadelphia archaeology program. Any opinions, findings, and conclusions or recommendations expressed in this material are those of the author and do not necessarily reflect the views of the National Science Foundation. We also received a grant from the Oakley-Lindsay Foundation of Quincy Newspapers, Inc., and its Subsidiaries, as well as financial and logistical support from the University of Illinois, the University of Maryland, and the Illinois State Museum.

The field seasons received tremendous support from the New Philadelphia Association and various other individuals and organizations. The people and organizations that have helped make this program a success include Sprague's Kinderhook Lodge, Gary Andrashko, Larry and Natalie Armistead, Darlene Arnette, Larry and Mary K. Bennett, Philip and Linda Bradshaw, Carnes & Sons Trailer World, Joe Conover, Tom and Joan Coulson, Carolyn Dean, Fat Boys Restaurant, Christopher Fennell, Lynn Fisher, Shirley Johnston, Cheryl LaRoche, Marvin and Pat Likes, Likes Land Surveyors, Inc., Claire F. Martin,

Terrance Martin, Carol McCartney, Robert Newnham, Oitker-Ford
Sales, Terry Ransom, Red Dome Inn, Wayne Riley, Marjorie Schroeder,
Karen Sprague, Vibert White, Robin Whitt, Mr. and Mrs. Roger Woods,
and Harry and Helen Wright. My apologies to anyone I have inadver-
tently omitted.

I appreciate the spirit of cooperation of many of the descendant and
community members, especially those who shared their memories of
the town and the surrounding area. I became acquainted with several
McWorter family members and relatives who have been very supportive of the overall program to promote and protect the legacy of New
Philadelphia, including Gerald McWorter, Kate Williams, Sandra Mc-
Worter Marsh, Allen Kirkpatrick, Shirley McWorter Moss and Stewart
Moss, Lonnie McWorter Vond Wilson, Patricia McWorter Sheppard,
and Karen Wall. I received the Daughters of the American Revolution
national award for historic preservation because of my work with New
Philadelphia, and I appreciate Karen Wall's efforts to nominate me
through her chapter. I also respect the strong drive of Juliet Walker to
promote and preserve the memory of Frank McWorter.

Claire Fuller Martin worked tirelessly with the students to transcribe
many of the historical documents relevant to New Philadelphia, and
these documents are now available to a wider audience, as we were able
to post them on our websites. Her curiosity and her ability to ask important questions of the historical data have enabled us to have a better
understanding of the context of the site and the relationships between
different community members. Linda Cunningham, executive editor,
Eleanor Smith, librarian, and Aaron Chambers of the *Rockford (Illinois) Register Star* were extremely helpful in finding people to transcribe the audio of part of the web page produced by the newspaper
(Chambers 2007b).

I owe a special gratitude to Joy Beasley and Tom Gwaltney. Over
several weekends in the fall of 2002 and the spring of 2003 they
worked diligently on the initial survey of the New Philadelphia town
site. They generated a catalogue and a GIS of the spatial distribution of
artifacts, which allowed us to move ahead and apply for a grant to the
NSF-REU program. The following organizations and people volun-
teered in this survey effort from various organizations: from the New
Philadelphia Association, Larry Armistead, Natalie Armistead, Philip
Bradshaw, Joe Conover, Carolyn Dean, Shirley Johnson, Marvin Likes,
Pat Likes, Carol McCartney, and Roger Woods; from the University of

Illinois, Lynn Fisher, Sridhar Gaddam, Sreekanth Vudumula, Vibert White; from the Illinois State Museum, Terrance Martin and Robert Warren; from the University of Central Florida, Vibert White; from the University of Maryland, Joy Beasley, Tom Gwaltney, Charlotte King, Cheryl LaRoche, Paul Shackel, and Robin Whitt; from the Illinois State Museum and Illinois State Historic Preservation Office; and local volunteers and students from Hannibal LaGrange College, Illinois College, University of Illinois–Springfield, and Lincoln Land Community College: Heather Bangert, Erin Brand, Greg Butterfield, Roberta Codemo, Jessica Dix, Brandon Eckoff, Sarah Edminston, Cinda Farris, James Farris, Lynn Fisher, Justin Garcia, Jeff Gheens, Tammy Hamilton, Michelle Huttes, Fran Knight, Ellen Marr, Norval McIntyre, Donald McWilliams, Elizabeth Netherton, Terry Ransom, Lisa Schnell, Tim Sorrill, Mary Thomas, Robert Warren, Debbie White, Heather Wickens, Seth Wilson, Lisa Winhold, Linda Woods, and Carolyn Wrightam. The three field schools include the following participants:

2004 NSF-REU Field School students: Cecilia Ayala, Dana Blount, Megan Cerasale, Richard Fairly, Kati Fay, Steve Manion, Jesse Sloan, Janel Vasallo, Laura Wardwell.

2004 NSF-REU Field School staff: Carrie Christman, Christopher Fennell, Charlotte King, Terrance Martin, Paul Shackel, William White.

2005 NSF-REU Field School students: Caitlin Bauchat, Kimberly Eppler, Shanique Gibson, Emily Helton, Jessica Jenkins, Hannah Mills, LaShara Morris, Andrea Torvinen, Megan Volkel, Jordan Bush (volunteer for ten weeks).

2005 NSF-REU Field School staff: Carrie Christman, Christopher Fennell, Charlotte King, Terrance Martin, Paul Shackel, Christopher Valvano.

2005 University of Illinois, Urbana–Champaign Field School students: Alison Azzarello, Michael Collart, Elizabeth Davis, Thomas Duggan, Maria Elana Frias, Hillary Iden, Kyle Johnson, Matthew Kane, Gail Kirk, Christina Puzzo, Leslie Salyers, Jill Scott, Liz Watts, Charles Williams.

2005 University of Illinois, Urbana–Champaign Field School staff: Christopher Fennell, Phil Millhouse, Eva Pajuelo.

2006 NSF-REU Field School students: Adeola Adegbola, Holly Brookens, Athena Hsieh, Jason Jacoby, Hillary Livingston, Angie

Maranville, Maria Nieves Colon, Shamia Sandels, Erin Smith, Megan Bailey (volunteer for ten weeks), Chris Stawski (volunteer for three weeks).

2006 NSF-REU Field School staff: Christopher Fennell, Emily Helton, Charlotte King, Terrance Martin, Paul Shackel, Christopher Valvano.

There were so many people involved in the project I apologize if I overlooked someone. Everyone was important to the program's success.

Barbara Little, Barbara Esstman, Marisa Deline, Charlotte King, Kristin Sullivan, and Judith Freidenberg provided insightful and constructive comments on different versions of this manuscript. Philip Bradshaw, Chris Fennell, Terry Martin, Charles Orser, and Jeffrey Hantman also provided in-depth comments on an earlier version of this manuscript. In writing portions of this book I was supported by the School for Advanced Research's Ethel-Jane Westfeldt Bunting Fellowship. Thank you to James Brooks, Nancy Owen Lewis, Laura Holt, and Leslie Shipman for making my stay pleasant and productive.

Barbara Little was supportive of my efforts throughout the entire New Philadelphia project, cheering me on when things were going well and giving me encouragement during difficult times. I also value my discussions with other scholars, including Randy Mason, Richard Leventhal, Robert St. George, Robert Pruecel, Barbie Zelizer, Phoebe Kropp, Don Mitchell, Amy Hillier, Craig Cipolla, Stephanie Ryberg, and Sara Rocca.

It has been a tremendous journey for me working with so many people on the project. I hope that our efforts have made us all learn and grow from our collective experiences. I believe that dialogue and cooperation can help make our world a better place.

CHAPTER I

The Settlement of
New Philadelphia

"The first white man in Hadley Township was a colored man." (Thompson 1967:151)

The founding of New Philadelphia in west-central Illinois by Free Frank McWorter is a compelling and heroic narrative about freedom and the entrepreneurship of an African American family. It is a story of an African American man who purchased his freedom and founded and registered a town, which developed into a multiracial community on the Illinois frontier before the Civil War. The town thrived for a while as a rural commercial center, and it later fought to survive in the post-Reconstruction era. The history and the archaeology of the place chronicle the community's pursuit of freedom and its struggle to endure while dealing with society's changing attitudes toward race.

Born in 1777 near the Pacolet River in South Carolina to Juda, an enslaved African American woman, and her white owner, Frank grew up and labored on his father's plantation. When Frank was about eighteen, George McWhorter, his father and owner, relocated him to Pulaski County in the Kentucky frontier. George McWhorter later purchased additional properties in Kentucky and Tennessee and left Frank behind to manage the farm in Pulaski County. The historian Juliet Walker (1983a), a fifth-generation descendant of McWorter, wrote a biography of Free Frank. Piecing together clues from various historical documents and oral histories, she traced his life and accomplishments.

In 1799 Frank married Lucy, an enslaved woman who resided on a neighboring plantation in Pulaski County. He became the father of four children: Judy, Sallie, Frank Jr., and Solomon. In 1815 George

McWhorter died without making any provisions for Frank's manumission. Two years later Frank had saved enough money operating a saltpeter mine after hours and on his days off to purchase his wife's freedom for $800. Since Lucy was pregnant at the time, his action ensured that their son Squire would be born free. After two more years Frank was able to purchase his own freedom from George McWhorter's heirs for the same sum. The document that declared his freedom stated that "a certain Negro man named Frank, a yellow man," was to be liberated. His former owners signed the document on September 13, 1819, in Pulaski County (Matteson 1964:2). In the 1820 U.S. Federal Census Frank's name is listed as "Free Frank." He continued to live in Pulaski County while he speculated on and expanded his saltpeter operations near the town of Danville. After he and his wife were free they had two more children: Commodore and Lucy Ann (Matteson 1964:1; Walker 1983a:28–48).

Frank continued to work hard to keep his family together and purchase the freedom of his children. In 1829 he traded his saltpeter enterprise for the freedom of his son Frank Jr. In 1830 Free Frank and Lucy decided to leave Kentucky, and he acquired a quarter section of land (160 acres), sight unseen, in Pike County, Illinois. Free Frank, Lucy, and their freed children arrived in Hadley Township in the spring of 1831 after spending the preceding winter in Greene County, Illinois. The McWorters were the first settlers in the township; others joined them two years later (Chapman 1880:216–17). I find it interesting that a Pike County history described the early settlement of Hadley Township this way: "The first white man in Hadley Township was a colored man" (Thompson 1967:151). Perhaps *white* was used to distinguish from *American Indian*. More likely the historian had a template for writing the county's history, and since the early settlers with land were always white, the author had some difficulty crediting an African American family for their accomplishments and the adversity they had to overcome to move to the area.

THE EARLY SETTLEMENT OF ILLINOIS

When the McWorters settled in Pike County in 1831 there had already been more than 150 years of European expansion, exploitation, and conflict with American Indians in the area. The French explorers Louis Joliet and Jacques Marquette investigated the Mississippi River, and France claimed the Illinois Country in 1673. The French took an early interest in the Illinois region, and by 1720 they were protecting their North American claims by constructing a ring of forts, posts, and missions from Quebec to the Gulf of Mexico. Illinois served as a strategic midpoint in this ring. The French had also imported about a thousand enslaved American Indians and Africans to work on the fertile American Bottom, an area in the southwestern portion of Illinois on the Mississippi River (Davis 1998:48–51; Simeone 2000:19). The Illiniwek, consisting of the Cahokia, Kaskaskia, Michigamea, Peoria, and Tamaroa, had occupied present-day Illinois, eastern Missouri, southern Iowa, and northeastern Arkansas since at least the middle of the sixteenth century (Warren and Walthall 1998). Disease, warfare, and dislocation perpetrated by the European settlers impacted the native populations. In 1660 the American Indian population located in present-day Illinois is estimated to have been about 33,000. By 1680 just under one-third of that number remained. The population dropped to 6,000 by 1700 (Davis 1998:42). These calculations are based on European perceptions of the region and of a people at a time when colonists worked diligently to separate the American Indian from their past, as well as from their land. Many Europeans devalued American Indians and their cultures from the beginning of contact, and in later decades they were not even considered worthy of being recognized in the decennial federal census. This bias continued until 1860, when a new form of discrimination determined how American Indians were counted on the census; only those who renounced their tribal rules were counted. It was not until 1900 that Indians were enumerated on reservations as well as in the general population.

After the British expelled the French from North America as part of the 1763 treaty to end the French and Indian War, the Illinois region was annexed to Virginia in 1778. It ceded the territory to the United States in 1783. The federal government recognized the "ancient laws and customs" of the region, and the 1787 Northwest Ordinance protected the private contracts previously formed, including the existence of slavery, although with some caveats (Simeone 2000:19). The Northwest Territory included the current states of Ohio, Indiana, Illinois, Michigan, Wisconsin, and Minnesota. Article 6 of the ordinance banned slavery and involuntary servitude, although there was an exception for French and Canadian settlers, as well as those who had previously sworn allegiance to Virginia, which was a slave state (Davis 1998:95–96).

After the War of 1812 immigrants began a steady migration to Illinois from the upland south via the Ohio River and settled mostly in the southern part of the state. In 1817 Congress set aside 3.5 million acres known as the "Military Tract" and allotted 160-acre tracts to veterans of the War of 1812 in an area between the lower Illinois River and the Mississippi River. The public also had the opportunity to purchase tracts of land in this area (Maissie 1906:42; Mazrim 2002:25).

The Illinois territory became a battleground between proslavery southerners and abolitionist northerners. No other state north of the Ohio River had as many enslaved people as Illinois, or came as close as Illinois to providing constitutional protection for slavery (Davis 1998:19–20, 161). When Illinois became a state in 1818 it had about forty thousand residents; over one-third lived in the greater American Bottom in southwestern Illinois. Some of the early nineteenth-century immigrants brought enslaved people with them, although in many cases their owners registered them as indentured servants. In the salines, or saltwater springs, enslaved laborers produced salt for export. They collected the water and boiled it down to extract the salt. By the early 1820s the salines generated about one-fourth of the state's tax revenue. The 1818 Illinois State Constitution allowed slaves to be imported into Gallatin and Jackson Counties (the salines) for one year in order to work in these facilities. The allowance, according to the Constitution, was to end in 1825 (Simeone 2000:25, 153). However, in all probability many of the enslaved people were recategorized as indentured servants and continued to work in the area. The Constitution allowed French citizens to own slaves. Indentured servitude, whereby African Americans were contracted to work for decades, was also legal for all citizens. The male children of indentured servants had to serve until they were twenty-one, the female children until they were eighteen (Davis 1998:165).

At the beginning of its statehood Illinois had a majority of its citizens emigrating from the upland south, an area that includes Kentucky, Tennessee, South Carolina, and western Virginia. However by the early 1820s northerners began their steady influx into the state; the majority of them were against the idea of chattel slavery. A traveler from the north recounted her experience with a woman from Tennessee who resided in Illinois. In 1822 she wrote that the Tennesseean remarked, "I am getting skeery about them 'ere Yankees; there is such a power of them coming in that them and the Injuns will squatch out all the white folks" (quoted in Simeone 2000:6; see also Tillson 1995:24–25). The influx of northerners brought new customs to the area. Previously business deals were typically sealed with a handshake. As one former Tennessean wrote, once the "Yankees" infiltrated the area they introduced a "system of accounts and obligations" that was looked upon by the southern community with great distrust. The Yankees used words and writing that intimidated "the white folks" (Buck 1917:291). It is interesting to note that the woman from Tennessee equated whiteness with southern customs and cultures, while others, including American Indians and European Americans from the northeastern states, were omitted from the white category. This is an example of the fluidity and flexibility of racial categories to create the "other." The racial category was a way to try to protect the hegemony of the customs of those from the upland south.

On August 2, 1824, a popular vote defeated a referendum for the legalization of slavery. Pike County overwhelmingly voted against the referendum (Davis 1998:167). However the proslavery faction gained many seats and the control of the State General Assembly. Illinoisans thus created a society that hampered the introduction of slavery, but nevertheless maintained an implicit white supremacy. Black Codes passed in 1819 denied African Americans basic civil and political rights and restricted their immigration to the state. In 1829 further restrictions required African Americans to produce a certificate of freedom and post a $1,000 bond in order to settle in the state (Simeone 2000:157). Yet there apparently were exceptions in terms of how evenly this regulation was enforced. Even though Frank McWorter acquired his land in 1830, there is no record of his posting bond. The deed of sale "shows that Free Frank paid Elliot $200 for the 160-acre tract" (Walker 1983a:66), only one-fifth of the bond. The 1829 Illinois *Revised Code of Laws* states, "Solvency of said security shall be approved of by said clerk" (109). Perhaps, as Walker (1983a:67) states, because McWorter owned valuable land he was able to demonstrate that he was self-supporting and would not be a charge to the community.

RACE AND THE WESTERN FRONTIER DURING THE SETTLEMENT OF NEW PHILADELPHIA

Before the American Civil War most free African Americans lived in urban areas and suffered deteriorating social and economic conditions. Despite the prohibition of slavery in the North and the greater freedoms allowed to African Americans there, political and social norms maintained by the European American majority still left many African Americans struggling to survive. Laws restricted their opportunities, and they often had irregular or seasonal employment. "They had a low incidence of property ownership in most cities, and were universally described by contemporary observers as in large part poverty stricken" (Curry 1981:122). As a result African Americans in urban areas increasingly called for reforms.

The American Colonization Society, made up mostly of white philanthropists, aggressively promoted the relocation of free African Americans to the west coast of Africa in a territory known as Liberia. Founded in 1817 the organization attempted to address the issue of what to do with freed African Americans. President James Monroe, Representative Henry Clay, and Chief Justice John Marshall all supported the plan to settle free African Americans in Liberia. The goal of the organization was not to settle the issue of slavery, but rather to export freed Africans from the United States. The Society believed that African Americans could not rise above their current condition and the members did not seek to alter the racial hierarchy. Although the colonization effort quickly lost momentum, by 1830 nearly two thousand people had been resettled in Liberia. Many abolitionists, such as William Lloyd Garrison, condemned the Society because it did not oppose slavery or support immediate abolition (Hutton 1983:376–89; Mausur 2001:48; Temperley 2000).

In response to the promotion of resettlement in Africa the Organized Negro Communities Movement proposed that separate agricultural settlements should be established for free African American families in undeveloped rural areas within the United States. The organization also encouraged the migration of such families to the frontier. The Communities Movement felt that these proposals would allow African Americans the opportunity to develop new economic opportunities for themselves (Pease and Pease 1962:19–34).

In 1819 the first manumission colony in Edwardsville, Illinois, stood as one of the most prominent settlements of the Organized Negro Communities Movement. The Edwardsville Settlement operated as a paternalistic endeavor by Edward Coles on land he purchased for thirteen freed African Americans so that they could develop farms. Other paternalistic settlements developed following Coles's lead. Many of the settlements failed, including Edwardsville. These planned agricultural communities usually consisted of farms that were too small or with too little capital to be self-sufficient (Mausur 2001:58; Pease and Pease 1963:23–24).

Unlike Edwardsville, other African American settlements did succeed. For instance, Sundiata Keita Cha-Jua (2000) describes the community of Brooklyn, Illinois, settled in 1830 by several black families adjacent to St. Louis. Five white settlers platted the area in 1837, and citizens incorporated the town after the Civil War. Because of racism and industrialists' unwillingness to establish businesses in the mixed-race town, Brooklyn struggled financially through the beginning of the twentieth century. Reverend Lewis Woodson believed that African Americans should establish separate communities, separate businesses, and separate churches. In 1830 his father's settlement, Berlin Cross Road, in Jackson County, Ohio, served as a prime example to show that separate African American communities could survive and prosper. By 1838 this all-black settlement was considered "socially independent" by outsiders, not needing the aid of white oversight (F. J. Miller 1975:315).

Beyond these issues regarding resettlement of freed African Americans and the development of mixed-race towns in the American frontier, the years prior to, during, and just after the Civil War were also characterized by threats of and actual incidents of interracial violence. In 1829, the year before the McWorters began their journey out of Kentucky, David Walker's *Appeal* created a great stir with its call for slaves to revolt against their masters. Whites were put on guard and any free African American traveling through the South was greeted with increased suspicion. A free black originally from the South, Walker wrote that whites had no more right to hold blacks in slavery than blacks had a right to hold whites in bondage. He rejected all gradual approaches to end slavery, and he called for Africans and African Americans to rise up and strike. Walker alerted Americans, "Your DESTRUCTION is at hand" (quoted in Mausur 2001:28). He also spoke out against the Colonization Society, stating that those of African descent had every right to settle in this land in which they had labored and built. Within a few months his pamphlet was found throughout the South. Southern states reacted strongly to this challenge to the institution of slavery and to white hegemony. The state of Georgia, for example, offered $1,000 to anyone who killed Walker. In the summer of 1830 he was found dead near the doorway of the shop in Boston where he sold old clothes (Mayer 1998; Zinn 2003:237).

When the McWorter family arrived in Pike County the following year there were more than two million enslaved people living in the South. Southern whites and many northerners convinced themselves that enslaved laborers were content in their situation and that slavery was a righteous institution. Such delusions proved difficult to sustain. On August 22, 1831, Nat Turner led an insurrection that resulted in the death of his owner and his owner's family. Many other plantation owners were also killed. Although this revolt ended two days later, incidents of antislavery violence clearly demonstrated that slaves were not content with their posi-- tions in life and that slavery was not positive for slaves and owners alike (French 2004; Greenberg 2003).

In addition to violent rebellions against slavery, intellectual resistance to slavery grew throughout the early and mid-1800s, as evidenced by abolitionist organizations and newspapers. In 1831, for example, William Lloyd Garrison, a prominent American abolitionist, journalist, and social reformer, began publishing *The Liberator,* an abolitionist newspaper. Garrison rejected Walker's call for violence as well as the efforts of the American Colonization Society. He believed that moral, nonviolent means would transform public opinion and end slavery. He demanded the immediate, unconditional abolition of slavery. He called for a revolution in public sentiment and stated that enslaved persons must have their freedom in life and not just in death. *The Liberator* began with twenty-five subscriptions, but by the 1850s there were over 100,000. By that time the antislavery movement had become a force. However, this force had as yet been unsuccessful in gaining political victories, and the laws of the nation continued to uphold slavery. In 1850 Congress passed the Fugitive Slave Act, the president signed it, and the Supreme Court upheld it. The Act required authorities in free states to return escaped slaves to their masters. Under this Act more than three hundred African Americans were returned to slavery; in one case a man was taken from his family in Indiana because a southern owner claimed that he had run away nine years earlier (Mausur 2001:29; Mayer 1998; Zinn 2003:237).

Other forms of legislation also seriously curtailed the rights of free African Americans. Black Codes established throughout the United States before the Civil War often restricted the freedom of African Americans, who frequently were left with no choice but to work on farms or perform menial tasks. Although a vacuum created by the expanding frontier allowed people to take risks on entrepreneurial activities, African Americans were not on an equal footing with white settlers in these endeavors. Not only did many European Americans have better financial bases from which to start entrepreneurial endeavors, but racist legislation such as Black Codes provided them with special privileges over African Americans.

Similar to other parts of the nation, free African Americans in southern and central Illinois met resistance from some local white populations.

For instance, about seventy miles south of New Philadelphia in the town of Alton, Elijah Lovejoy ran his abolitionist newspaper and founded the Illinois Anti-Slavery Society. An angry mob attacked his newspaper in 1837, one year after the founding of New Philadelphia. They killed Lovejoy while he tried to protect his press. The mayor could have asked for military troops to quell the uprising, much as the mayor of Norfolk, Virginia, did in 1831 after the Nat Turner uprising. Instead he believed Lovejoy's activities had created disorder, and he allowed the mobs to take control of the situation (Dillon 1961; Tanner 1881).

Only thirteen miles east of New Philadelphia in the town of Griggsville violence broke out after an 1838 antislavery meeting. Many people at the meeting signed a petition calling for the abolition of slavery in Washington, D.C., and for rejecting the admission of Texas into the Union as a slave state. Proslavery citizens were agitated by this resolution. Some of them met at the local grocery store and passed their own resolution, stating, "The parties who signed this obnoxious petition should be compelled to erase their signatures from it" (Chapman 1880:516). The proslavery men seized the document and "then waited upon those parties and demanded of them that they should immediately erase their names" (516). Hearing this news, the abolitionist people of Griggsville and the surrounding area came to town that evening armed in order to defend their petition. They informed the proslavery contingent that they "must disband, or else they would be dealt with harshly, and that the first man who dared to intimidate another petitioner would receive a 'fresh supply of ammunition' " (516).

The 1845 Illinois Supreme Court decision in *Jarrot v. Jarrot* terminated the institution of slavery in Illinois for all time. Still, state delegates voted 137 to 7 to deny suffrage to blacks. In addition Article 14 of the state's new constitution prohibited the immigration of blacks to Illinois (Davis 1998: 413). In 1853 the General Assembly implemented the provision, which is considered to be one of the harshest codes passed in the United States (along with comparably restrictive provisions in Indiana, Iowa, Oregon, and the New Mexico Territory). It forbade free African Americans from settling in the state (Gertz 1963:466).

Unlike other northern states, Illinois did not resist the Fugitive Slave Law of 1850 by passing personal liberties laws (Davis 1998:289). The Fugitive Slave Law also created a dilemma for those African Americans trying to unite with family members. This law made it even more difficult for McWorter family members to enter Illinois after being purchased and freed. In 1862, during the Civil War, Illinois defeated the proposal for a new state constitution; however, Article 18 of the proposed constitution was voted on separately and won by an overwhelming majority. It read, "No negro or mulatto shall migrate to or settle in this State, after the Adoption of this constitution, [and] No negro or mulatto shall have the right of suffrage, or hold any office in this State" (Gertz 1963:467). Although Illinois opposed slavery, it refused to grant equality to African Americans. Free African Americans were not on equal footing with whites, which makes the development of a multiracial community like New Philadelphia an even more compelling story.

BUILDING NEW PHILADELPHIA

While establishing their farm in Illinois, Frank and Lucy McWorter left three children, sons- and daughters-in-law, and grandchildren behind in Kentucky. Despite the fragmentation of the family McWorter acquired over five hundred more acres in Illinois. On this land the McWorters grew wheat, corn, and oats and raised cattle, hogs, horses, mules, and a mixed variety of poultry (Matteson 1964:5; Figure 1). A county historian noted that Frank McWorter was a "reputable, worthy citizen, kind, benevolent, and honest. He labored hard on his Hadley acres, accumulating little by little until he owned a considerable body of land" (Thompson 1967:152).

In 1835 Free Frank traveled back to Kentucky and purchased his son Solomon's freedom for $550 (Walker 1983a:89). In an extraordinary event several citizens from Kentucky and Illinois vouched for Free Frank's character in order to help pass a legislative act to change his name to Frank McWorter, taking the surname of his former owner and father while altering its spelling. The act also gave him the right to "sue and be sued, plead and be impleaded, purchase and convey both real and personal property in said last mentioned name" (Laws of the State of Illinois 1837:175). He was now able to purchase land and protect it in a court of law, a right that most African Americans did not have in this era. The law also stated that his children would take the name of their father.

The Illinois legislative act made note that Frank had laid out a town in 1836 "which he calls Philadelphia, and understanding and believing that the said Frank has laid out the town intending to apply the proceeds of the sales for the purchase of his children yet remaining slaves, two young women about twenty years of age—The said town is in handsome country, undoubtedly healthy" (General Assembly Records 1837).

FIGURE 1. Artist's rendition of Free Frank McWorter overseeing his land in New Philadelphia in Pike County. The Illinois Emancipation Centennial Commission commissioned Anna McCullough to do the painting in about 1960. Courtesy of Abraham Lincoln Presidential Library & Museum.

However, when Frank McWorter established New Philadelphia he also faced discrimination on many different fronts. For instance, 1831 Illinois legislation calling for the incorporation of towns declared that the inhabitants had to be white: "whenever the white males over the age of twenty-one years, being residents of any town in the state, containing not less than one hundred and fifty inhabitants, shall wish to become incorporated for the better regulation of their internal police" (Laws of Illinois 1831:86). Two-thirds of the qualified voters (which meant white males over twenty-one) could dissolve the incorporated town (86).

New Philadelphia is the earliest known town founded, platted, and registered in a county courthouse by an African American in the United States. While Illinois laws made it difficult for Frank McWorter to incorporate his town, he did go as far as he could by platting and registering it with the county. He created the forty-two-acre New Philadelphia from an eighty-acre parcel of land that he acquired in 1835 for $100 (Walker 1983c:23). He platted twenty blocks, most of them with

FIGURE 2. An 1860 atlas details the layout of "New" Philadelphia and the owners of land surrounding the town. Image by Jim Helm, Illinois State Historical Society. Courtesy of Abraham Lincoln Presidential Library & Museum.

eight lots. In total there were 144 lots, each measuring 60 by 120 feet. There were two main thoroughfares, Broad and Main Streets, each platted as 80 feet wide; secondary streets were 60 feet wide, and alleys measured 15 feet wide. Although an African American founded the town, both European Americans and African Americans purchased property in and around New Philadelphia (Figure 2).

The 1830s served as one of the most speculative eras in Illinois land sales. The Blackhawk Wars ended in 1833, and American Indians were forced to forfeit the last of their lands in the state. Thanks to wild speculation numerous towns were platted between 1835 and 1837. Some town plans remained only on paper, and many others barely developed before they folded. Along with this wild speculation came the "Panic of 1837," when land sales dropped and many investors lost considerable capital. Supplies of materials and labor also decreased significantly (Davis 1998:236, 272–73).

The creation of New Philadelphia was part of this great optimism for growth and expansion on the western frontier, and it outlived many of these Illinois boom towns. Frank McWorter paid a surveyor and took a great chance by removing a portion of his lots from potential agricultural activities with the hope that the lots would eventually be purchased. Because New Philadelphia was a new village with great potential to become an economic hub for an agrarian community with craftspeople and merchants, some influential residents of the Pike County community helped to realign a major roadway away from the town, aided by 1840 state legislation (Laws of the State of Illinois 1840:129). New Philadelphia lost a main artery that connected it to commercial centers, an event that probably seriously hampered its initial growth. It appears that the McWorters had little influence in keeping the road in place. Whether this act was an economic choice or one based on racism is unclear, but it was the first of many acts that, along with the lack of political power that came with the darker skin color of many of the residents, hurt the future growth of the community.

There was active trading both inside of New Philadelphia and between New Philadelphia and other towns and cities; in 1839 the community had a grocery. It was connected to eastern markets through nearby ports on the Mississippi River, such as Hannibal and Quincy. Although New Philadelphia did not rival eastern cities in size, its location meant it had some potential for economic advantages. LeGrange Wilson carried mail in the 1840s and described New Philadelphia as a "bustling metropolis of the early day and the largest town on his mail route. There were three houses in Philadelphia" (Thompson 1967:151). By all accounts New Philadelphia was a prime area for expansion.

Pike County, where New Philadelphia is located, is only one of two counties in Illinois bordered by both the Mississippi and Illinois rivers. The first steamboat arrived in St. Louis in 1817. After 1835, with advances in steam technology, both commerce and population boomed in the area. By 1840 the steamboat served all navigable waters. Soon thereafter the national road and railroads were being constructed throughout Illinois. The state's population became increasingly diverse, and they had little trouble accessing consumer goods (Davis 1998:413). The archaeology shows that its residents had all of the modern conveniences of the time. Material goods came to the western frontier from manufacturers in Pittsburgh, Wheeling, Cincinnati, and Louisville via the Ohio River. By the mid-1820s Illinois residents could purchase the most fashionable goods, including printed Staffordshire tea sets within a year of the sets being introduced in eastern markets (Mazrim 2007:28).

The completion of the ninety-six-mile Illinois and Michigan Canal in 1848 created new ties to the north and helped to transform the Midwest "from a southern nexus economy to a northeast orientation of agricultural exports and imported goods" (Taffee and Gauthier 1973:54–58). The new canal connected Lake Michigan to the Illinois River, and Illinois trade and migration shifted from north-south along the Mississippi River to also include east-west movement, connecting the Midwest to New York and New England. By the 1850s the number of railroad lines had increased significantly, connecting Chicago and St. Louis to major east coast cities. The transportation of goods and people became quicker and easier (Conzen and Carr 1988; Ranney and Harris 1998). Enthusiasm for more economic growth increased in 1853, when the Pike County Railroad Company (1853:1), made up of prominent farmers and businessmen in the area, met to create a route for a new railroad line. At that point the railroad had the potential to go through New Philadelphia.

New Philadelphia remained a small rural town through the 1850s and existed in a context of widespread racial tensions. It offered African Americans an alternative to isolated rural farmsteads and the hostile environment of urban enclaves. Frank and Lucy McWorter did not live in the town proper, but to the north and adjacent to the town. The 1850 U.S. Federal Census indicates that the town had fifty-eight residents living in eleven households. There was a Baptist preacher, a cabinet maker, a laborer, two merchants, two shoemakers, a wheelwright, and four farmers. About one-quarter of the town's residents were born in Illinois. The 1850 Census listed people according to racial categories, as white, black, or mulatto. Twenty residents are listed as black or mulatto, while the majority (thirty-eight individuals, 62 percent) are categorized as white. Some of the town residents with surnames of McWorter, Burdick, Clark, and Hadsell planted deep roots in the community, and their families would stay for several generations. Five years later the 1855 state census notes eighty-one town residents. The eighteen African American residents account for only 22 percent of the town's population, and the rest are registered as white (King 2006; Walker 1983a:133).

Frank McWorter died in 1854 at seventy-seven years of age. He not only purchased the freedom of himself, his wife, his four children, and two of his grandchildren before he died, but his will also provided for the purchase of six of his grandchildren who were then enslaved. Two of his two sons, Solomon and Commodore, carried out the provisions of his will (Matteson 1964:10; Walker 1983a). Frank McWorter created a strong foundation for the town to grow and his family to prosper over the next generation, despite the growing racist attitudes in the region.

CHAPTER 2

Expansion and Decline

Despite the strict 1853 Black Codes, which forbade the immigration of African Americans to Illinois, several landowning African American families moved to the outskirts of New Philadelphia and became prominent members of the community. In fact some of the heads of households were mentioned in short biographies in the 1872 *Atlas Map of Pike County, Illinois*. For instance, the *Atlas* includes John Walker, born enslaved in Louisa County, Virginia, in 1798. In 1834 he purchased his freedom for $300. Four years later the owner of his wife and children moved to Missouri, so John also moved to Missouri to be close to his family. There he purchased eighty acres for farming. In 1850 he purchased the freedom of two of his children for $400 each, and in 1858 he purchased the freedom of his wife, Lucy, and his son Oregon, who was eighteen years old, for $1,100. In 1861 he owned 460 acres and livestock: horses, mules, cattle, and hogs (*Atlas Map of Pike County* 1872:58).

Living in a slave state during the beginning of the American Civil War must have encouraged Walker to sell his land and livestock in 1861. He then purchased a farm adjacent to the north side of New Philadelphia. By 1872 he owned "500 acres of good land, with very good buildings, where he and his family [lived] in comfort" (*Atlas Map of Pike County* 1872:58). Like Frank McWorter, Walker ventured back to his former residence in Missouri and purchased the freedom of family members (58). He was one of the wealthiest men in Pike County, with an estate worth at least $40,000. The nineteenth-century perspective of the *Atlas* is evident in its description of Walker: "[He is] a man of strict moral and religious habits, and he has always lived quietly and peaceably with all men. He has no animosity towards any person, has always recognized the right to hold slaves where it was allowed by law, and says he never received any cruel treatment from any of his masters. He is very highly respected in the neighborhood in which he lives, and his word is considered as good as his note" (58). This treatment is telling of the racist attitudes of the time. According to the *Atlas* he was respected, but with the caveat that he did not oppose slavery or complain about it.

James Washington also established his farm close to the New Philadelphia. Enslaved on a plantation in Missouri, he found himself at the age of six working with other children in the fields. By his eighth birthday he was handling a team of horses. In 1865, while working in the fields, he and his fellow enslaved workers learned that the Civil War was over; his owners dismissed the workers without the day's second meal. His mother took him and his nine other siblings to her brother's place until her husband returned from the war. His father purchased a farm, and the children went to school for a few months every year (Triplett 1929). When Washington married he rented a farm in Missouri, but racist laws did not allow them to stay in the state for an extended amount of time, so he brought his family to Illinois and settled near New Philadelphia. His first wife died, and he later married Mary E. McWorter, daughter of Solomon and Frances Jane McWorter (Matteson 1964:26; Triplett 1929).

The 1872 *Atlas* indicates that Thomas H. Thomas, the son of Thomas Thomas, a former slave, lived in section 33, southwest of New Philadelphia. The senior Thomas came to Pike County in 1857 after obtaining his freedom (Matteson 1964:29). Shortly before he went to Illinois he purchased the freedom of his wife, Sophia Patiese, a woman of French descent (30). Thomas H., the eldest son, married Desara Ann Lawson of Natchez, Mississippi, born October 24, 1850. The 1872 *Atlas* states that they had two children and that Thomas was a Methodist and a Republican. He owned 320 acres of valuable land (30).

Ansel Vond came to Pike County in 1857 from Monroe County, New York, where he was born in 1828. He married Frank McWorter's daughter Lucy Ann in 1858. They had three children, Lucy, George E., and Frances Nero. Vond owned eighty-two acres of cultivated land just north of New Philadelphia. Lucy Vond died in 1902, at age seventy-seven, and is buried in the New Philadelphia cemetery (Matteson 1964:30).

The 1860 U.S. Federal Census shows that New Philadelphia's town population had increased to about 114 individuals. A blacksmith, a carpenter, a physician, and a schoolteacher along with thirteen farmers resided in the town proper. On the eve of the American Civil War ninety-three (82 percent) of the residents were listed as white and twenty-one as black or mulatto. An increasing proportion (43.9 percent) of the town came from other Illinois communities (King 2006).

On February 4, 1865, after the Emancipation Proclamation and at the close of the Civil War, all of the Black Codes of Illinois were repealed; African Americans were subsequently free to migrate into Illinois (Angle 1967:74). Many new African American families had settled in and around New Philadelphia during the Civil War era; the town's population peaked in 1865 with 160 individuals residing in twenty-nine households. The census takers categorized 104 (65 percent) as white and fifty-six (35 percent) as black or mulatto. The African American population increased threefold in five years, although at about the same proportion as the white population. The influx of African Americans resulted from the northward migration of formerly enslaved persons leaving slave states (King 2006).

According to several oral history accounts recorded by Matteson (1964:19), New Philadelphia had separate schools for African Americans and whites in the town before 1874. "A schoolhouse for colored people [stood] near the center of the town of Philadelphia. . . . It was vacated some time before 1881" (19). Irene Brown, a former resident of New Philadelphia, believed that a schoolhouse once existed on the east side of the square, probably in block 9. The deed records show that in 1858 a 30 by 21 foot section of the southwest corner of block 8, lot 1 was sold to the school district, which is on the east side of the square and adjacent to block 9, lot 5 (Pike County Deed Book 1858 54:5). Some people remember the one-story building as the "black schoolhouse" or the "Negro schoolhouse," although at present there are no documents to confirm this fact. The second New Philadelphia schoolhouse known in recent memory is not shown in the 1872 Pike County atlas. However, many people believe it was built in 1874. No person interviewed by Matteson could be certain about the exact date of its erection, although it stood on about one acre of land on the southeast corner "of the Art McWorter Farmstead" (Burdick 1992: n.p.). One informant claimed that he heard Arthur McWorter say that it was constructed the year he was born, 1874. Both white and black students attended the school, and

FIGURE 3. A class at the New Philadelphia schoolhouse in the 1920s. Students are from the surrounding community. Courtesy of Pike County Historical Society.

it functioned into the 1940s (Matteson 1964:19–20; *Pike County Illinois Schools* 1996:153; Figure 3).

Throughout New Philadelphia's history all of the town lots were sold, some as many as a dozen times. The high turnover rate is noticeable especially during the early speculative period of the town. Perhaps while the town existed as a small rural community serving the immediate hinterlands many others prospected on town land with the hope of making significant amounts of money if the railroad line was laid adjacent to or through the town. There are many cases of small-town speculations in Illinois in the 1850s, when properties adjacent to the railroad doubled in value; in some cases the values increased by as much as nine times the original price (Davis 1998). However, the fortunes that accompanied railroads did not occur for the New Philadelphia speculators.

Beginning in the early 1850s business interests in Hannibal, Missouri, promoted the construction of a railroad across Pike County to connect Hannibal to the railroad town of Naples, located on the Illinois

River. With this action Hannibal would develop into a major commercial hub of the region (Fennell 2010). In 1853 the Pike County Railroad Company began planning a route for a new line. Local businessmen set out "to adopt such measures as might be thought practicable for the construction of a Rail Road across said County, from a point on the Mississippi River, opposite or nearly opposite the City of Hannibal in the State of Missouri" (Pike County Railroad Company 1853:1). The majority of the original subscribers to the railroad—those with at least forty shares—were from Griggsville and Barry. Other interested investors came from Pittsfield and Springfield (Pike County Railroad Company 1853). It appeared that those communities would stand to benefit the most by this new capitalist venture. The interests of New Philadelphia were not represented on the board. The construction and completion of the railroad occurred only after the end of the Civil War. The new enterprise, the Hannibal & Naples Railroad, was routed north of New Philadelphia by about one mile (Chapman 1880:904; Matteson 1964:9). The railroad constructed a spur to Pittsfield, the county seat, the following year. The location of two main transportation arteries away from New Philadelphia—a main road in 1840, and now the railroad in 1869—severely hindered the town's growth, and its population began a steady decline (Figure 4).

Why did the railroad line arc its northern route around New Philadelphia? Could it have been racism, an intentional act of avoiding an African American enclave, or was it the greed of a few landowners who had shares in the company and wanted to route the line closer to their properties so that they could profit? Certainly the fact that William Pine, who had a farm about four miles northeast of New Philadelphia, donated land to the railroad was an inducement for the company. (The town, known as Pineville, later became known as Baylis; Walker 1985:62). However, the story is probably more complicated. Chris Fennell and his team of graduate students at the University of Illinois have pored through the newspapers and the corporate records of the Pike County Railroad Company and its successor, the Hannibal & Naples Railroad Company. New Philadelphia residents are not mentioned, nor are they stockholders or board members. John McTucker was appointed liaison to Hadley Township by the railroad company. I am sure that it is no coincidence that the area's new depot, Hadley Station, was established on a parcel of his land, just about one mile northwest of New Philadelphia. The route bypassed New Philadelphia to the north and through prairie; this route was not practical because the railroad

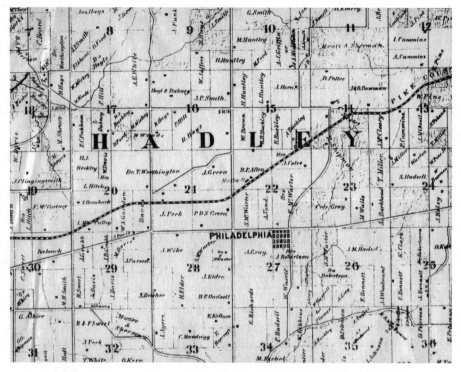

FIGURE 4. Atlas map of Pike County, Illinois, in 1860 showing the anticipated route of the railroad, north of "Philadelphia." *Atlas Map of Pike County, Illinois,* 1860.

needed a booster engine to push the train on the incline that bypassed the town (Fennell 2010).

At the time New Philadelphia had a population of 160 people, significantly larger than Pineville and Hadley Station. In fact Hadley Station developed on farmland with the hope that a town would develop there. Other black towns, such as Nicodemus, Kansas, shared New Philadelphia's fate. The town of Nicodemus, founded in 1879, grew to about seven hundred people. In 1887 the Union Pacific Railroad's decision to bypass the town was a devastating blow. The African American Registry (2005) notes, "In a fate shared by the majority of Black towns that failed to attract a rail line, Nicodemus soon dwindled and died."

Walker (1983c) explains that white Pike County founders used their influence to hinder New Philadelphia's connection to the broader markets. In one instance they persuaded the Pike County commissioners to approve roads that would benefit their communities. In 1840 they ordered the relocation of part of an east-west road, which ran through New Philadelphia. Walker writes, "[This] provides one example of the limited influence of a black town founder in influencing county road-building activities. . . . That Illinois law prevented blacks from voting or holding office limited Free Frank's influence as a town proprietor, however. Lacking political clout, the black town founder was at a dis-advantage. County and state officials were disposed to act favorably in the interests of town proprietors who could offer some political reciprocity"(38–39). The routing of the railroad around New Philadel-phia in 1853 took advantage of McWorter's lack of political and eco-nomic clout, and race most likely had a role in the decision, much as it did in the rerouting of the road away from the town in 1840.

After the railroad line opened in 1869 people began to slowly move away from New Philadelphia to larger cities and less developed land west of the Mississippi River. In the early twentieth century, when New Philadelphia had about six households remaining in town, the railroad realigned the tracks about a half-mile south of its initial location. Cars and engines could traverse a more even grade in the topography with-out a booster engine. This change in course, however, came too late to save the town (Fennell 2010). Although the railroad now lay less than half a mile from New Philadelphia, many of the town's residents had already relocated.

One county historian wrote of New Philadelphia in 1880, "At one time it had great promise, but the railroad passing it a mile distant, and other towns springing up, has killed it. At present there is not even a post office at the place" (Chapman 1880:740–41). In 1880 New Philadelphia had about ninety-three residents. The town included fourteen farmers as well as a blacksmith, a schoolteacher, a storekeeper, eight farmhands, and nine general laborers. The majority of the residents (fifty-four, or 58.1 percent) were Illinois natives, and thirteen individuals (13.97 percent) came from Ohio. The federal census lists sixty-eight (73.1 percent) as white, twenty-two (23.7 percent) as mulatto, and three (3.2 percent) as black (King 2006).

It is important to look at the depopulation of New Philadelphia in relationship to the rest of Pike County. Once we do this, it becomes ob-vious that the population growth trends were similar in the town and the county. While the county experienced rapid growth before the Civil War, this trend slowly reversed in the 1870s. By the end of the century urban areas and western lands drew people away from Pike County

(C. R. Smith and Bonath 1982:74–76). New Philadelphia fits this general trend.

All of the town lots were purchased and sold many times, and a newspaper report in 1876 provides highlights of some of the consequences of these transactions in the community. The *Barry Adage* of June 10, 1876, reports, "The village of Philadelphia . . . has been readjusting lines, and it is found that most of the people are on other than their own lands. There will have to be some moving of property lines or a general compromise" (quoted in Fennell 2010). The easternmost portion of the town appears to never have been settled, or at least was unoccupied after the Civil War; Ansel Vond had this land in agricultural use. Agricultural lands are assessed a lower tax; Vond went through the process to get blocks 1, 10, 11, and 20, as well as the eastern half of blocks 2, 9, 12, and 19, declared vacant and subsequently no longer legally part of the town in 1885. Canton Street and Maiden Lane were removed, and Queen Street became known as Stone Street. The platted land of the former town had shrunk from 42 acres to about 27.5 acres (Walker 1983a:167–69). The New Philadelphia area had both a white and a black cemetery, and the black cemetery was deeded to the county in 1883. African American community members continued to be buried in the cemetery until 1950.

NEW PHILADELPHIA IN THE EARLY TWENTIETH CENTURY

Farm values and farm sizes in Pike County increased significantly during the first decade of the twentieth century. From 1900 to 1910 the average farm size increased from about 123 acres to 134 acres. At the same time, the rural population slowly declined. The number of individually owned farms decreased from 4,000 to 3,500, and the total number of improved acreage declined slightly from 388,000 to 385,000. Pike County experienced a greater rural decline when compared to the other counties in the state. On the whole, people did not migrate to the larger villages of the county, but moved away from the area to larger metropolitan areas such as Chicago, St. Louis, and Springfield (Main 1915).

Floyd Dell, a well-known writer in the first half of the twentieth century, lived in Barry, Illinois, several miles from New Philadelphia, for a significant portion of his childhood. He described Pike County as "vaguely permeated by Southern influences—a touch of laziness, quite a lot of mud, and like the scent of honeysuckle, a whiff of the romantic attitude toward life" (1933:3). While many Americans experienced prosperity during the 1920s, farm income decreased dramatically. Dell wrote, "The Pike County farmer believed that land was gold; they could not imagine that in a few years it might be as worthless as those abandoned New England farms . . . sweated over generation after generation, only to be sold for taxes" (354). For many farmers in Pike County it appears that the decreasing land values and income meant that the Great Depression actually started a decade earlier.

Other narratives add texture to the town's twentieth-century history. For instance, temperance was a burning issue in the community at the turn of the century. Carrie Nation, the popular American temperance agitator who began breaking up saloons with a hatchet in the early 1900s, was invited to the area. George Gibbens, a preacher who lived in Hadley Township, and Arthur McWorter, a religious man, invited her to come to their community and give a lecture. A meeting was held in a clearing in the grove southeast of New Philadelphia and was attended by a very large crowd—a noteworthy event for the townspeople (Matteson 1964:21–22).

Other stories help to reconstruct the town's landscape and show that in the early twentieth century it existed as a small village. Mary Jo Foster, interviewed in 2004, remembered the town in the 1920s: "There were a few buildings left in New Philadelphia when I was a kid, and a few streets. The buildings didn't have any paint on them and the ones I remember were down that street [Broad]." Throughout the twentieth century several maps still designated the area as "Philadelphia" or "New Philadelphia." Oral histories of several former residents recorded in the early 1960s indicate that a multiracial community survived into the 1930s, although the land was virtually abandoned by the 1940s (Matteson 1964). Only the Burdick family remained (Figure 5).

In 1964 Grace Matteson compiled a history of the McWorters based on personal interviews with residents and former residents of the town. She also used personal records loaned by Thelma Kirkpatrick of Chicago, a great-granddaughter of Free Frank. Irene Butler Brown, born in 1881, lived in New Philadelphia until 1906, when she moved to Jacksonville, Illinois. Brown remembered that the remaining families lived in the town surrounding a square. Besides her own family, the Butlers, who lived on the east side of the square, were the Kimbrews; "Squire McWorter's family lived on the north side of the square; and the family of Jim McKinney (who had come from Oklahoma) on the south side, all of whom were col-

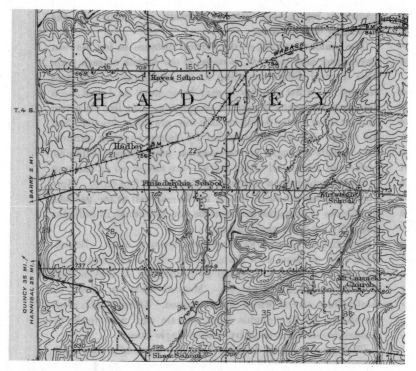

FIGURE 5. The location of the New Philadelphia schoolhouse and a few remaining houses in a 1926 topographic map. The former town is located beneath the letter *S*. U.S. Geological Survey. Courtesy of the Map and Geography Library of the University of Illinois at Urbana-Champaign.

ored; and the Venicombes on the west side, and the Sylvester 'Fet' Baker family, Caucasians" (Matteson 1964:18–19). Larry Burdick, one of the last residents of the town, wrote of his recollections of the town in a manuscript that is on file at the Pike County Historical Society. His map shows that "the Park" (no. 2 in Figure 6), also referred to by others as "the square," consisted of block 8, lots 1–8 and was probably so named because no buildings existed on it and houses stood on all of its four sides, thus creating an open green space between the houses (Burdick 1992).

Irene Brown remembered the grocery store on the north side of New Philadelphia as the only remaining business in town; it was operated by Mr. Kellum (Matteson 1964: postscript). This building stood to the west of Broad Street on block 4. To the east stood a blacksmith shop on block 3 that was operated by Squire McWorter (Frank and Lucy's son). The foundations of the blacksmith shop still remained in the 1960s, although

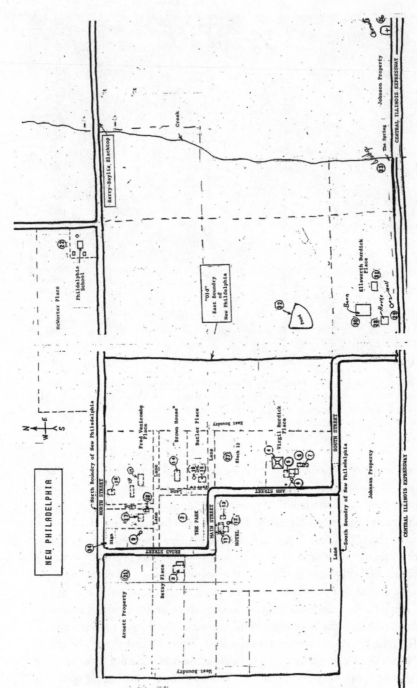

FIGURE 6. Larry Burdick's map of New Philadelphia, drawn from memory in the 1970s. Each number on the map corresponds to a known occupant or feature from the 1920s. "New Philadelphia: Where I Lived," on file at the Pike County Historical Society.

they are not visible today (Matteson 1964:19; see Figure 6). On the same Block the Venicombes built a house in New Philadelphia in about 1900 (no. 17 in Figure 6). There was "no reason to believe it was part of the original town" (Burdick 1992: n.p.).

On the east side of the "the park" (on block 9, lot 5, or block 8, lot 1) stood the "Negro schoolhouse." That building fell into disrepair after a new integrated schoolhouse was built across the road on the northeastern edge of the town. Two brothers, George and Martin Kimbrew, purchased the older school building, renovated it, and used the structure as their residence (Matteson 1964: postscript). To the west of the park stood the Betsy Place (no. 3 in Figure 6), a small house with a front room addition. Interviewed in 2005 Harry Johnson, one of the local descendants, remembered, "There was just on the west side of this road up here there was a little old shack there, I think it was Venicombe's mother who lived there [in the early twentieth century]. She would set up in the yard there in the chair smoking her pipe. If anybody came along, well, that pipe went under the grass so nobody would see it. She was just a little old lady." In the 1930s they used the grounds to raise chickens and operate a truck garden (Burdick 1992).

The Burdick family owned property in New Philadelphia as early as 1846, and in 1941 the family decided to stay in the town and build a new home (no. 5 in Figure 6; Burdick 1992). The old Burdick house stood on a limestone foundation. Larry Burdick remembers, "In the winter the winds sifted between the rocks, chilled the floors enough to make your teeth chatter. The walls were not boxed in. My mother used to say that the only thing between us and the outside was a little bit of weatherboard" (n.p.).

Squire and Louisa McWorter's House, originally built in 1854, was called "the hotel" by the early twentieth-century residents. The house (no. 11 in Figure 6) stood as the largest building in New Philadelphia, a two-story house situated near the intersection of Broad and Main Streets. A barn and a well also existed on the property (Burdick 1992). The house burned to the ground on December 7, 1937. "The man who rented the house at the time set a metal can of cylinder oil on the stove to heat to pour into his old car to get it started. The oil overheated and exploded and set the building ablaze" (n.p.).

The Brown house (no. 14 in Figure 6) had a single story with wood frame construction and a gabled roof on the east and west ends. Fred Venicombe owned the property in the 1930s, and the building served to store grain. Like many of the other places in town, "the house decayed and fell in. The structure was removed and the land was converted to farmland in the late 1940s or early 1950s" (Burdick 1992: n.p.).

William Butler (no. 15 in Figure 6), an African American from Louisville, Kentucky, served as an orderly for a Confederate general during the Civil War. He moved to New Philadelphia when he was nineteen, probably in 1865 or 1866, after migrating from Marion County, Missouri. One rainy night, while traveling through Pike County, he stopped at Solomon McWorter's home, where the family invited him to stay overnight. Apparently McWorter and Butler hit it off, and McWorter offered him a job and an invitation to live with the family. When Solomon died, Butler remained with the family to help Frances with the farm and supervising the children. Butler married "a lovely young full-blooded Caucasian woman" named Catherine Wright, who originally came from Missouri. She settled in the New Philadelphia area with a European American family named Wagoner (Matteson 1964: postscript).

Irene Brown, one of William Butler's daughters, recalled that he owned the entire public square (block 8) and that the Butlers lived on the east side of it (block 9, lots 5 and 6). The Butler house stood vacant in the 1930s and began to deteriorate. "The house was respectable looking, not a shack," explained Burdick (1992: n.p.).

People remembered the many annual fairs at the New Philadelphia schoolhouse near the north edge of the town, which served as a community center. Events included contests, races, exhibitions of home arts, "and all the things that go with a fair" (Matteson 1964:21). One thing that stands out in Eleanor Kelly Lightle's memory is the school float that the students decorated under the direction of their teacher, Hazel Blake. The float was entered in the Fall Festival Parade held in the village of Baylis in the fall of 1942 and won first prize (*Pike County Illinois Schools* 1996:153). Mary Jo Foster, interviewed in 2004, remembers using the schoolhouse for community meetings: "Once a month, we'd had community meetings at night and people would take refreshments and then on the last day of school, we just had a regular big blowout, you know, with all kinds of [food]. Sophie Washington, LeMoyne's mother, was such a nice woman and they lived in the neighborhood, and she would bring food just like the rest of us did and some of them would go around looking to see what she took out because they didn't want to eat anything a Negro woman made, and I'd be going around asking what the recipe was because she was a wonderful cook, but that was the attitude."

Reverend Mason, a Baptist minister, frequently held church services at the schoolhouse (Matteson 1964: postscript). Larry Burdick remembers attending, "all eight years of grade school in this building. It was closed in 1947 when the county consolidated its rural schools" (1992: n.p.). Children who once attended the one-room schoolhouse before the consolidation afterward attended a larger central school built in Barry. In 1949 the land of the old schoolhouse was sold and the building torn down. There were some school reunions held in the 1950s, which many of the former students, teachers, and families attended (*Pike County Illinois Schools* 1996:153).

Community members realized the importance of New Philadelphia and its place in history. A road sign stood at the site of New Philadelphia beginning in the 1950s commemorating the multiracial town and the achievements of the McWorter family. Only the Burdick family remained on the original town site.

The history of the town and the development of the multiracial community is an intriguing story. Race is such a haunting American legacy, I thought it would be worthwhile to learn more about the place and, through archaeology, to examine the changing role of race in the American heartland.

CHAPTER 3

It Was Never Lost

In 1998 Jane Buikstra, now at Arizona State University, invited me to the Center for American Archaeology (CAA) to help the staff identify historic sites that might be of interest for a future research program. The headquarters of the CAA is in Kampsville, Illinois, in Calhoun County, adjacent to and south of Pike County. The area has tremendous prehistoric resources, as American Indians settled and exploited these rich riverine environments of the Illinois and Mississippi Rivers. I have known Buikstra since 1979, when I participated in a field school that worked ahead of a road construction project for the development of U.S. Route 72 that connected Springfield, Illinois, to Hannibal, Missouri. Coincidently the new road passes immediately to the south of New Philadelphia. I worked on the Elizabeth Mounds located on the western banks of the Illinois River, above Napoleon Hallow in Pike County. It was an experience that changed my life. I became enthralled with knowing more about the past and the thrill of discovery. Ever since that time I have worked hard to become an archaeologist and have been in occasional contact with Buikstra, meeting from time to time at national conferences for brief chats.

When I arrived at Kampsville, Buikstra was out of town, and Cindy Sutton and Jody O'Gorman, both working for the CAA, showed me several possible sites in Calhoun and Pike Counties. I also did some archival work. At the end of my stay I suggested to them that if the CAA wanted to make an impact in historical archaeology they needed to think about working on a nationally significant place. I identified three places that fit that criterion.

One project focused on the development and decline of the button industry in Pearl, Illinois. Pearl thrived for a short time as a small industrial town, stamping shell buttons, thus becoming part of the larger story of industrialization and clothing manufacturing in the United States. This project could be tied to the rise and decline of the garment industry and the eventual outsourcing of manufacturing to other regions and other countries. The second project involved an abandoned settlement known as Mormon Town, which is located in a cornfield outside of Pittsfield, the county seat of Pike County. Mormons settled the region in 1839 after fleeing Missouri, and they established their capital in Nauvoo, along the Mississippi River and about eighty miles north of Hannibal. In 1846 they were forced to abandon these settlements, some moving to Missouri and others moving to Utah. Their story is important in developing an understanding of the history of intolerance in the United States. The third site that I identified was the town site of New Philadelphia. The local people in Pike County knew about the town, and many were aware of the heroic story of the McWorter family. I thought that a project at this site could highlight the achievements of African Americans, the quest for freedom, and the history of race and racism in the United States.

The Center for American Archaeology made several overtures to the New Philadelphia Association (NPA) over the next several years. The NPA was established in 1996 as a nonprofit organization to promote the story of Frank McWorter and New Philadelphia. At that time the association consisted of about a dozen white community members, professionals and farmers. The CAA could not convince the NPA that they had the resources to sustain a research program at New Philadelphia.

Over the next several years I continually mentioned New Philadelphia to my historical archaeology class, which I taught once a year. Cheryl LaRoche, a graduate student in one of my classes, who has since earned her Ph.D., applied for a CAA summer internship to see if she could help develop ties with the New Philadelphia community. Even though LaRoche met with the NPA and the CAA staff, the NPA decided to partner with the University of Illinois at Springfield rather than with the CAA. They were attracted to the university connection and the potential for a long-term commitment with funding. LaRoche instead focused her energies on Rocky Fork, an African American community located outside of

St. Louis in Illinois. It served as a station on the Underground Railroad, and her research became part of her dissertation.

I believed New Philadelphia had a unique history that needed to be remembered in the larger public memory, but I thought the project dead from lack of funds. So imagine my surprise when I received a phone call from Vibert White. In a tone of excitement and urgency he informed me that he was holding a conference in Illinois about New Philadelphia and he invited me to attend. Then chair of the African American Studies Program at the University of Illinois–Springfield, White told me that he had received a $50,000 grant from his institution for seed money to develop a project with the NPA to explore the research potential at New Philadelphia. Cheryl LaRoche, who met White at a history conference, explained to him that I had been interested in the place for at least a few years. White invited me to the University of Illinois on June 21 and 22, 2002, for the conference and workshop with other scholars, practitioners, and members of the NPA to start thinking about how to develop a research program for this site.

I immediately accepted White's invitation to join the conference, titled "Researching and Preserving African American Frontier Settlements." White had connected with Philip Bradshaw, the president of the NPA and a politically astute pig farmer with connections to local and state politics. Bradshaw had been involved in the construction of Federal Highway 72, which passes New Philadelphia, and at the time of its construction in the 1990s he vowed to help preserve the town and its cemetery and bring it to greater public recognition. The archaeology that I did in 1979 was performed to prepare for this road and the twin bridges that cross the Illinois River into Pike County. Thus I already had a long connection with Bradshaw, although I had not formally met him.

White had already commissioned a local architecture firm to develop drawings for a reconstructed New Philadelphia, and the NPA also had a vision of reconstructing the town, much like New Salem. New Salem is now an Illinois State Park with fabricated buildings that give the appearance of the 1830s town in which Abraham Lincoln lived before moving to Springfield. However, there was little documentation on which to base the reconstruction of New Salem. There is a long history of scholarship criticizing the rebuilding of particular historic places, including New Salem, Williamsburg, and many buildings in national parks. There is also a long history of scholarship criticizing the rebuilding of any historic place, based on how these recreations mislead the public's perceptions of the past. Such conjectural buildings sit on the landscape and present a sense of reality and authenticity, when in fact they are fabricated, sometimes incorrectly, and visitors rarely are told that they are looking at reconstructions (Bruner 1994; Handler and Gable 1997; Leone 1981; Moyer and Shackel 2008; Shackel 1994).

This conference was a great opportunity to get involved in a very important project, and I thought I still had some time to prevent these organizations from making the same mistakes of fabricating a town with little or no evidence. We were joined by Spencer Crew, director of the Underground Railroad Museum in Cincinnati, and Terrance Martin, curator of anthropology at the Illinois State Museum, among many others.

Given fifteen minutes to address the group, I took the opportunity to inform the audience about two issues: the perils of reconstructing the town and the importance of placing the town site on the National Register of Historic Places. I suggested that they should avoid reconstructing the town, especially as it was impossible to accurately interpret the way the town once looked. What did the buildings look like? Were they one story or two? Were they clapboard or log? It would be especially difficult to accurately restore the town if we did not know the location of buildings. Furthermore the town had existed for about one hundred years, so they would have to choose which time period to rebuild and interpret. To reconstruct the town as it looked in one time period would neglect other histories and other events. For a short-term goal it was important to place the town on the National Register of Historic Places, a designation that honors locally, regionally, and nationally significant places and archaeological sites. More than eighty thousand sites in the United States are listed on the National Register. Fewer than 7 percent of these are archaeology sites (B. J. Little 1999), and fewer than nine hundred sites are connected to African American, Asian American, or Latino heritage (Kauffman 2004).

The representation of traditional peripheral groups on the American landscape has changed significantly since the Civil Rights Act. Until that time there was very little on the national landscape that could memorialize minority groups in the national public memory. Places like Woman's Rights National Historical Park, the Frederick Douglass House, and Lowell National Historical Park now tell the stories of women, African Americans, and labor, respectively. Yet the telling of stories of traditionally marginalized groups is becoming even more important on the national scene with the redevelopment of many inner cities. Traditional minority communities are being displaced from the landscape with gentrification and the development of transit schemes, such as highways and metros. While the heritage of minorities can still be found in traditional folkways, the places in which these ways of life were practiced are increasingly being erased, and historic parks are one of the few places where minority stories can be told and passed down over the generations (Kauffman 2004). New Philadelphia was one site that could make our national heritage more representative of the entire nation, and archaeology was one tool to help create a more inclusive past.

I suggested to the New Philadelphia Association that once the town site was listed on the National Register, the organization should next think about going for National Historic Landmark (NHL) designation. National Historic Landmarks are nationally significant historic places so designated by the Secretary of the Interior because they possess exceptional value or quality in illustrating or interpreting the heritage of the United States. They are outstanding places that have meaning to all Americans, and there are fewer than 2,500 sites in the entire United States that have NHL status. While this designation does not guarantee that it will become a national park, national parks usually have NHL status before being accepted into the national park system. The state or federal government would be more likely to accept a donation of the land if there was sufficient documentation that indicated its national importance.

Terry Martin spoke about the importance of doing historical archaeology and the necessity of doing it in a systematic and professional fashion. He reiterated the importance of going for the federal designations. Others, such as Spencer Crew, spoke about the importance of the site and tied it to the Underground Railroad.

Members of the New Philadelphia Association watched and listened. They came away with the feeling that their plans to save and commemorate New Philadelphia were important, and they resolved to move ahead and work on the project. However, they now had some doubt about whether reconstruction was the proper way to commemorate the town. At the end of this meeting I had a conversation with Terry Martin for the first time. We spoke about developing a strategy to move ahead and begin an archaeological survey. He promised support from the Illinois State Museum, and we agreed to keep in touch as we developed plans to help the University of Illinois and the NPA to commemorate New Philadelphia.

I told Chuck Orser, who was then at Illinois State University, of my plans to work at New Philadelphia, partly because of my long relationship with Orser, who is one of the discipline's most prolific scholars, and partly because I would be working in his backyard. Orser told me that he had tried to develop a program at New Philadelphia in the early 1990s but had received some negative vibes from one of the descendants. He was now entrenched in his work in Ireland, and he wished me luck. He also graciously sent me some of the information that he collected on the place, including maps, notes, and some typed manuscripts.

THE BEGINNING

While sensitive to the issues of race and racism throughout my life, I have noticed that some scholars are not attuned to the fact that archaeology can help address racism in the past and the present. For instance, in 1999 the University of Maryland sponsored a one-day symposium titled "Commemoration, Conflict and the American Landscape: An Archaeology of Battlefield and Military Landscapes." One of the participants was emphatic that national battlefields should be preserved not for interpreting the relationship of the Civil War to race and slavery, but only for interpreting battlefield tactics. His suggestion that we ignore the larger social and historical context was puzzling to me and helped to strengthen my resolve to focus my scholarship on issues related to race. I have since published several articles, one in *American Anthropologist* (Shackel 2001), and later wrote a book, *Memory in Black and White* (2003) on the importance of developing more inclusive interpretations at national historic sites. I thought that New Philadelphia could be a project that addressed these issues.

During the late summer of 2002 I asked Joy Beasley, a recent graduate from the University of Maryland's applied anthropology program, and Tom Gwaltney, a graduate of the geography department's program, to help out with the archaeological survey. In fact they ended up running it. At the same time, Terry Martin and Lynn Fisher of the University of Illinois at Springfield began to coordinate volunteers for the program. There was a lot of energy going into this effort because we all believed that the town was nationally significant because of its place in American history.

Our goal was to systematically walk the fields, locate and map artifacts, and identify the areas where people once lived during the town's existence. I asked Phil Bradshaw for help with the project. "Let us know what you need and we will do our best to help," he answered. I thought to myself, What a great response! This project had the potential to make the place a part of the national public memory and at the same time be a lot of fun, as we would be working closely with the local community. After all, it's not every day that a community will create an immediate partnership with an archaeology team and provide them with tremendous support.

New Philadelphia is located on gently rolling hills with plowed and fallow fields. Some prairie grass grows on the north side of the former town, and a few cabins and a shed from other parts of the county have been placed over existing foundations. A gravel road bisects the town and passes the unoccupied Burdick house. We needed to systematically walk over the fields and look for artifacts. Locating and mapping these artifacts would give us a good idea about where people once lived and deposited refuse. Studies in experimental archaeology have shown that artifacts in plowed soils tend to stay close to their original deposited location.

However, I was concerned that the town once stood in an area now covered with grasses with only about 10 to 20 percent visibility of the soil. These conditions would make it difficult to produce reliable results if we did a walkover survey of the property. So I used my first favor and asked Phil to coordinate a shallow plowing of the fields, but only land that had been plowed in the past. The plowing would expose the soil and provide better visibility for finding artifacts, and because the area had not been plowed for fifty to a hundred years one more plowing would not make a significant impact on the archaeological record, especially if the plowing was relatively shallow.

The plowing, however, was easier said than done. Various farm bills passed by Congress over the past thirty years or so have endeavored to preserve America's farmlands. New conservation methods, including no-till agriculture, are encouraged. Many farmers in the area began abandoning their plows in the 1980s in favor of drilling seeds, making no-till agriculture the dominant planting method in much of the Midwest. Now just finding a plow was not easy.

In August 2002 I was on the phone with Terry Martin almost every day, planning two walkover surveys. Commitments to school, teaching, and family forced us to limit our work to two long weekends in October and November. Joy and Tom, who would be responsible for the survey work, suggested this long weekend arrangement. Terry and Lynn Fisher began announcing our plans to students and contacting longtime volunteers. Vibert White agreed to use part of his seed money to help defray some of the costs associated with the project. At the same time I received a small grant from my university to help defray some of the costs.

Joy, Tom, and I planned to visit the site at the end of September to look at the plowed fields prior to our walkover survey. We booked our flights, and Phil Bradshaw called for a news conference at the site. However, Phil was having some difficulties in getting the field plowed. He spoke to me on the phone a week before our trip, explaining that Roger Woods, a neighboring farmer, was dusting off his old plow. He promised that all of the fields would be plowed by the time we got to the news conference. Phil paused for a short moment and said, "I hope!"

Phil said that he was happy to leave the decisions about archaeological methods and interpretation to the archaeologists. However, he had his doubts about plowing the field to find the town site. Over several phone conversations he always asked me if this was really going to work. I assured him that it would. And I followed a short pause with "I hope."

Phil is a well-known pig farmer in the region and is highly respected in the national and international arenas for his farming expertise. He travels around the world for various humanitarian food programs, representing the United States on the soybean board. Despite his prominence, the weekend before we arrived at Pike County Phil rode alongside Roger Woods on the tractor, ready to assist when needed. He had to hop off a few times to clear the plow blade, and as he did so he noticed a few window glass fragments, and in another area a couple of pieces of broken ceramics as well as a few corroded nails.

We arrived at the site in the last weekend of September for the news conference. The New Philadelphia Association was well represented. Larry and Natalie Armistead, caretakers of the New Philadelphia Land Trust, did all they could to make the event a success, but when the television camera lights were on they faded to the background. Local newspaper reporters and a staff writer from the *Quincy (Illinois) Herald Whig* roamed around the site talking with Tom and Joy. Television crews from Quincy, a small city of fifty thousand that is about thirty-five miles to the northwest of New Philadelphia, interviewed Joy and several community members. Phil arrived with a big grin and we shook hands. He admitted that he hadn't believed me when I said that we would find artifacts related to New Philadelphia, but the place was loaded with nails, glass, and bits of pottery. He let out a small chuckle. That was terrific news, and Joy and Tom grinned. We knew we were at the right place, and now we had committed ourselves to a task that seemed to grow with every hour.

FIGURE 7. 1998 aerial photograph of New Philadelphia site with an overlay of the block, lot, and street boundaries. The large numbers are the blocks and the smaller numbers are the lots. Image courtesy of USGS archives. Overlay by Christopher Fennell.

Next I asked Phil if he knew of a local surveyor who could help out with the initial layout of the town. Within days he introduced us to Tom and Marvin Likes, local land surveyors, who have always lived in the area. Pat, Marvin's wife, was on the NPA board and was a big supporter of the archaeology project. She may have twisted the arms of Likes Land Surveyors, Inc. of Barry, Illinois, to help us out. I'll always remember Tom and Marvin as easygoing people who get the job done right. They located the original plat and imposed the town plan over the existing topography, marking the outer boundaries of the town on the landscape, as well as a few streets, blocks, and lots. They then produced a map that Tom Gwaltney overlaid onto the existing aerial photograph (similar to Figure 7), and that in turn guided our archaeological survey (Gwaltney 2004). We were set for the next phase.

THE ARCHAEOLOGICAL SURVEY

Some type of survey is necessary at any archaeological site in order to indicate if anything remains of that site, such as building foundations, trash dumps, wells, or privies. In the case of New Philadelphia the artifacts found in a plowed field indicated that more substantial remains existed below the surface. The plow usually scrapes the top of features—cellar pits, wells, trash dumps, and privies—and brings a few artifacts to the surface. Finding not just a few items but a cluster of artifacts on the surface meant that there was a good chance of locating other material below the plow zone. Furthermore any clustering of artifacts would indicate where people had lived within the forty-two-acre town.

Archaeologists usually survey plowed fields by laying a grid over the land (e.g., 10 meters by 10 meters, or larger) and systematically collect artifacts on the surface within each designated square. The number of artifacts gathered in each collection unit indicates roughly where the main settlement occurred at a site. For example, finding ceramic sherds might indicate a domestic space, while finding scraps of metal and slag might be evidence of a former blacksmith shop. However, when Joy, Tom, and I first developed a field strategy, we thought it would be best, time permitting, to piece-plot each artifact. Piece plotting involves noting every artifact's location and placing this information in a Geographical Information System (GIS). We thought piece plotting could provide a nice visual that would identify discrete areas of occupation, because residents would have tossed trash in areas close to where they lived. Naturally piece plotting would take longer than collecting in a grid, but the benefit would be more precise data. Before we started the walkover survey we thought that surveying the forty-two-acre town site would take two long weekends (October 11–14 and November 8–10, 2002) and that we would find a few thousand artifacts.

Terry Martin and Lynn Fisher rallied the volunteers, and each day we had about a dozen field workers, including students from local colleges and members of the community. The New Philadelphia Association erected a large tent, had a portable toilet at the site, and brought us a hot meal every day. Larry and Natalie Armistead always made sure that we had the supplies we needed to guarantee a successful project. Natalie eagerly helped us walk the fields, as she had done so over the past several years and already knew the location of some of the hot spots. This survey, while cost-effective, also brought together the local community and outsiders, all working on a common cause.

As we worked on those two weekends our fingers and toes were chilled by the cool autumn mornings; a thick fog hung over the fields each day until the sun burned it off in the late morning. One day the fog was so thick we never saw the sun. Pike County is one of the windiest areas in the country, and every day we had a ten- to twenty-mile-an-hour wind. If we didn't get sunburned we got wind burned during our autumn surveys. But that didn't stop the volunteer crews from showing up each day. We were excited to find window glass, broken pieces of ceramics, and nails. We knew that they marked the ground floor of something bigger, and we worked from sunrise to just after sunset.

As we walked the plowed fields we marked each artifact with a pin flag. After finishing each transect we repeated the process. Each pin flag marked an identified artifact and received a provenience identifier number. Archaeologists logged the artifact in the field and placed each artifact in a bag for collection. The spatial location of each target was recorded using a laser transit and electronic data recorder that Tom downloaded every night. Several nice patterns developed, with clusters of artifacts forming within the boundaries of town lots. This phenomenon was no coincidence. The overlay was exact, and our survey data corresponded nicely with the information from the Likes survey. It was nearly a perfect execution of a field survey. Maybe it was too perfect, because we realized by the middle of the second survey weekend in November that there were many more artifacts than we had previously estimated. By end of the November 2002 survey we had collected about four thousand artifacts, and we had surveyed only about two-thirds of the town site.

The large number of artifacts we discovered meant that we were unable to complete the survey in November 2002; we had to schedule another Pike County visit to finish this preliminary work. However, winter was upon us and it could now snow at any time. Snow not only means uncomfortable and even unsafe conditions for surveying, but also difficulties in visually locating artifacts. To complete the next survey we needed to find a time after the winter broke but before the farmers planted their crops. Planting in the area usually happened during the first week of April, depending on weather, moisture, and type of crop. So I pulled out the *Farmers' Almanac* and picked a weekend in March that it predicted to be dry with above normal temperatures. I phoned Phil Bradshaw and asked him if he put much faith in the *Almanac*. He told me that his father had often used it, but for the most part farmers today see it as entertainment and depend on the Weather Channel and TV forecasts instead. I tried to get some sense from him about how much I could rely on its predictions. He hedged around a bit and seemed noncommittal. I remembered that several years ago the *Almanac* had predicted nine of ten snowstorms in my area—to the day. I thought that was a good batting average, so at that point I said to myself, What the heck! It was the only tool we had for long-term planning. Joy, Tom, and I had to buy plane tickets in advance, Terry and Lynn had to coordinate volunteers, and the New Philadelphia Association coordinated lunchtime meals. So if it didn't work out, I could always blame the *Almanac.*

To begin our work in 2003 I planned a mid-March survey trip to New Philadelphia. When I told Joy and Tom they expressed some reservations since the area would not quite be out of snow season. If snow covered the fields we would lose surface visibility, squandering a plane ticket to central Illinois, and Terry and Lynn's organization of volunteers would be wasted. Maybe we got lucky, or maybe the *Farmers' Almanac* is accurate in predicting the weather. As forecasted by the *Almanac,* the temperatures were above normal, and we successfully completed our work with little time to spare.

By the end of the survey the archaeology team had identified, flagged, and collected 7,073 artifacts. This figure includes about six thousand historic artifacts (including forty-three faunal items) and slightly more than one thousand prehistoric artifacts. Over the course of the next six months volunteer labor at the Illinois State Museum worked with Terry Martin to clean and prepare the artifacts for the next step. By the end of the summer all of the artifacts were carefully processed, and we were ready to contract Tom Gwaltney to catalogue and enter the data into a database.

The crew carefully identified the type of materials of each artifact (ceramic, glass, metal), as well as its function (plate, window, nail). Next the artifacts received a functional category designation (architectural, domestic, kitchen, personal). For instance, artifacts in the architectural category included nails, brick, mortar, roofing slate, structural spikes, window glass, and door and window hinges. Kitchen artifacts included objects related to storage, serving, and food preparation, such as glass and ceramic vessels and serving and eating utensils. Personal artifacts included clothing-related items such as buttons and buckles, coins, and sewing-related items. Domestic artifacts included housewares and containers that did not fit into the kitchen or architectural categories (Gwaltney 2004). With the artifacts coded with these labels on a database, Tom then downloaded this information into GIS software and the spatial data were co-registered with the site's aerial photograph and the historic town plat.

New Philadelphia Historic Material Distribution

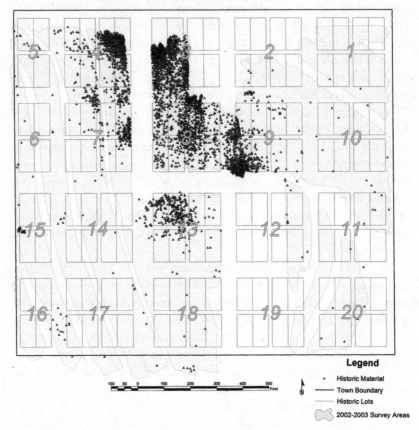

FIGURE 8. Distribution of historic artifacts found during the pedestrian survey at New Philadelphia. Source: Gwaltney 2004.

Important spatial, temporal, and functional patterns emerged. Artifacts clustered around Broad Way and Main Streets, the major streets in town. The presence of both domestic and architectural artifacts indicated that these places served as domestic sites. Few work-related materials, such as blacksmithing tools, were present in the assemblage (Gwaltney 2004; Figures 8 and 9).

Based on the information entered into the catalogue system, the manufacturing dates are known for 35 percent of the artifacts. The average date for blocks and lots are calculated in Table 3.1. All of the blocks date close to 1860, about when the town's population peaked.

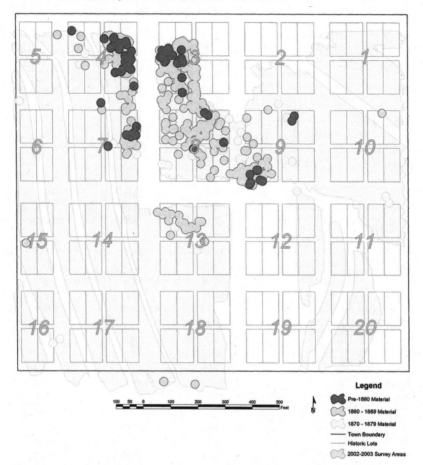

New Philadelphia Dateable Ceramic "Time View"

FIGURE 9. Time sequence and distribution of all datable artifacts found during the pedestrian survey at New Philadelphia. Source: Gwaltney 2004.

Blocks 3, 4, 7, and 9 have ceramics that date to the earliest part of the nineteenth century, and blocks 8 and 9 have the earliest average date, closer to the middle of the century. Block 13 has one of the latest dates (1864). This information is reassuring since we know from the historical records that Squire and Louisa McWorter settled on block 13 after 1854 and that this area was occupied until 1937.

The archaeology work—from the walkover survey to the computer-generated spatial data—also produced impressive results. Our survey

TABLE 3.1   MEAN DATE ESTIMATES FOR BLOCKS AND LOTS BASED ON MEAN
CERAMIC DATES OF MATERIALS RECOVERED DURING THE PEDESTRIAN SURVEY

Block: Lot	Dateable Artifact Count	Mean Date	Earliest Mean Ceramic Date	Latest Mean Ceramic Date
3:3	31	1864	1835	1870
3:4	25	1850	1805	1870
3:5	31	1865	1845	1878
3:6	26	1861	1804	1874
3:7	3	1864	1863	1865
3: Alleys	60	1862	1805	1873
Block 3	**176**	**1861**		
4:1	26	1859	1804	1870
4:2	43	1860	1808	1878
4:3	1	1870	1870	1870
4:4	4	1854	1810	1878
4:5	1	1878	1878	1878
4:6	1	1860	1860	1860
4:7	4	1862	1850	1870
4:8	23	1844	1800	1878
4: Alleys	17	1855	1804	1878
Block 4	**120**	**1856**		
7:1	23	1854	1805	1873
7:8	5	1868	1863	1878
7: Alleys	8	1859	1805	1878
Block 7	**36**	**1857**		
8:1	7	1860	1835	1870
8:2	22	1863	1845	1873
8:3	7	1864	1863	1870
8:4	11	1865	1860	1878
8:5	2	1870	1870	1870
8:6	2	1868	1863	1873
8:7	6	1865	1863	1870
8:8	4	1864	1860	1870
8: Alleys	14	1864	1863	1873
Block 8	**75**	**1865**		
9:2	3	1844	1805	1878
9:4	2	1863	1863	1863
9:5	30	1859	1805	1878
9:6	6	1853	1805	1863
9:7	1	1870	1870	1870
9: Alleys	1	1863	1863	1863
Block 9	**42**	**1858**		

TABLE 3.1   *(continued)*

Block: Lot	Dateable Artifact Count	Mean Date	Earliest Mean Ceramic Date	Latest Mean Ceramic Date
13:2	2	1862	1860	1863
13:3	12	1864	1863	1873
13:4	7	1864	1860	1870
13:7	2	1871	1863	1878
13: Alleys	1	1866	1866	1866
Block 13	**23**	**1864**		

SOURCE: Gwaltney 2004:22–23.

work indicated that there was a high probability of locating the past, domestic occupations of the town. With these reassuring results, we had enough enthusiasm to begin writing proposals to build a long-term research project that included universities, the Illinois State Museum, the NPA, and other local and descendant stakeholders.

CHAPTER 4

From Grass Roots to a National Movement

By the time we completed the walkover survey we realized we were at the beginning of something big. Artifacts found in discrete locations at the former town site were a good indication that archaeological remains could be found under the plow zone. The site was significant to the local community and descendants, and now it was potentially significant because of its archaeological value. At this point it was important to figure out a way to secure funding to do additional archaeology and research on the town.

CONGRESS TO ST. MARY'S CITY

Since the incorporation of the New Philadelphia Association in 1996 the organization had tried to increase awareness of the place and raise a significant amount of money to save New Philadelphia from future development. However, by 2003 the NPA had accumulated only a small amount of cash, enough to pay for incidentals but not enough to buy land. Phil Bradshaw remained adamant that he did not want to go to the local, state, or federal government for grants or for any other form of assistance. He believed that the government should not intervene in community affairs and that private citizens should raise the money to preserve the place. But this small nonprofit group made up of about a dozen people was running out of options. Approaching private foundations for support just led to more disappointment. The NPA believed that personal contacts would help them raise money, but they often reached dead ends.

It became apparent that the NPA needed to find other solutions to help with their fund-raising efforts. Despite the NPA's stance against receiving government funds, I received a call from Vibert White in the summer of 2003, while I was back at the University of Maryland. He explained that we needed to find a way to help the NPA and that creating a coalition of Republicans and Democrats, both conservatives and liberals, would make any legislation for helping the project much stronger. He was in contact with Senator Peter Fitzgerald's office and had made an appointment to see Congressman Jesse Jackson Jr., both from Illinois. Vibert said that he was going to Washington to meet them and he insisted that I come with him.

What a strange combination, I thought. Fitzgerald is a conservative Republican who served in the Senate from 1999 to 2005 after defeating Carol Moseley Braun, who was dogged by corruption charges. Throughout his career he battled with the state Republican Party and filibustered a funding bill that would have benefited the building of the Lincoln Presidential Library and Museum in Springfield because the bill lacked competitive bid wording. With little party support Fitzgerald declined to run in 2005, and Democrat Barack Obama easily won the election. On the other end of the political spectrum, Jackson is a liberal Democrat who served as a field director for the Rainbow/PUSH (People United to Serve Humanity) Coalition prior to being elected to office. Vibert also tried to make an appointment with Ray LaHood, the district's congressman, who is well respected as a moderate Republican; however, the congressman's schedule was full. LaHood was elected in 1994 and was part of the "Republican Revolution," although he was one of three Republicans who did not sign on to Newt Gingrich's "Contract with America." Local fund-raising had gotten nowhere in seven years, and Vibert saw this initiative as a way of forcing the community to look at other funding options.

I met Vibert at National Airport in Washington and brought him to my house, where we had dinner and talked politics through the evening. In 2003 Senator Fitzgerald nominated him and Vice President Richard Cheney appointed him to serve on the White House Commission on African American Leadership. He received national attention when he published *Inside the Nation of Islam: A Historical and Personal Testimony by a Black Muslim* (White 2001). In his book White suggests that Farrakhan's Nation is a cult that utilizes black nationalistic and religious dogma that exploits poor and working-class black Americans for the leaders' economic and political gain. He has since been contacted by the national media to comment on cases related to the Nation of Islam and was interviewed by Fox TV's Bill O'Reilly.

The following day Vibert and I went to Capitol Hill. Previously I had spoken to a lobbyist who gave me a few pointers. She predicted we would see a congressional aide and that we would have no more that fifteen minutes of his or her time. We should condense our material to one or two pages in outline form, highlighting the important points. Anything more would be overwhelming, and busy congressional schedules would relegate materials to a pile in the corner of the office. Our visit to Capitol Hill foreshadowed the type of political support we would have for the project over the next few years.

We followed one of Jackson's aides to his office, packed to the ceiling with letters, files, and boxes and no place to sit. Those piles of papers were probably all of the unread supporting materials that I was warned about. We stood around a large round table in the reception area, next to the front door of the office and in close proximity the secretary. The congressman remained in his office with the door open, talking to staff members and making telephone calls. We had fifteen minutes to inform the aide about our project, and then we were politely dismissed. We had no idea if our two-page petition for support would reach Jackson's desk.

We then ventured to Fitzgerald's office, where we waited for about half an hour. The senator was held up in a vote on the floor, and we never got to speak with him. Instead one of his aides met with us, this time in a well-furnished office without clutter. Once again we had no guarantee that the senator would get our information. Disappointed that we did not have a one-on-one with a congressman or senator from Illinois, we left the building and began our hike to the Metro station.

Back at my house we deconstructed the day and figured out what to do next. I thought it was important to reconfirm that it was not good preservation practice to rebuild, especially in a place like New Philadelphia, where no structures and no photographs exist of the original town. For the next two days we visited several places where archaeology played a role in interpreting the landscape. At Monocacy National Battlefield, about forty-five miles north of Washington, Joy Beasley and Tom Gwaltney, now employed by the National Park Service, showed us several archaeological excavations with exposed features that included foundations and the top of a stone-lined privy. They demonstrated the utility of using a Geographic Information System to organize data and show patterns of artifact distributions. We then drove to Harpers Ferry National Historical Park and saw outlined house foundations and the remains of ruined walls that gave visitors a sense of what had once stood on the landscape.

The following day we drove to southern Maryland. First we met Kirsti Uunila at Jefferson Patterson Park and Museum. She brought us to Sukeek's Cabin, a site once occupied by an African American family. Kirsti demonstrated the importance of telling the African American stories in a part of Maryland where this group's heritage is slowly disappearing from the landscape. A sign next to a path described the history of the site and the importance of African American history in the region. The path led us to the archaeology site, where rubble from the cabin's remains tells visitors of a past occupation. Next we visited St. Mary's City, where Silas Hurry showed us some of the new interpretive techniques used at the place. St. Mary's City is the former seventeenth-century capital of Maryland; nothing of the original settlement remains above ground. Ghost structures, or timber frames, are placed over sites where buildings once stood. They provide the visitor with a sense of the height, bulk, and spatial layout of a settlement. The ghost structures do not try to interpret the architectural details of a building, since they will never be known. However, they do give a sense of place, providing an estimation of density and the height and bulk of buildings.

St. Mary's City Commission is also intensively involved in rebuilding, even though they do not have much site-specific evidence for how the town might have appeared in the seventeenth century beyond deed records and buried archaeological features. The characteristics of individual buildings are based on similar period buildings found elsewhere. The Commission had moved a nineteenth-century building off the site because it did not fit into the interpretive time framework of the place.

At the end of Vibert's three-day visit he appeared willing to accept the concept that reconstruction of New Philadelphia could not accurately display the long-term history of the place and that there were other ways to interpret New Philadelphia to the public. In July 2003 Vibert moved to the University of Central Florida as the director of the Public History Program and associate professor in the Department of History.

I began working with Terry Martin on proposals to help fund an archaeology project at New Philadelphia. At this point we thought it was important to recruit other professionals to help with the research program. Christopher Fennell joined the project. He was teaching at the University of Texas at Austin. Well-known for his work in African

American archaeology and issues related to the African diaspora, he is also editor of the *African Diaspora Archaeology Newsletter*. He played a pivotal role in getting the archaeology project off the ground.

BASING THE RESEARCH DESIGN IN LOCAL HISTORY

As we developed our research design a strong starting point focused on talking to community members and understanding the way they remember New Philadelphia. The place and its significance was, for the most part, an element of the local community's memory. The 1872 *Atlas Map of Pike County* highlights Solomon's McWorter's achievements, after mentioning his parents, Frank and Lucy. In an 1876 centennial address at the county seat in Pittsfield, William Grimshaw provided an overview of the history of Pike County and mentioned Frank McWorter and the founding of New Philadelphia (Grimshaw 1876:31). However, some early histories of Pike County's communities written at the turn of the century do not mention New Philadelphia, perhaps because the town had withered to about six dwellings by then. For instance, William Maissie's county history, published in 1906, has a section titled "The First White Men in Pike County." Frank McWorter is not mentioned as one of the area's first settlers, nor are any of the white residents of New Philadelphia (Maissie 1906:52). The title Maissie uses is particularly exclusionary and would not, by definition, consider the African American residents of New Philadelphia. In a speech delivered at the Old Settlers' Meeting in 1907, Judge Harry Higbee recollected the early settlement and development of Pike County. He mentioned some of the early settlers and visitors, including Abraham Lincoln and Stephen Douglas, but he did not mention Frank McWorter or New Philadelphia (Higbee 1907:7). The Jim Crow era encouraged a type of amnesia with regard to the accomplishments of the McWorters, their neighbors, and the development of a multiracial town.

The story of New Philadelphia was never extinguished from the memory of the local community, however. In the mid-1930s, with only about two households remaining in town, Jess Thompson (1967:152) wrote, "Some of the descendants still live in Hadley Township, in the vicinity of the vanished town of Philadelphia, founded by their noted forebear." Although New Philadelphia was largely abandoned during the Depression, the town's one-room schoolhouse continued to operate into the late 1940s. Both white and black students attended classes, and the memory of the place by older members of the community had not faded. A historic marker stood on the town site from the 1950s. In the 1960s Grace Matteson began to gather stories of the place. She described a multi-racial town and noted that many of the families "were a mixed race: some of them were part French, some part Indian, some Irish, and many of them part Caucasian. It will be recalled that Free Frank himself was described as 'a yellow man'" (Matteson 1964:20–21). Matteson's construction of identity divides the town's population into ethnic groups (Irish and French) and racial categories (Indian, Caucasian, and a mix of Euro and African American, which she calls "yellow man"). While this may have been a unique feature for a small rural town, she also wrote that the white and the black families lived in harmony with each other in the community (21). Interpreting what harmony meant in the antebellum and postbellum eras in west-central Illinois became a point of contention later on in the project.

Less than two decades later Helen McWorter Simpson (1981), the great-granddaughter of Frank McWorter, wrote about her family members and also described life in New Philadelphia. She wrote about going back to the family home outside of New Philadelphia in the early twentieth century. She described the farm and the house that her grandfather, Solomon McWorter, built. It stood as a two-story wood building with a stone-lined cellar across the road from New Philadelphia and on the south side of his farm. It replaced the family home originally constructed by his father, Frank (40). Juliet Walker (1983a), a fifth-generation descendant of Frank McWorter and professor of history at the University of Texas–Austin, wrote a compelling biography of Frank McWorter, documenting his early days of enslavement in the Carolinas and Kentucky and his founding of the town of New Philadelphia. In 1988 Walker successfully placed McWorter's gravesite on the National Register of Historic Places, one of only three gravesites in Illinois placed on the Register, the other two belonging to Abraham Lincoln and Stephen Douglas. Two years later she completed a 370-mile walk from Kentucky to Pike County to highlight Frank McWorter's original trek in 1830–31. In an interview Walker said, "I did this as a personal tribute to Free Frank, but also to demonstrate the economic enslavement of black Americans. Black entrepreneurs were there [on the landscape], but like so many others, Free Frank's history has been preserved only by his family and by local county historians" (Coulson 1990).

In 1996 Pike County citizens incorporated the New Philadelphia Association, a nonprofit group, for the preservation of the New Philadelphia community. The by-laws state, "The purpose of the corporation is

FIGURE 10. Image of New Philadelphia before field season, with cabin and sheds. Photograph by Paul A. Shackel.

the commemoration, preservation, exposition, research, and teaching of Pike County, Illinois, history in general and specifically that of the settlement of New Philadelphia, platted in 1836, and that of its creator, Free Frank McWhorter *[sic]*, a former slave."

During the summer of 2002 I conducted background research at a variety of state and local repositories and libraries: the Illinois Historical Society, the Illinois State Library, the Pike County Court House, the Pike County Historical Society, the City of Barry Library, the Barry Historical Society, the Hull Historical Society, the Western Illinois University Library, and the Library of Congress. This initiative helped to develop a social history of the entire town, from 1836 through the 1940s. A collection of oral histories (performed by Carrie Christman) of the local and descendant community members furnished additional insight into the town's early twentieth-century composition and sheds light on issues of race relations in the community. Deed research (performed by Robin Whitt), state and federal census records (by Charlotte King), and township tax records (by Claire Fuller Martin) have been compiled and are listed on our web pages (www.heritage.umd.edu; follow the links to New Philadelphia). The community became involved in understanding some of the conclusions we were about to develop about the growth, development, and eventual demise of the town (Figure 10).

ARCHAEOLOGICAL RESEARCH QUESTIONS

While the historical record can focus on an individual, the questions archaeology can address are usually much broader, and they tend to be more general in nature. Understanding the historical context is important for our development of the research questions. Our focus was not on one man or one family; instead we wanted to understand the development and eventual demise of the entire town. Our goals were (1) to understand the town's founding and development as a multiracial community; (2) to explore and contrast dietary patterns between different households of different ethnic or regional backgrounds; (3) to understand the townscape and town lot uses of different households; and (4) to elucidate the different consumer choices residents made on the frontier and understand how household choices changed with the increased connection to distant markets and changing perceptions of racism.

Some of the most important stories of New Philadelphia are about the quest for freedom, life on the frontier, confronting racism, and the struggle of a small multiracial rural town to survive for a while in Jim Crow conditions. The residents of New Philadelphia were from diverse backgrounds. The census enumerators noted that 65 to 70 percent of the entire population was white, and 25 to 35 percent was black or mulatto. Most of the early settlers came from the upper South, and by the middle of the nineteenth century the majority of the residents migrated from the east coast and the Midwest.

Ethnicity can be tentatively identified through historical records, and we believed at the beginning of the project that we should center our archaeological explorations on group boundaries. However, it is clear that ethnic boundaries are fluid, and perhaps archaeology can illuminate what forces have transformed these boundaries over time (McGuire 1982:161; Rodman 1992). In a place like New Philadelphia, which developed as a multiracial town, defining these boundaries becomes increasingly difficult because in small communities neighbors tended to support and trade with each other. It was probable that some form of local hierarchy existed that was based in part on racial categories, class, and gender.

Placing our archaeological work in the context of the changing meaning of race, class, and gender was essential to knowing how groups in this community became identified and how racial conflicts have shaped American society (Omi and Winant 1994).

Many studies in African American archaeology and material culture have dealt with the pre-emancipation era (Epperson 1999; Ferguson 1992; Kelso 1986; Upton 1988; Vlach 1993). Recently there has been a new emphasis on archaeological explorations that focus on social uplift and achievement, and they are becoming more prominent in our national public memory. These stories include the archaeology of the Underground Railroad (Frost 2007; Levine, Britt, and Delle 2005) as well as surviving and prospering in a racialized and segregated society (Leone, LaRoche, and Babiarz 2005; Mullins 2004). These types of stories, as opposed to histories of bondage and enslavement, appear to have greater public support from the descendant communities.

New Philadelphia allows archaeologists the opportunity to examine the development of this community on the western frontier during the pre- and postemancipation eras. I remembered an important book that I read in graduate school, and I thought many of the observations about behavior and material culture on the frontier made by Mary Douglas and Baron Isherwood (1979) several decades ago could also apply to New Philadelphia. They note that on a periphery, such as a frontier, differences and deviations from the norm are acceptable. However, once those frontier situations become part of the core or semiperipheral area, material culture and behavior often become standardized. Loren's (2001) study of dress styles and Shackel's (1993) work on dining and etiquette on the colonial frontier echo these observations. The same may be true for the frontier situation of New Philadelphia. The town developed as a multiracial town during the antebellum era, a situation that was not the norm in the core area of the eastern states. But when the Illinois frontier closed, racism set limits to the town's growth. Racism influenced the social and economic interactions between residents within the community as well as between residents and the county and state at large.

Understanding the role of consumerism and consumer choices is a key issue for this study. Several scholars have examined how ideals of consumerism filtered into rural and frontier communities (Purser 1992; Schlereth 1989). Consumption practices varied across regional boundaries as well as ethnic, class, and gendered groups. Mullins (1999) shows how an urban postbellum African American community chose to participate in consumer society as a way to avoid local racism and confront class inequalities. An analysis of rural consumption in New Philadelphia can reveal the complexities of how mass-produced and mass-advertised products infiltrated the rural community. It may show us how consumption patterns changed as the concept of racism changed.

I wrote the bulk of the research design for the grant proposal and Terry Martin and Chris Fennell added sections and gathered résumés from professionals and faculty members who would teach in the program. In August 2003 we submitted two proposals through the University of Maryland, each highlighting questions associated with doing archaeology at a multiracial site. The first was submitted to the National Endowment for the Humanities Collaborative Research Program. The proposal emphasized these questions as well as the importance of the joint effort between universities, the Illinois State Museum, and the New Philadelphia Association. The proposal received several good reviews, but in the end the agency did not fund it. We were all disappointed because we thought we had a project that could not miss because of its national significance. Perhaps it did not meet the rigor the NEH panel was looking for, or perhaps it was difficult during a conservative administration to support ethnic histories that emphasize race in the United States.

During the recent Bush administration there was a growing emphasis on funding traditional celebratory histories through such programs as "We the People." Some scholars remind us that during the Reagan and George H. W. Bush administrations Lynne Cheney, chair of the National Endowment for the Humanities, argued in her report to Congress that scholars were occupying themselves with issues related to gender, race, and class. She discouraged funding projects that encouraged a pluralistic view of the past and sharply curtailed any projects dealing with women, labor, or racial groups or any project that might conflict with the national collective memory. Cheney packed the NEH Advisory Council with critics of multiculturalism, and they rejected proposals that questioned consensus history (Nash, Crabtree, and Dunne 1997:103).

During the George W. Bush administration Cheney also had a powerful role in the NEH and helped to develop the "We the People" initiative. In a CNN interview in 2003 she suggested that the NEH could be used to help foster an "American history that's taught in as positive and upbeat a way as our national story deserves" (M. Jacoby 2004). On the surface the NEH's "We the People" initiative is about supporting the teaching of history in schools, but Eric Foner, a history professor at Columbia University and longtime Cheney critic, has some reservations. "I strongly support their effort to promote the better teaching of history at the high school level. But the danger is that this 'We the People' thing could become a merely celebratory history," he said. "We don't need to teach history that smashes America. But if you put forward a version of American history that it began perfect and has been getting better ever since, you're not equipping students to think critically." Cheney, Foner added, "always saw history in terms of generating a kind of patriotism for the country" (quoted in M. Jacoby 2004). I bring this point up to give us something to reflect upon when we think about the connections between politics and the research supported by the federal government. New Philadelphia is about race and ethnic history, and it runs counter to consensus history.

We submitted a second proposal to the National Science Foundation—Research Experiences for Undergraduates Program (NSF-REU). Whereas our NEH proposal had emphasized minority history, the NSF proposal emphasized undergraduate education for minority students. The REU Program provides support for the education of undergraduates who are traditionally underrepresented in the sciences, including ethnic minorities and women. We thought it was a natural fit because one of our goals from the beginning was to get minority students involved in a project about minority history.

It's difficult for me to pinpoint the moment I became aware of minorities and issues of race, but growing up in the Bronx I know it came at a relatively early age. My neighborhood in Pelham Bay contained people who were mostly of Italian decent. In 1957, several years before I was born, my father, along with his friends Jack Gootzeit and Walter Oldham, founded the Institute of Applied Human Dynamics, Inc. The organization now serves the Bronx and Westchester County with the goal of enhancing the lives of people with developmental disabilities and dual diagnoses, their families, and those who work with them. They developed this program in addition to their nine-to-five jobs, working nights and weekends. My parents socialized with the cofounders and their families, and my father is still in touch with Mr. Oldham, although they live about a thousand miles apart. The Oldhams left New York to work for Tuskegee University in the early 1970s. They are African American, and my parents are of eastern and southern European descent. I learned at a very early age, during the height of the civil rights movement, that people of different backgrounds could work and socialize together. While thinking about applying for the NSF-REU grant I recalled how these gentlemen had developed a program together. Wouldn't this be a wonderful opportunity to recruit students of different backgrounds and have them work and live together for at least ten weeks during the summer? Perhaps they could take this experience back with them and help build communities that are tolerant and inclusive of different people and different views. The NSF-REU program was one such mechanism to make this happen.

Just before Christmas we received word that the NSF would fund our project for three years for a total of $226,500. Everyone involved in the project was ecstatic, but there was not much time to celebrate. We had to put together our research team, begin advertising for students, and get ready for the summer.

CONTESTING THE PROJECT

We had a project that was to take form in less than half a year and we had the support of the local community and a few descendants who were in the region. Chris Fennell began making contacts with several people who would be important to the success of the project. He sent an email to Sundiata Cha-Jua, one of Walker's former graduate students who is now teaching at the University of Illinois in the African American Studies and Research Program. Cha-Jua (2000) is the author of *America's First Black Town: Brooklyn, Illinois, 1830–1915*. Chris also contacted a known descendant, Abdul Alkalimat (Gerald McWorter), a great-great-grandson of Frank McWorter. At the time he was a professor of sociology and director of the Africana Studies Program at the University of Toledo. He is now at the University of Illinois, Urbana-Champaign. When asked about participating in the project, Gerald sent a brief response to Fennell to the effect that he was interested in the town and wanted to study its political economy some time in the future. Chris also sent an email to Juliet Walker, informing her about the grant and saying that he wanted to discuss her involvement in the project:

> I'd love to stop by your office sometime in the coming week to discuss this project and start working with you to realize the most we can from these opportunities and new resources. This new source of funding and academic research should contribute substantially to achieving your goals of attaining the greatest recognition of the national heritage of Free Frank and New Philadelphia. (January 19, 2004)

Walker responded positively and noted that she would be happy to meet and hear more about the project (email, Juliet Walker to Christopher Fennell, January 19, 2004). A meeting would be very convenient since, at the time, both Fennell and Walker were teaching at the University of Texas.

Chris developed several ideas to engage Walker for participation in both long-term and short-term scenarios; he also wanted to extend these opportunities to Gerald McWorter and Sundiata Cha-Jua. These scenarios were meant to be a starting point to include more scholars and more descendants.

Fennell and Walker met on January 27 in her office for over two hours; his attempt to convey the need for collaboration was not well received. Walker later wrote in an email that she was unhappy that we did not invite her to be a principal investigator in the archaeology project since she considered herself a specialist in the history of Free Frank and New Philadelphia. She felt that she had not been given the proper respect and attention during the proposal's development and made it clear that she was not willing to collaborate with the archaeology project in any way (email, Juliet Walker to Christopher Fennell, January 28, 2004).

We were not prepared for this negative reaction toward our proposal and felt a bit overwhelmed with our dilemma. We had strong support from the local community and many descendants of the town, especially those who lived in the local area. Perhaps we were naïve to count on one hundred percent support from descendents. We thought that people would appreciate our attempt to help bring the place to national attention. We had developed a proposal to the NSF based on our support from the local and descendant communities. In hindsight we should have made a broader attempt to reach more descendants before we planned the project. We consulted with the New Philadelphia Association about this situation, and they urged us to carry on our cooperative work. We continued our planning for the summer project.

May 2004 came and we were all very anxious to participate in the archaeology project. Although the response from Juliet Walker put a damper on the project and the situation was far from perfect, we continued our efforts because of the persistent energy and enthusiasm demonstrated by the many other descendants and the local community. We thought it was important to help the community to work toward making all of New Philadelphia and its many histories part of the national public memory.

CHAPTER 5

The First Field Season

Each summer we recruited nine students from diverse backgrounds from around the country to work with us on the archaeology research project. The many interested members of the local community greeted us warmly. In 2004 and 2006 we had a staff of about fifteen people, including undergraduate and graduate students. In 2005 the number doubled as a University of Illinois field school joined the project for six weeks.

A COMMUNITY EFFORT

There was an outpouring of support from the community. Everyone was excited that we would work toward developing a more in-depth understanding of the growth, development, and eventual demise of New Philadelphia. The New Philadelphia Association and Hannibal LaGrange College provided us with a van to transport students to the archaeology site from the Kinderhook Lodge, where we resided during our five-week fieldwork in the summers of 2004 through 2006. Pat Likes and Carolyn Dean worked with local restaurants and a grocery store to provide us lunch each day, and someone from the New Philadelphia Association was always at the site to greet visitors. Natalie Armistead, one of the landowners, worked with the students, both in the field and in the on-site lab with Charlotte King.

Terry Martin's position as curator at the Illinois State Museum places him at the center of Illinois archaeology. He has good connections with many of the midwestern archaeologists and is respected for his expertise in faunal analysis. He is also well liked by the professional community for his friendly demeanor, cooperative attitude, and his willingness to be a team player. Archaeologists sometimes quarrel over turf issues or make public their disagreements with competing interpretations; despite being known for its midwestern hospitality, Illinois archaeology is no different. However, the professional community greeted us warmly, especially when they stopped by to visit the project.

Before we started the field project Terry enticed Michael Hargrave of the U.S. Army Engineer Research and Development Center, Construction Engineering Research Laboratory to test out his geophysical equipment on a historic site. Most of Hargrave's work is conducted at military installations, looking for buried munitions. He also has an impressive résumé working on prehistoric sites throughout the country. Working at our site appealed to him because it would broaden his knowledge of the recent past. He greeted Terry's invitation with enthusiasm.

Geophysical surveys help to create maps of subsurface archaeological features that are nonportable, such as foundations, privies, wells, and other disturbances in the soil. It is a noninvasive and nondestructive technique. Geophysical instruments can detect buried features when their electrical or magnetic properties contrast measurably with their surroundings. Readings taken in a systematic fashion become a data set that can create maps that show electrical or magnetic resistance (Hargrave 2006a).

Hargrave used two instruments for the survey work. First, the electrical resistance work performed at the site was conducted with four probes mounted on a rigid frame and inserted into the ground. Archaeological features show up in readings where there is higher or lower resistivity than their surroundings. A stone foundation might impede the flow of electricity, whereas the moisture in organic deposits, such as privy fill, might conduct electricity more easily than surrounding soils. Second, magnetometer field gradiometry was used to measure the gradient of the magnetic field. All materials have relatively unique magnetic properties, and magnetometers react very strongly when they encounter iron, brick, and burned soil. Many types of rock are also magnetic. Sometimes it is possible to detect very subtle anomalies caused by disturbed soils or decayed organic materials (Hargrave 2006a).

Hargrave worked closely with students for three days at the beginning of each field season. He focused his efforts in areas where we had located the greatest concentration of artifacts during the pedestrian survey, the immediate eastern and western sides of Broad Street and the intersection of Main and Broad. His scientific instruments detected the presence of subsurface anomalies (irregularities in the soil that are buried beneath the surface). His work further narrowed our focus on areas where we would likely find potentially important features (Hargrave 2006a).

The geophysical survey results, historic maps, old aerial photographs, and oral histories helped us to develop an excavation strategy. After the geophysical survey our next step was to verify these anomalies and then see if archaeological remains were intact below the plow zone. Collecting artifacts from these features and then performing analyses of the materials would be the first step to help address some of our research questions. In general we had a good sense of who had owned each lot. A review of the deeds, tax records, and the federal and state census records also helped in developing context for each area we excavated. Based on the documentary evidence, archaeological survey, and geophysical survey, over the three-year grant period the archaeology team chose to work in specific areas in blocks 3, 4, 7, 8, 9, and 13 (Figure 7).

CASIAH CLARK AND WILLIAM BUTLER'S HOMESITE

During the first field season we started our excavations in the southwest corner of block 9, lot 5. A man named William Butler owned the lot from 1888 until the 1930s, and there was a good chance that we would also find earlier remains related to Casiah Clark's ownership of the property. In 2004 we met Ron Carter, a descendant of William Butler, who became an enthusiastic supporter of the project and a New Philadelphia Association board member.

Frank McWorter sold block 9, lot 5 to Kizie (also known as Kessiah, Kasiah, and Casiah) Clark in 1854. Casiah was born in Kentucky in about 1806 and was later married to John Clark, a millwright in Kentucky. Her husband died before they arrived in Illinois, but his father, John Sr., lived in her household until the 1850s. Census enumerators described Casiah as mulatto with seven children. She acquired property in Pike County for farming in 1845, about 1.5 miles east of New Philadelphia. Although she does not show up in the 1855 state census records, she is noted in the 1850 federal census. Her daughter Louisa (listed as Eliza in the 1888 *Portrait and Biographical Album of Sedgwick County, Kansas*) married

Squire McWorter; they built a house and outbuildings on block 13, lots 3 and 4. For three decades Casiah lived with Louisa, at least part of the time, until Casiah's death in 1888. The 1860 federal census shows Louisa and Casiah living together in Quincy, Illinois, a major abolitionist town on the Mississippi River, which bordered the slave state of Missouri. The *Garden Plain, Kansas* (1984) centennial publication also claims that Simeon Clark, Casiah's son, participated in the Underground Railroad. Simeon also lived in Quincy in 1860, and perhaps they worked together in the abolitionist movement.

Casiah purchased the town lot in 1854 for $5; it had $25 in improvements in 1867, and in 1868 the improvements decreased to $3. In 1871 the improvements were again assessed at $25. This information suggests that a small structure existed on the property, perhaps a cabin. Casiah's son Thomas, listed as eleven years old in the 1850 federal census, inherited the lot after his mother's death. He sold it to William Butler in 1888, when it included a small structure or some other type of improvement.

Matteson (1964: postscript) recalls that William Butler came from Louisville, Kentucky, and that he "had served as an orderly for a Rebel general in the Civil War." After emancipation he worked in Marion County, Missouri, for several years, then he "bought himself a mule and headed for Illinois." According to oral history, he happened to stop at the McWorter place on a rainy night, and they invited him to stay overnight. Solomon McWorter gave Butler a job, and he remained in the New Philadelphia area. After Solomon died in 1879 Butler helped run the McWorter farm (postscript).

In 1880 William Butler married Catherine Cartwright, a white woman. Matteson writes, "Her father brought her from Missouri to Illinois. She had come to Philadelphia to stay with a white family by the name of Wagoner" (1964: postscript). The 1880 federal census indicates that William, twenty-seven years old, and Catherine, twenty-two, had a one-year-old daughter named Mary. The census shows that both William and Catherine came from Missouri and that Mary was born in Illinois. They had a total of three children, and Irene Butler Brown, daughter of William and Catherine, is Ron Carter's relative. Ron helped to settle Irene's estate after her death, and working through her records helped to stimulate his interest in the New Philadelphia project.

Catherine had died by 1900, when the federal census lists William Butler as sixty years old and living with his daughter Dora (twenty-five years old) and his son Golden (twenty-two). They were all categorized as black. It is interesting to note that the 1900 U.S. Federal Census dropped the category "mulatto," classifying people as either black or white. The elimination of the mulatto category is a reflection of the heightening of Jim Crow attitudes. Any form of interracial mixing would have categorized a person as black.

Many of the local residents remember Butler because he was one of the last landowners in New Philadelphia. One local resident recalls, "Several of the fellas, the Negro men, helped my dad. They worked for him, but I remember there was one man they called Butler, I think that was his last name. He was really strong. They told [a story] about a wagon wheel—something was wrong with it. They had to replace it or repair it and this Negro [Butler] held the wagon up all by himself, while they fixed the wheel. Then, he took a sack of wheat in his teeth and flipped it over in the back of the wagon. He was a strong, strong man" (Hughes 2004).

THE ARCHAEOLOGY OF CASIAH
CLARK'S HOUSEHOLD

The geophysical survey did not show a strong anomaly in block 9, lot 5, the place where the Clarks and Butlers lived; however, an overlay of the 1939 aerial photograph shows the remains of a building in the southwest corner of the lot. During the pedestrian survey we found a large quantity of artifacts in the area, and it is one of the few places that had datable artifacts that predated the Civil War era.

An excavation team led by William White, then a graduate student at the University of Idaho, placed three excavation units in the approximate location of the structure identified on the aerial photograph. We had a hunch that the building in the photograph might be a remnant from the nineteenth- or early twentieth-century occupation. Until we excavated we could not be sure if it was related to the Clark or the Butler occupation. Our first task was to identify the depth of the plow zone, the soil disturbed by plowing and planting. Throughout the town site it normally existed to a depth of about one foot. It is somewhat deeper in places where filling occurred. In other places, where soil has been eroded, the plow zone is shallower. We hoped to find undisturbed features underneath the plow zone, such as pit cellars, wells, privies, and foundations.

In the southwest corner of the lot we excavated large quantities of brick and plaster fragments and household debris that came from the plow zone. The bits of plaster, or what remains from the interior walls of a house, are an archaeological signature that indicates a good chance of finding the remains of a domestic structure. Under the plow zone archaeologists noticed a darker colored soil compared to the surrounding undisturbed subsoil. When completely revealed the feature measures about 5 by 5 feet. The archaeology team bisected the feature, leaving the eastern half in place. It has a concave shape and extends to a depth of about 0.5 feet below the plow zone (Figures 11 and 12).

The feature has the typical shape, depth, and form of a cellar pit found on the Illinois frontier. These usually lacked stone or wood walls and were used to keep a few items cool. Rebecca Burlend's 1830s description of her Pike County house included some detail about a cabin with a pit cellar: "It was a fair specimen of a log-house. . . . There were two rooms, both on the ground floor separated from each other with boards so badly joined, that crevices were in many places observable. The rooms were nearly square. . . . Beneath one of the rooms was a cellar, the floor and sides of which were mud and clay." She also recalled seeing in the cellar "two or three large, hewn tubs, full of lard, and a lump of tobacco" (Burlend 1936:47–48, 50).

Our strategy for the entire project was to sample all of the features at New Philadelphia, including this pit cellar, removing about half or less of the feature fill. By following this strategy we had enough information to date the feature and to make some conclusions about the lifestyle and diet of the former occupants. We left a substantial amount of the feature in place so that undisturbed archaeological remains continue to exist at the site and the archaeological record is intact and considered significant.

We were all very excited at this initial discovery for several reasons. First, we had located undisturbed archaeological materials below the plow zone. Retrieving significant information about past lifeways and keeping enough archaeological information in its original undisturbed context (in the ground) allowed us to start thinking about nominating the town to the National Register of Historic Places. Second, the recovered materials from the feature date from the 1850s–1860s and are associated with the short occupation of this lot by Casiah Clark's family. The 1875 tax records show that there are no improvements on the lot, meaning that Casiah's house was probably dismantled before that date. After the structure was dismantled, refuse from the surrounding area was deposited into the cellar pit. The artifacts in the cellar fill correspond nicely with Casiah's occupation and eventual abandonment of the site.

Charlotte King supervised the identification and cataloguing of the retrieved materials, and Christopher Valvano worked with students

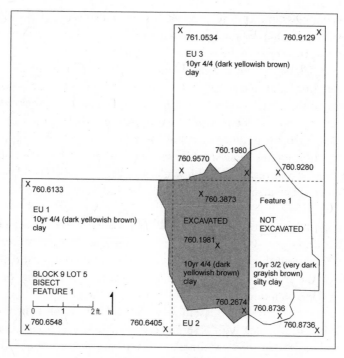

FIGURE 11. Plan view of feature 1, the cellar pit attributed to Casiah Clark and her family. Drawing by Christopher Valvano.

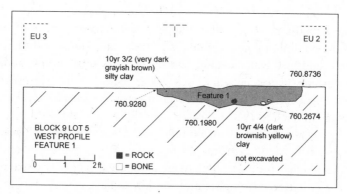

FIGURE 12. Profile of feature 1 bisected. The feature fill dates to about the 1850s. Drawing by Christopher Valvano.

identifying glass and ceramic vessels. Students also worked with Terry Martin to perform the faunal analysis, and Marge Schroeder supervised students in the floral analyses.

Casiah Clark's ceramic assemblage consists of a variety of pieces that were once plates, teacups, bowls, and storage jars. There is no sign that any of the ceramic pieces were part of matched sets, tableware, or tea sets. Interestingly there are a low proportion of both stoneware and unrefined earthenware, meaning that there are few items that represent storage and cooking vessels. Glass storage containers became popular in the late 1850s, yet we found few glass storage vessels. The glass vessels that could be identified include medicine and snuff bottles. An aquamarine glass sherd is part of a scroll flask that was made in Louisville, Kentucky, between 1840 and 1860 (Bauchat and Helton 2006; Figure 13). We know that Casiah came from Kentucky; however, since New Philadelphia and the Pike County region were well connected to trade routes by the 1830s, it is easy to imagine her trading, bartering, or purchasing these containers in New Philadelphia in the 1850s.

The faunal analysis at Casiah Clark's homesite is also intriguing. Terry Martin, working with NSF-REU student Andrea Torvinen, noted the number of identified specimens, minimum number of individuals, and biomass. The biomass is the amount of tissue and meat associated with a specific bone. For example, the biomass of a cow rib will be significantly larger than that of a fish rib. The biomass for each taxon was estimated using an allometric scaling technique developed by Reitz and Wing (1999:70–72).

The faunal assemblage from the cellar pit consists mostly of swine, chicken, small mammals (rabbits, squirrels, opossums, and rats), fish (buffalo and freshwater drum), and birds (bobwhite, turkey, and passenger pigeon) (Torvinen and Martin 2006; T. Martin and Martin 2010). Passenger pigeon is found in nineteenth-century archaeological assemblages, but their presence decreases after the middle of the century, and they are extinct in Illinois by about 1900 (Schorger 1973). This assemblage lacks any significant amount of cattle, sheep, goat, or white-tailed deer. The higher proportion of swine compared to cow is a strong example of what archaeologists and folklorists have classified as an Upland South diet. Families from the southern hill country—Kentucky, Tennessee, western Virginia, and the Carolinas—practiced small-scale subsistence based farming (Torvinen and Martin 2006; C. Martin and Martin 2010). They had diets with a high proportion of swine and chicken, along with wild game, such as white-tailed deer, rabbit, squirrel,

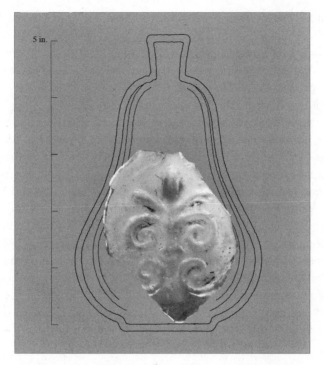

5 in.

FIGURE 13. Scroll flask manufactured in Louisville, Kentucky, from about 1840 to 1860, found in Casiah Clark's pit cellar. Photograph by Christopher Valvano.

and fish. When these families migrated many of them brought these traditions with them (Mazrim 2007:76–77; McCorvie 1987).

THE "BETSY HOUSE"

We thought it would be good to place a few excavation units in block 7, lot 2. The 1939 aerial photograph shows the remains of a house there, and the results of the walkover survey produced a large cluster of artifacts in the area. According to the township tax records, a building stood on the property by at least 1878.

Larry Burdick's manuscript and an oral history interview with Harry Johnson identified the structure as the "Betsy House." It was a small house that was abandoned by the 1930s. A local farmer stopped by the site and asked me why we were digging in the area. I told him that we were looking for a house that we identified on the 1939 aerial photograph.

He told me that we were never going to find it. He sounded definitive, so I had to ask him why. In his Pike County drawl he explained that he was a boy during the Great Depression and had aided with the removal of the house's foundation after it was destroyed. The goal was to make the land usable for agriculture. He dumped the foundation stones near the local creek, probably where they were originally retrieved.

At that point I slowly walked over to the excavation area and talked to Carrie Chistman, then a graduate student at the University of Maryland, who was leading this area excavation. She optimistically responded by saying that I shouldn't worry, they were a tough team and they were going to find something important. The next day Carrie's team uncovered foundation stones below the plow zone, about a foot below the surface. Apparently our visitor and his fellow workers had helped to remove the foundation to a depth where it would not interfere with the plow but left the deeper fieldstones. We had found the remains of a second homesite at New Philadelphia, and this one dated to the postbellum era. It seemed that some people were interested in living in the town even though the railroad had been routed around it. Subsequent excavation in 2008 uncovered more of this late nineteenth-century foundation.

UNEXPECTED EARLY SETTLEMENT IN PARK AREA

Michael Hargrave identified several geophysical anomalies in the western portion of block 8, lot 4 as a result of the electrical resistance survey. We labeled one of them anomaly A2 (A for anomaly and 2 for the second identified anomaly), and at this point we decided to see if the geophysical survey could accurately identify subsurface features in New Philadelphia. First we performed a core sample survey to ground-truth anomaly A2. We placed a grid in the area of the anomaly that consisted of three rows of nine cores. The coring device is one inch in diameter, and we probed to a depth of two feet, well below the plow zone. As we worked we detected resistance as the core encountered stone, brick, and mortar in ten of the twenty-seven cores. The resistance clustered in one area.

These findings are intriguing because Larry Burdick (1992) recalls block 8 as being unoccupied through the twentieth century; he referred to the area as "the park." The impression that many former twentieth-century residents have of the area is that block 8 was never occupied but served as the town square or commons. The impression that a town square existed from the beginning has almost become common knowledge among those who know the history of the place. A review of the earliest surviving records also confirms this impression and shows that block 8, lot 4 was not improved. The earliest known deed transaction for the spot dates to 1871, when James Vokes sold it to Solomon Mc-Worter. However, an 1867 tax assessment shows Solomon McWorter being taxed on this lot, although it had no improvements. No improvements existed on the lot through the rest of the century and into the next. The 1865 state census had Solomon McWorter with five people in his household and with livestock valued at $500; however, it is improbable that he lived on the lot. Solomon did not live in the town in 1870, but on a parcel to the north, adjacent to the town. There are eighteen transactions for block 8, lot 4 from 1871 to 1930 without any signs of major improvements on the land.

Because of the positive results of the coring and because the historical records do not indicate settlement on the lot, we thought we had a chance to discover an early and undocumented part of New Philadelphia's history. Therefore Christman and her crew opened three excavation units (EU 1, 2, and 3) in the 2004 season. They located a large concentration of brick fragments and stones that measured 0.25 to 0.5 feet in diameter. This large concentration of debris is anomaly A2 that Hargrave detected in the geophysical survey (Figure 14). Needless to say, Hargrave was ecstatic that we had so productively ground-truthed one of his identified anomalies. This buried feature contained debris and artifacts that date to about the 1850s. The western portion of feature 4 was exposed in 2004, although it was not until 2005 that they exposed the entire feature.

In 2005 the archaeology team excavated several more units and determined that the feature, which we labeled feature 4, measures about 12 feet east–west and 12.5 feet north–south. The feature soil is very dark grayish-brown silty clay and is noticeable because it is a bit darker than the surrounding lighter, undisturbed soils. The team bisected the feature and removed the eastern portion in half-foot arbitrary levels, thus keeping separate the materials found near the bottom from those found near the top (Figures 15 and 16). Generally the feature sloped down toward the middle, and its cylinder shape provided a clue that the original function of the feature was a cistern or a well.

Marjorie Schroeder at the Illinois State Museum supervised the student analysis of the macrofloral remains from this feature. Macrofloral remains are plant parts that can be seen with the naked eye and include charred or uncharred remains of seeds, charcoal, wood, and other plant parts. These remains are usually recovered by immersing soil samples into a tank of

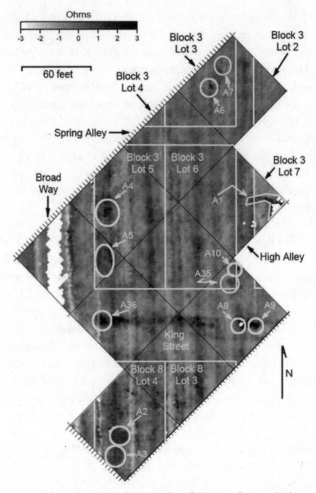

FIGURE 14. Geophysical survey identified anomaly A2, which is associated with feature 4 in block 8, lot 4. Map by Michael Hargrave. Overlay by Christopher Fennell.

water. The plant remains tend to rise to the surface while the soil sinks. Macrofloral remains can provide evidence of diet and environment.

Schroeder and the students detected few organic materials. There was also a lower than expected frequency of faunal material and domestic trash identified in the feature. Rock, mortar, and brick are located throughout the feature fill. These findings are clues that the feature was not open for a long enough period of time to accumulate much trash. After it was no longer in use, community members rapidly filled the feature.

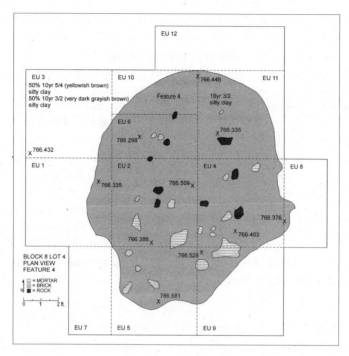

FIGURE 15. Plan view of feature 4 in block 8, lot 2. Drawing by Christopher Valvano.

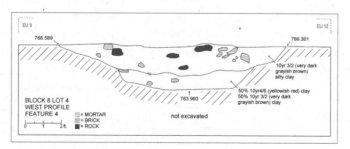

FIGURE 16. Profile of feature 4 bisected. The feature fill dates to the 1850s. Drawing by Christopher Valvano.

Even though the earliest known deeds for block 8, lot 4 date to 1871 and the tax records from 1867 show that the lot was not improved, the archaeological evidence shows that the area was probably used for domestic space decades earlier. The artifacts found in this feature date to the 1850s, and we believe that the well, dismantled and abandoned by the 1850s, is related to the early development of the town.

Although the town's descendants remembered the entire block 8 as being unoccupied and serving as a park or a town square, the archaeological survey, the electrical resistivity survey, the coring, and the excavation show that the area was occupied during the town's earliest settlement. The archaeology began to show that the landscape was much more complex than revealed in a synchronic snap shot of porous historical records, and that the built landscape was constantly changing. Therefore these findings made it much more difficult to reconstruct the town's landscape at any one time period, since, as with any town, there was always building, decay, and demolition.

CONSUMERISM IN A FRONTIER TOWN

NSF-REU students Kimberly Eppler and Emily Helton (2006) worked to analyze the ceramic and glass vessels under the supervision of Charlotte King and Christopher Valvano. The assemblage from feature 4 on block 8, lot 4 had an equal amount of refined earthenware vessels (such as dinner plates) and utilitarian wares (such as stoneware crocks). A teacup and sugar bowl from the same set have a Romantic scene that includes a tree and a building. This design was popular from about 1831 to 1851 (Samford 1997). A second teacup and a plate have a similar blue transfer printed design. Otherwise all of the plates are of different patterns.

The presence of only two potentially matched vessels suggests that maintaining a complete set of tableware was not a priority for this household. Frontier homes were less likely to have matched sets of dishes. Excavations at other early homesteads across the South show a similar pattern of mismatched plates and cups (Huddleston and Poplin 2003:6). The presence of tea ware in feature 4 indicates at least some specialization of vessel forms, but does not mean that they were used in the ways that others used them in socially competitive urban areas during the Victorian era.

There is a preponderance of stoneware storage vessels compared to yellowware and a complete lack of redware storage vessels in this assemblage. The preference for stoneware over unrefined earthenware (redware and yellowware) was not necessarily an economic choice since stoneware was more difficult to produce and commanded a higher price than red-ware or yellowware. However, stoneware vessels were more durable, and they eventually dominated the container market until glass became cheaper and more available in the third quarter of the nineteenth century (Eppler and Helton 2006).

Among several glass vessels from this feature is a small vial embossed with "KBERRY." "BLACKBERRY" is commonly found on a patent medicine bottle. The other identifiable vessel in the glass assemblage is a square aqua green inkwell with the embossed letters "J. J. BUTLER/CIN." The J. J. Butler Company was an ink manufacturing company in Cincinnati (Eppler and Helton 2006). This particular bottle was manufactured only from 1854 to 1860, thus helping to provide a date for the feature. The ink bottle is also located a few lots away from a school lot used in the antebellum era.

HINTS OF ANOTHER LATE NINETEENTH-CENTURY OCCUPATION

Block 3, lot 4 is another area where we found a large concentration of domestic artifacts in the walkover survey. In 1838, in one of the first lot sales by the town's founder, Frank McWorter sold the lot to Henry Brown. There are ten transactions involving the property throughout the following century. The Clark family owned the site until 1865, and the Cobb family made some improvements to the property before 1867, but by 1868 buildings no longer existed on the lot. The Hadsell families owned the lot and lived in New Philadelphia for most of the 1870s. William Welbourne purchased the lot in the twentieth century, although he and his family lived in New Philadelphia by at least 1880. Welbourne, his wife, Josephine, and their three children are classified as white in the 1880 federal census.

Under Terry Martin's supervision the archaeology team excavated a total of six units in this lot. Diagnostic artifacts from the plow zone include cut nails (with dates ranging from 1790 to 1880) and ceramic whitewares (1820–1900). Four of the units (EU 3, 4, 5, and 6) formed a larger block that measures 10 by 10 feet and enabled the team to fully expose feature 2, a lime slaking pit. This feature measures 2.8 by 4.4 feet; it was dug into the soil and clayey subsoil and served as a basin for hydrating quicklime, resulting in the production of calcium hydroxide, which is used in mortar, plaster, and whitewash. The edge and top of the feature is about 0.4 feet higher than the deepest part of the basin.

FIGURE 17. Excavations of the lime slaking pit in block 3, lot 4. Photograph by Paul A. Shackel.

Artifacts in close proximity to the lime pit are from the plow zone and have a mean ceramic date that ranges from 1805 through 1870. The existence of the lime pit indicates that a structure with plastered walls once stood nearby (Figure 17). Additional excavations in the area during the 2008 field season uncovered a stone feature that served as a base for a hearth. Nearby was a cellar filled with 1890s debris.

We were very pleased with the outcome of the first field season. We had worked successfully with Michael Hargrave and ground-truthed several anomalies. We located undisturbed features existing below the plow zone, some of them related to the early settlement of the town and others dating to the very late part of the century. We were thinking that these results could help us place the town site on the National Register of Historic Places. We also had a significant amount of local, regional, and national newspaper coverage, and we now had an opportunity to discuss the history of race and racism in the community.

CHAPTER 6

Race and the Illusion
of Harmony

Race and ethnic identity are charged with meaning and develop in different ways. Orser (2007:8) explains that ethnicity is created from the inside, whereas race is imposed from the outside based on perceived biophysical differences as well as cultural practices and religious beliefs and traditions. Racialization is the process of assigning people to groups based on physical or cultural characteristics, which helps create the perception of inferior or socially unequal groups. Racialization creates racially meaningful groups that previously did not exist. Those classified as "other" are seen as inferior to the group creating these classifications (Omi and Winant 1983:51; Orser 2007:9).

RACE AND THE POWER OF ILLUSION

The term *race* had no clear meaning until the eighteenth century. While the English were busy conquering the world, they developed attitudes that had not appeared before in Western history. They created a new kind of understanding and interpretation of human differences. For instance, while relegating the Irish to a subordinate group, the English developed and institutionalized the concept of *savagery,* a term that became very prominent in the early evolutionary theories of nineteenth-century thinkers. The English expressed a hatred of both Irish culture and people, a sentiment that reached its peak during the sixteenth and seventeenth centuries when the English began their settlement of North America

(Smedley 1998:694). This hatred, considered an early form of racism, provided an "other" that could be compared to the constructed identity of the "civilized" English. The concept of savagery carried with it many negative and stereotypical characteristics that contrasted with the sense the English created of their own uniqueness (Allan 1994).

Race thus emerged as a social classification by which to create "otherness" in much the same way that the concept of savagery developed. Theodore Allan (1994) and many others (e.g., Breen and Innes 1980; Handlin and Handlin 1950; W. Jordan 1978:278; Kulikoff 1986; Morgan 1975) discuss the invention of the white race, using the Chesapeake region to examine the development of racism in the New World. Racism was not codified during the first half of the seventeenth century in the Chesapeake region because the demands and rewards of the tobacco economy unleashed a sense of individualism that worked against the social cohesion necessary to forge highly structured hierarchies (Breen and Innes 1980:49).

Until the 1660s statutes applied to enslaved blacks were similar to those for white servants. Legislators applied stiff penalties to blacks and whites equally for running away, drunkenness, and carrying arms. Over time these regulations grew less stringent for white servants, but little changed for blacks (Handlin and Handlin 1950:244; Morgan 1975). Differential treatments of blacks and whites developed as early as 1662 and were codified in provincial laws. Within several years of the 1676 Bacon's Rebellion, an insurrection of small planters, indentured servants, and enslaved blacks, a Virginia law established "An Act preventing Negroe Insurrection" and stated that "negroes" and slaves could not own guns (Breen and Innes 1980:27). In 1681 a Maryland act described mixed marriages as a "disgrace not only of the English butt also of many other Christian Nations" (quoted in W. Jordan 1978:277). After 1691 marriages between enslaved people and free Africans or African Americans became illegal. Consequently by the end of the seventeenth century much New World legislation was couched in terms of race, and especially in terms of black and white.

Racialization continued through additional legislation during the eighteenth and nineteenth centuries (Shackel 2003). The new racial ideology that developed in Western Europe and the Americas structured political, social, and economic inequalities as countries from these regions conquered and exploited a large part of the world. This new racial ideology contradicted the development of Renaissance ideals that promoted freedom, democracy, equality, and human rights. Europeans naturalized their new racial attitudes by focusing on physical differences and concluded that Africans and Indians were, by the laws of nature or God, a lesser form of human beings (Smedley 1998:694). Whites relegated blacks to a low status and constantly portrayed them as "culturally backward, primitive, intellectually stunted, prone to violence, morally corrupt, undeserving of the benefits of civilization, insensitive to the finer arts, and (in the case of Africans) aesthetically ugly and animal like" (695). Race identity took priority over all other forms of identity that had once guided socialization and group interaction.

Anthropology's roots existed in the Western natural history tradition that encouraged social observers to classify and compare human populations. In the 1830s Samuel Morton became the authority on explaining racial differences with his book *Crania Americana* in 1839 (Thomas 2000:38–42). Later, E. B. Tylor and Lewis Henry Morgan became proponents of social Darwinian theory, which aided in creating and reinforcing human racial typologies. Their work added a veneer of scientific rationality to bigoted, socially constructed conceptions of race.

While the outcome of the American Civil War reunited the United States and slavery was legally dissolved, racial ideologies remained and the barriers that prevented African Americans from integrating into American society still existed. After the war, a time when the United States was transforming itself into a major industrial power, a labor shortage existed in the North. African Americans had a unique opportunity to be integrated into the industrial mainstream. However, white Americans continued to paint black Americans as inferior, and instead relied on white European immigrants to fuel late nineteenth-century industry. Whites prohibited blacks from learning new skills that would allow them to compete for industrial jobs. With the exclusion of African Americans from northern industries and southern agriculturalists dependent upon African American labor to produce cotton, African Americans returned to the fields as tenant farmers and sharecroppers (Horton 2000). As the work of Tylor (1874) and Morgan (1877) demonstrates, nineteenth-century science and social science also helped to reinforce these racial views.

While many anthropologists backed these racial typologies, some scholars worked to dismantle these racial views. In 1897 the anthropologist Franz Boas questioned the premise behind unilinear evolution and challenged the notions that race was biologically fixed and permanent and that people could be ranked in proximity to apes (Mukhopadhyay and Moses 1997:518). Some anthropologists see Boas's *The Mind of the Primitive Man* (1911) as an important publication that made cultural relativism and multiculturalism important concepts in anthropological thinking. In this book Boas stressed the importance of environment over heredity in creating human populations. The work challenged the celebration of Western civilization and stressed the importance of other cultures and experiences as valid cultural expressions (Visweswaran 1998:70; Roseberry 1992:848). In *Changes in Bodily Form of Descendants of Immigrants* (1912), Boas demonstrated that morphological features, including such core racial indicators as head form, could change in a single generation because of nutritional, environmental, or cultural factors (Blakey 1987; Mukhopadhyay and Moses 1997:518). Paul Rabinow (1992:60) claims, "Boas' arguments against racial hierarchies and racial thinking have thoroughly carried the theoretical day." However, it would take several generations before his observations would have a significant impact on twentieth-century views of race.

Despite the efforts of people such as Franz Boas, racial typologies persisted in anthropology as well as in mainstream twentieth-century culture. Nazism, and the genocide its proponents carried out in the name of creating a racially pure society, spurred anthropologists to reexamine racial typologies more critically. In 1938 Boas persuaded the American Anthropological Association to pass a resolution denouncing Nazi racism (Visweswaran 1998:71). After World War II American anthropologists argued against the old classifications of racial construction and supported a socially and culturally constructed form of race. In 1952 the United Nations Educational, Scientific, and Cultural Organization rejected the linkage between sociocultural differences and biology (Mukhopadhyay and Moses 1997:519). Yet although race is no longer a scientifically credible position in anthropology, racism has hardly disappeared from the American landscape (Rabinow 1992:60). Examining the historical context of race allows us to place the meaning of New Philadelphia in a new perspective.

Every summer we had an open dialogue with the field school students and members of the local and descendant community to discuss historic and contemporary issues of race and racism. Community members were invited along with the students to view in three parts a 2003 PBS special on race, *Race: The Power of Illusion*. The film explains the history and development of race and dismantles the myths associated with its construction. Students discussed the following points outlined in the companion guide to the documentary:

1. **Race is a modern idea.** Ancient societies, such as the Greeks, did not divide people according to physical differences but according to religion, status, class, or even language.

2. **Race has no genetic basis.** Not one characteristic, trait, or even gene distinguishes all of the members of one so-called race from all the members of another so-called race.

3. **Human subspecies don't exist.** Unlike many animals, modern humans simply haven't been around long enough, nor have populations been isolated enough, to evolve into separate subspecies or races. We are one of the most genetically similar of all species.

4. **Skin color is really only skin deep.** The genes for skin color have nothing to do with genes for hair form, eye shape, blood type, musical talent, athletic ability, or forms of intelligence.

5. **Most variation is within, not between, "races."** Of the small amount of total human variation, 85 percent exists within any local population. About 94 percent can be found within any continent. That means, for example, that two random Koreans may be as genetically different as a Korean and an Italian.

6. **Slavery predates race.** Throughout much of human history, societies have enslaved others, often as a result of conquest or debt, but not because of physical characteristics or a belief in natural inferiority. Due to a unique set of historical circumstances, North America had the first slave system where all slaves shared a common appearance and ancestry.

7. **Race and freedom were born together.** The United States was founded on the principle that "all men are created equal," but the country's early economy was based largely on slavery. The new idea of race helped explain why some people could be denied the rights and freedoms that others took for granted.

8. **Race justified social inequalities as natural.** The belief in white superiority justified antidemocratic actions and policies like slavery, the extermination of American Indians, the exclusion of Asian immigrants, the taking of Mexican lands, and the institutionalization of racial practices within American government, laws, and society.

9. **Race isn't biological, but racism is still real.** Race is a powerful social idea that gives people different access to opportunities and resources. The government and social institutions of the United

States have created advantages that disproportionately channel wealth, power, and resources to white people.

10. **Color blindness will not end racism.** Pretending race doesn't exist is not the same as creating equality.

In an open discussion one white student expressed amazement that blacks did not have an extra muscle in their legs that allowed them to run faster, as she had learned while growing up in a rural community. An African American student told of his experiences being profiled and harassed by St. Louis City Police on several occasions. While we created a productive dialogue, whereby everyone had a chance to speak about their perceptions of race, we were also able to imagine similar stereotypes and physical assaults in a historic context between people of different color.

We talked about the uniqueness of the integrated town, but also pointed out that racism did exist in various forms and that the types of racism changed through time. There are historical and oral accounts that discuss racism in the area in the nineteenth and twentieth centuries. For example, the memory of Ku Klux Klan activities is forgotten or repressed by some in the community. "Sundown towns" prohibited African Americans, including the McWorter family, from appearing outside of their community after sunset. Separate cemeteries based on skin color were a way to maintain separate races through eternity. These conversations were often spirited, as a few students struggled to rethink approximately twenty years of their learned and preconceived notions of race. Students expressed their anger that racism existed in the past and that it still survives today, and that no matter how hard people struggled to overcome racism, barriers and new definitions kept groups of people separated and ranked based on biophysical characteristics.

Several students approached me after the second episode of the video and told me that they were mad that racism is still alive. This was a teachable moment. We discussed ways they could change this attitude in the United States. One student explained very carefully that racism could change only if individuals worked through it on a case-by-case basis; we need to change the world one person at a time. Another student said that we need more government legislation to help level the playing field and to create more antidiscrimination laws. This student explained that the safety net that helped minorities gain an equal footing began to disappear during the Reagan administration. As President Reagan dismantled domestic programs that had a disproportionate impact on African Americans and the poor, he also diminished the role of the Civil Rights Division of the Justice Department. He initially approved tax exemptions for private segregated colleges. During Reagan's term job training and antipoverty programs were dramatically reduced. She explained that since Reagan it is even more difficult for minorities to gain an equal footing (see Fields 2004).

In the early years of the twenty-first century the attitude of the government seemed to be drifting back toward the discredited ideals of social Darwinism, which championed racial categorizations and hierarchies and the concept of survival of the fittest. Many minorities tend to be poor and nonwhite and to have minimum wage jobs, and various forms of racism keep many of them at a disadvantage.

Several field school students created an action plan and a call for justice. They stated that they could begin change by dealing with this matter on an individual level and by making issues related to race and racism part of the school curriculum. Many students said that they were more self-aware about race and racism in the world after our discussions. They said that they could be better citizens by acknowledging that we should create a color-conscious society rather than a color-blind society, and that it was important to explain the misperceptions of race whenever possible.

RACE RELATIONS IN EARLY PIKE COUNTY

Some believe racism was milder in a frontier situation, where whites and blacks had to rely on each other for survival. Many local Pike County residents today project this sentiment when thinking about their community's past. For a long time the New Philadelphia Association stated on their website that the town was a place "where white and black Americans lived together peacefully on the antebellum Illinois Frontier." Many of the local stories and newspaper articles repeated this conclusion so many times it has become fact in the community's narrative of the place. Pike County was different, claimed the newspapers and the local residents. Everybody got along, and whites and blacks lived together in peace. Pike County, I began to think, could be a place where we could learn and teach about racial harmony. However, my idealism was short-lived as I read more about the area's history and we gathered oral histories from the local and descendant communities.

The situation in nineteenth-century Pike County was not as peaceful and harmonious as many want to believe. Early county historian

Charles C. Chapman (1880) recalls that in the early 1830s a black man known as Bob went to the southern part of the county and wanted to marry a white woman, the daughter of a Mr. Guernsey. The prospect of an interracial marriage upset many of the locals, and Chapman stated that Bob's proposal "aroused the indignation of the whites, and as soon as he saw the citizens after him he took to his heels and ran away so fast the 50 men couldn't catch him!" (217). Although this story is light in tone, in it we see not only white indignation regarding interracial marriage but also the threat of violence against a black man.

In 1833, while Frank, Lucy, and their three children were taming the frontier lands of Hadley Township, the Illinois General Assembly passed "An Act Respecting Free Negroes, Mulattos, Servants, and Slaves." The new law stated that blacks and mulattos could not settle or reside in Illinois unless they could produce a certificate from a judge or clerk that verified that they were free. Another section of the law stated that no one could bring slaves into the state for the purpose of emancipation. If any citizen wanted to give a slave his or her freedom, a bond must be posted first (Revised Laws of Illinois, 1833:457–59, 465).

The 1845 Illinois Supreme Court decision in *Jarrot v. Jarrot* terminated the institution of slavery in Illinois for all time. However, Illinois did not resist the Fugitive Slave Law of 1850 (Davis 1998:289). Though Illinois was considered a free state, in 1853 the state legislature passed "An Act to prevent Immigration of Free Negroes into this State." Highlights of the act follow:

> Sec I. That if any person or persons shall bring, or cause to be brought into this State, any negro or mulatto slave, whether said slave is set free or not, shall be liable to an indictment, and upon conviction thereof, be fined for every such negro or mulatto, a sum not less than one hundred dollars, nor more than five hundred dollars, and imprisoned in the county jail not more than one year, and shall stand committed until said fine and costs are paid. . . .
>
> Sec III. If any negro, or mulatto, bond or free, shall hereafter come into this State and remain ten days, with the evident intention of residing in the same, every such negro or mulatto shall be deemed guilty of a high misdemeanor, and for the first offense shall be fined the sum of fifty dollars. . . .
>
> Sec IV. If said negro or mulatto shall be found guilty, and the fine assessed be not paid forthwith to the justice of the peace before whom said proceedings were had, it shall be the duty of said justice to commit said negro or mulatto to the custody of the sheriff of said county . . . ; and said justice shall forthwith advertise said negro or mulatto, by posting up notices thereof in at least three of the most public places in his district, which said notices shall be posted up for ten days, and on the day and at the time and

place mentioned in said advertisement, the said justice shall, at public auction, proceed to sell said negro or mulatto to any person or persons who will pay said fine and cots, for the shortest time; and said purchaser shall have the right to compel said negro or mulatto to work for and serve out said time, and he shall furnish said negro or mulatto with comfortable food, clothing, lodging during said servitude. . . .

Section X. Every person who shall have one-fourth negro blood, shall be deemed a mulatto. (Purple 1856:780–81)

Several years later, in 1858, the famous Lincoln-Douglas debates for the state's U.S. Senate seat highlighted the issue of race. These famous debates held in Illinois came after the 1856 national election in which a growing number of Irish voted for Democrats and the antiabolitionist movement. The Know-Nothings ran Millard Fillmore, who commanded the loyalty of native-born workingmen who feared immigrants, the introduction of new cultural ideals, and the debasement of their craft with the introduction of cheaper wage labor. Douglas ran on a platform of "Negro inequality" (Johannsen 1973:571). He spoke about "preserving not only the purity of [white] blood but the purity of the government from any . . . amalgamation with inferior races" (quoted in Roediger 1999:142). Douglas noted that the mixing of whites, Indians, and blacks in Mexico led to the country's inferior population; thus they were easily defeated in the Mexican War. He assured his audiences that Mexican War veterans could back his claim of racial impurities. Douglas called Abraham Lincoln a race mixer and challenged Lincoln's belief that the Declaration of Independence applied to all people of color of the United States (Roediger 1999:142). According to Douglas, the political attitudes within Illinois varied from north to south. He declared the northern part of the state as "pretty black," the center of the state as "pretty mulatto," and added, "It is almost white when you get down to Egypt [southern Illinois]" (quoted in Roediger 1999:142).

Lincoln insisted on a white republicanism that gave blacks a chance to profit from their labor and gain a very limited and temporary citizenship prior to their resettlement. The arrival of newly freed slaves into Illinois at the beginning of the Civil War drew criticism from many residents. The phenomenon was seen as a betrayal of white labor. Illinois soldiers voted in 1862 for an amendment to the state constitution to stop the immigration of African Americans into the state (Roediger 1999). A mass meeting of an estimated three thousand met at Court House Square in Pittsfield in Pike County on Saturday, September 11, 1862. Resolutions were passed expressing fear of the blacks invading the state and particularly the fear that white men would lose their jobs ("The Mass Meeting of Saturday," *Pike County Democrat,* October 16, 1862, cited in Waggoner 1999:67).

The *Pike County Democrat* attacked the preliminary Emancipation Proclamation announced after the Battle of Antietam in September 1862, and the paper continued to denounce it for the rest of the war. On January 1, 1863, Lincoln issued the Emancipation Proclamation, which freed only those slaves in portions of the South not under Union control. The idea of fighting a war to preserve the Union was the reason many Pike County residents enlisted; fighting a war to free the enslaved was not a popular idea. The *Pike County Democrat* railed against the changing nature of the war and strongly opposed a war to "liberate the niggers" (*Pike County Democrat,* June 25, 1863, cited in Waggoner 1999:79).

The attitude of Union soldiers toward African Americans was sometimes hostile. Henry Hoskins of D Company and the Ninety-ninth Illinois Regiment wrote to his mother and father from Vicksburg in 1863:

> You want to know what I thought of the nigger regiment. Well, I think that they are a poor excuse. You can't get ten steps here without seeing ten or twelve niggers laying in the shade. There have been two of three nigger regiments got up down here. But I think they are an expense to the Government for nothing. If they were to get into a fight the rebels would take their arms from them: and I hope would kill them. ("From the 99th Regiment," *Pike County Democrat,* May 29, 1863, cited in Waggoner 1999:79)

Clearly the strong public animosity of Pike County and Illinois residents toward blacks could not have made the place comfortable for African Americans in New Philadelphia and for those who wanted to settle in the area. While there are no recorded incidents of interracial violence during the antebellum era, the passing of Black Codes and the new provisions in the state's constitution reinforced the idea that African Americans should live as second-class citizens. From a white person's perspective there was no violence, but from a black person's perspective blacks had few legal rights. I remembered a passage in Henry Louis Gates Jr.'s (1994:92) memoir when he explained growing up in rural West Virginia in a small biracial community: "Nobody ever *talked* about race, but it was there in the lines drawn around socializing. . . . Obey [the rules] and everything will be fine. We'll all get along."

CONSTRUCTING A HISTORY OF HARMONY

So why does the New Philadelphia Association insist on perpetuating the idea that people lived in harmony on the antebellum frontier? It has been explained to me that from their perspective the lack of violence is proof that prejudice did not occur, and therefore implies harmony. However, the community oral histories and conversations with local residents provide a different perspective. After I was living in the community for a few weeks, several of the county's residents began to confide in me. They told me many stories about racial inequalities that have been part of the community's collective amnesia for decades. They are stories that would make anyone sad and disappointed in humankind, and they do not reflect an atmosphere of peace and harmony. They are accounts that were probably typical for the time in many communities throughout the United States.

All of the children went to small one-room schoolhouses in Pike County until the 1940s. The New Philadelphia school, an integrated one-room schoolhouse, existed from about 1874 into the 1940s. The schoolhouses closed in the late 1940s, and children from many neighboring communities then went to a local centralized school in Barry, Illinois. People of the era generally did not challenge corporal discipline in schools in the 1940s and 1950s, but in one case it went too far. I heard about a schoolteacher who beat an African American boy who died within a few days, probably from injuries related to the beating. The newspapers reported the child's death as the result of an illness. No one brings up this story when they talk about race relations in Pike County, and I am sure the community is trying very hard to repress it.

I was also told about an African American schoolteacher who was recruited to teach in a nearby community in about 1960 or 1961. She lasted in the position for only about six weeks; after some members of the all-white community burned a cross on her lawn one night, she packed her bags and left town. The threat of the Klan must have been terrifying, especially for the only African American in this all-white community. After all, Illinois had one of the largest contingents of Ku Klux Klan members in the United States until the 1970s.

Despite these events, or maybe because of them, in 1964 Grace Matteson described a racial harmony that may not have been congruent with the overall racial tensions found in Pike County. Her typescript manuscript is on file in the Pike County Historical Society and the State

Historical Society's library, now housed in the Abraham Lincoln Presidential Library. She wrote that racial discrimination did not occur in New Philadelphia, that the white and the black families lived in harmony with each other in the community. They "worked and ate together, and attended school, church services and social functions as friendly neighbors. They visited in each other's homes and were accepted for what they were and not on the basis of their racial ancestry and color of complexion" (21). I think it is important to place her claims for racial harmony in a larger context. They come at the height of the civil rights movement and they mask the racial tensions in the area in an attempt to create a unique memory of the place. She helped to create a memory that is supported by the local community into the twenty-first century, and the New Philadelphia Association continues to maintain these claims on their website (www.newphiladelphiail.org).

One neighboring family reinforced this idea of harmony in an oral history. "I don't think we had any trouble, you know, problems that way. Philadelphia was a settlement, and they lived peacefully. Barry was growing up and they had their own problems" (Hughes 2004). At the same time, a board member of the New Philadelphia Association acknowledges the racism of the twentieth century, but says that it may have been different in the nineteenth century: "I think locals in the 1920s and 1930s saw a black race and a white race. I don't know what it was like in the beginning. I suspect it was different from the way it finally ended up" (Likes 2004).

I found that many of the elders, compared to the younger community members, were more willing to talk about the race inequities they experienced growing up in the community. For instance, an oral history of one woman born in the 1920s describes a different past: "Some people from our area were really against the Negroes. Those black kids went hungry. Sometimes all they had to eat was blackberries. A few times they took things from our dinner buckets; they stole them. The white boys in our school were good to the Negroes during the school day, but after school they would shun them. I remember adults who shunned the black people altogether. But many of the school children got along" (Foster 2004).

An African American member of the New Philadelphia Association board and descendant of a resident of New Philadelphia tells a family story in which relatives suspected that a doctor intentionally killed a baby from a mixed marriage. He points to a picture of a married white

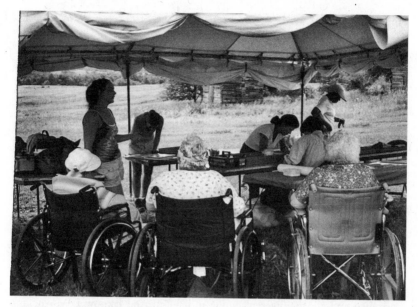

FIGURE 18. Members of the local senior citizens home visit the site and share stories with the archaeologists. Photograph by Paul A. Shackel.

woman, Catherine Wright, and a black man, William Butler, who lived at New Philadelphia:

> Now, this lady obviously doesn't look Afro-American. And she had a child, could have been this child right here [pointing at a picture]. The baby got sick. This was back, maybe . . . 1875. . . . She called the doctor for the baby and the doctor was a white doctor. He went in the room and said, 'I got to shut the door.' So, he shuts the door and they stayed outside. I don't know why he said, 'Stay outside,' but the baby died. It's suspected that he might have killed the baby. I don't know. That's what they suspected. The doctor didn't like it because of her husband [who was black]. I have the picture right here. That's her husband. That's William Henry Butler. They suspected that he didn't like this and this [pointing to a picture of William Henry Butler and Catherine Butler]. (Carter 2004)

A few of the older residents willingly spoke about some of the tough issues related to racism and the role of the Ku Klux Klan in the area. Apparently a group of the Klan existed in Barry, only a few miles away from New Philadelphia. One neighbor explained the importance of telling some of the more painful histories associated with the region's history: "I had two uncles in the Ku Klux Klan. I loved them to death, but I didn't like it when I found out, but that's the truth. Why hide the truth? Some families don't want the truth to come out, but it's the truth" (Duke 2004). Expressing both the good and the hurtful helps people become more aware of the history of racism, and it gives them the tools to develop an understanding of multiculturalism in the present.

Another community elder admits, "Barry had a Ku Klux Klan" (Foster 2004). The town was a sundown town, meaning that African Americans were not allowed in the town after the sun set. "When the McWorters used to go into town, they wouldn't let them go after dark" (Duke 2004). Several community elders recalled a story of a Klan ride and cross burning close to New Philadelphia:

> We were in there visiting and dad looked up and said, "Well, there they come" and they were coming out of Barry. The Ku Klux Klan was coming out because they'd moved in a big tent with women, about twenty-eight to thirty, to cook for those men who were putting the highway [Highway 36] through. They had horses and lights and sheets all in front of the things. Oh, it was scary looking. . . . Well, they weren't going to have that at all, Negro women and all, they weren't going to have it. And I know LeMoyne and they [the Washingtons] were scared and they just lived less than a half a mile up there, where they lived all their lives. They didn't bother them at all because they were natives, but they were scared anyway. And at that time, my mother said they wouldn't let the Negroes stay overnight in El Dara [a nearby town]. They didn't even want them coming in the daytime. Of course, they made sure you got out before nighttime. Now, that's just a little town down south of here. (Foster 2004)

Another community elder remembered other Klan activity in the area: "Our house was fairly close to the road and we could hear them coming, they rode past the house on the horseback, with the white sheets. And my dad would turn out the lamps and we'd watch out the window when they went by, but we didn't know where they went or what they did, but we had seen them several times." She remembered another incident:

> There was an old black fellow that lived along the river, that was the same place where we saw the Ku Klux Klan, and he just lived in a little house, and he used to garden and raised a few chickens for his own use, and he never bothered anybody and nobody ever bothered him, or you know, they got along, people in Naples, that wasn't a real big town, and, and they didn't, you know, they got along all right with this old fellow, but he just disappeared, and no one ever knew what happened to him. So I think they always thought maybe the Ku Klux Klan did something, but nobody ever said that. (Roberts 2005)

CREATING A PLACE FOR LEARNING

The forms of racism that existed in Illinois and Pike County changed significantly over the past two centuries. Through most of the nineteenth century legislation dictated a clear racial hierarchy. Laws reinforced a white-dominated society that discriminated against African Americans. Whites had the luxury of overlooking these restrictions and painting this era as a time of peaceful coexistence. Although discriminatory laws were illegal immediately after the Civil War, racism still existed and sundown towns developed. The KKK proliferated after World War I, and skin color continued to reinforce community hierarchy. By the late twentieth century African Americans were almost nonexistent in the New Philadelphia area and the county. As a result many whites will claim that racism does not exist in the area.

Clearly many members of the community want to believe in a harmonious past when in fact some of the community elders remember a very different story of the place. What we remember and how we remember allow us to see how public memory develops. A consensus history often occurs when we leave others out of the picture. After understanding the various views of New Philadelphia's past it became even more important to me that this historic site could become a place to learn about and understand contemporary social and political issues.

Valmont Layne (2008) discusses a similar case in District Six, located in Cape Town, South Africa. This area is known for some of the worst circumstances of the South African apartheid system. It is also a story of forced removal. What makes District Six so prominent in the memory of many citizens is that the forced removals occurred toward the end of apartheid, and people have maintained close ties to the community and have been able to fight for its remembrance. Layne notes, "The pre-apartheid era does risk becoming mythologized as an era of total harmony, preventing us from learning from and celebrating the challenges of how marginalized people confronted inequality and injustice within their own communities" (55).

There are some places in the United States that serve to make us aware of social justice issues, and I think they can also serve to frame the New Philadelphia projects. For example, the National Park Service sponsored a *Community Study Report* (Bowser 2000) that highlights its recent experience helping to organize community and park cooperation to celebrate diversity. The report contains many stories that show how the NPS connects with diverse communities and promotes pluralism. At

Alcatraz the NPS explored the history of the American Indian occupation of the island and related it to the current activism within American Indian communities. It is part of a larger program called "Promoting Tolerance" that "brings emerging leaders from Eastern and Central Europe to the United States to learn about techniques to strengthen pluralism and respect for diversity" (Bowser 2000:20). Representatives came from Russia, Bosnia, Estonia, Rumania, and Bulgaria, countries where democracy is a relatively new concept. The program demonstrates how differences can be reconciled and how minority groups can become part of the political process. The program uses a historic park to teach about democracy with the goal of promoting it throughout the world (20).

The difficult stories of our past are not always part of our national heritage (B. J. Little 1994; LaRoche and Blakey 1997). When studying the heritage of any place we need to understand that significant biases and prejudices regarding race, ethnicity, religion, language, age groups, class, sex, and physical disabilities are all part of our past. As we work at the site it is important to promote New Philadelphia as a multiracial place with a past that has stories of heroism, courage, and freedom, but it is also a place where racism existed. All of these stories can become part of a message and a learning experience for visitors and the local and descendant communities. To accomplish this goal we need to critically analyze and expose racism in the past and present and to dismantle the structures of oppression where we can. We need to recognize race and provide a historical perspective of racism when telling the story. We need to explore diversity in the past and to promote it in the present. You have not dismantled racism if you have only like-minded people participating in the project. We need to build a multicultural organization. We need to explore and identify the dividing walls, in the past and in the present. For us, the organization is the field of American archaeology and we hope that our efforts will help build diversity through the discovery of a variety of perspectives. We need to create a color-conscious past rather than a color-blind past in order to recognize cultural and ethnic differences and to provide a richer perspective of the past and the future.

Recruiting students of different ethnic backgrounds to participate in the project is one way to achieve these goals. As they entered the very white community of Pike County during the summer field school, they changed the community's complexion for a few weeks. One local community member commented, "When you are a stranger, every head turns." Although no one had heard any negative comments about the racial makeup of the students, this resident remarked, "I suspect there are some racial comments floating around."

One evening during the summer I addressed a local all-white community organization in Pike County and spoke about race being a historical construction. I told them that there was no relationship between race and biology. As I discussed racism many eyes looked down and away from me. I wondered, are they uninterested, or are they not willing to face a racist past? Several people in the audience commented that they did not experience racism in the local community, yet when they spoke about African Americans they sometimes used a patronizing tone, saying that African Americans were "good, nice and hard working" and "a lot smarter than people give them credit for." One student who lived in a nearby all-white community explained that she was never aware of racism since it was not part of her daily experience, especially in a place where no blacks lived. In much the same way, the evening's audience believed that they did not experience racism because no blacks lived in the area. However, African Americans did live in Pike County and the surrounding areas at one time, but during the Jim Crow era they left for larger towns or moved to the west in an attempt to escape racism.

The silence I faced regarding racism in Pike County and west-central Illinois is not unique to this area. It is emblematic of the conversations about race in much of America today. Issues related to race have gone unspoken, misremembered, distorted, or forgotten over the generations. It is a type of amnesia that makes many Americans believe that race is someone else's problem.

I believe that rewriting the past and addressing some of these tough issues related to race is important to ensure a more tolerant, inclusive, and hopeful future. I saw a significant opportunity in Pike County to develop a plan and discuss racism in the community. Weaving this discussion into the archaeology program could work with the right chemistry. It was important that we research and excavate places in New Philadelphia that were once occupied by African Americans and those of European descent so we could begin talking about the development and survival of this multiracial town that lasted for a hundred years.

CHAPTER 7

The Apple Festival
and National Significance

After the first five weeks in the field in 2004 we received a tremendous amount of publicity related to the archaeology at New Philadelphia. We were settling into our five-week laboratory routine at the Illinois State Museum in Springfield when articles began to appear in national newspapers. Deborah Husar of the *Quincy (Illinois) Herald Whig* wrote several stories about our work in the field and in the lab. An Associated Press news release titled "Researchers Want Ill. Town Named Historic" was picked up by the *Baltimore Sun, New York Newsday,* the *Atlanta Journal Constitution,* and the *Seattle Post Intelligencer,* to name a few. The article with variations of this title appeared in sixty other newspapers in the last week of June. The *St. Louis Post-Dispatch* ran an article on the front page titled "Illinois Farm Field Is Mined for Treasures of Racial History: Team Excavates First U.S. Town Incorporated by African American." The publicity prompted other descendants to take note of the project and even think about visiting the place.

THE BARRY APPLE FESTIVAL

For many years the Barry Apple Festival featured members of the McWorter family as representatives of the community's founder. Some McWorters had continued to attend the festival, even after they all moved away from the area. However, they had been absent for a while, so Natalie Armistead and the other members of the New Philadelphia

Association invited them to the 2004 festival and to visit New Philadelphia. Many family members accepted the invitation and were excited about returning to Pike County.

Terry Martin had a great idea for the Apple Festival. He suggested that the McWorter family members first meet at the archaeology lab at the Illinois State Museum on Friday afternoon, the day before the festival, so we could explain the goals and products of the first season's work at New Philadelphia. Terry arranged artifacts in the lab along with a collection of maps, drawings, and photographs of the summer's activities. I flew out from Maryland and arrived only a few hours before the family. At about 3 o'clock the McWorter family began to arrive from California, Texas, Ohio, and Illinois. They included Stewart Moss and Shirley McWorter Moss, Gerald Arthur McWorter (Abdul Alkalimat) and Kate Williams, Allen Kirkpatrick II (Thelma's son and Juliet Walker's brother), Sandra McWorter Marsh, and Lonie McWorter-Vond Wilson.

Terry laid out newspaper reports of the previous season on one table and a selection of artifacts on another. We discussed some of the fieldwork and the importance of working with the NSF-REU students. A miniature pewter tea set that we found at Casiah Clark's house lot drew the most attention. After an hour the family and archaeologists sat around a large table and the family fired away with questions.

"Can you find evidence of the Underground Railroad?" This is a tall order, we explained, since the Underground Railroad left few physical traces. Runaways hid in cellars and barns as well as in hiding places within houses. Although we can find some of these features, it will be difficult to link them to the Underground Railroad, which was meant to be invisible. However, in places like Lancaster, Pennsylvania, Jim Delle and Mary Ann Levine's work suggests that a modified cistern may have housed escaped slaves. Work in Syracuse, New York, where archaeologists found a sculpted face in clay beneath the former Wesleyan Methodist Church, the home of a noted abolitionist congregation, was perhaps created by escaped and hiding African Americans (Armstrong and Wurst 2003:19–37; Levine et al. 2005:399–414).

Another family member asked if we could find evidence of Africanisms. We acknowledged that archaeologists working on sites once inhabited by African Americans sometimes find artifacts that have strong ties to Africa and African culture. For instance, in Annapolis, Maryland, archaeologists led by Mark Leone found crystals, pins, and ceramics in a cache near doorways, possibly signs of the use of hoodoo, African

American traditional folk magic that was imported when mainly West Africans were enslaved and brought to the United States. In other places archaeologists have found small pieces of ceramics, about the size of an adult's thumbnail, that look water-worn. These are probably gaming pieces related to a game known as mancala, a game that is somewhat similar to backgammon, but has its roots in the Middle East. Pieces of mancala have been found at many plantation sites where African Americans lived, and they were also identified at the Robinson House, the site of a free black family that is now inside Manassas National Battlefield (Fennell 2007; Leone et al. 2005: 575–98; E. K. Martin et al. 1997: 155–75).

"What do you hope to find?" asked another family member. Our goal from the onset of the project was to do an archaeology of the entire town. Chris Fennell and Claire Martin are collecting names of former inhabitants of New Philadelphia and so far have found at least 200 different families associated with the town. They are contacting genealogy websites with the hope of reaching more New Philadelphia descendants. The goal of the archaeology is to get an idea of where people lived and figure out who lived where in the town. We want to get an idea about how people lived and survived in this rural town and trace the development of this multiracial community from 1836 until its ultimate demise in the 1930s in a racially charged area of the country.

"What will be the end product?" We want to have a strong presence on the Internet. We believe that we are being as transparent as possible by placing all of the data we collect on our websites. We want our archaeology to be a democratic process. Whoever wants to comment on our work or use the data we collect is free to do so. We invite others to add to and critique our work and conclusions. Eventually a site report and edited volumes will be produced from this work.

No one brought up the tension between the New Philadelphia Association, the archaeology program, and Juliet Walker's feeling of exclusion; however, the family's cautious approach made it clear to me that they were all aware of the confrontation. Everyone seemed a bit tentative during our first two-hour meeting at the Illinois State Museum.

Gerald McWorter, a fifth-generation descendant of Frank McWorter, broke some of tension by complimenting the archaeology program for placing our research and data on the Internet. By the end of our meeting there was a better understanding between some of the McWorter family members and the archaeology program. Terry Martin and I felt a bit relieved because it seemed that the attending family members were open to the goals of the project. We were working with the local community and descendants and trying to make this site and its story part of the national public memory.

The following day Terry and I drove seventy miles west of Springfield and met the McWorters at New Philadelphia. We took them on a tour of the fields and gravel roads that now comprise New Philadelphia and described the work from the previous field season. Walking from the northern end of the town and traveling south on Broad Street, we described the development of the town as a small rural commercial center. It was a living community, with houses being built and others being torn down. We reached the intersection of Broad and Main and pointed southward toward an empty field, the location of Squire and Louisa McWorter's house. Traveling west on Main Street we pointed to the area where Casiah Clark and later William Butler resided. We described New Philadelphia as a multiracial town that struggled to survive in the Jim Crow era. Butler died in the 1930s; he represents the last African American to reside in the town proper. Racism had taken its toll on the New Philadelphia landscape. The McWorter family also toured the family cemetery and returned to the town proper about an hour later. They were all concerned about the overgrown conditions of the cemetery.

After the tour the McWorter family, the archaeology team, and the New Philadelphia Association gathered in the meeting hall of the local Baptist church in Barry, the same church that Frank and Lucy Mc-Worter once belonged to. Gerald McWorter spoke for the family members who gathered there that day and reaffirmed the family's connection to the place. "We are the children of the last generation that was born and grew up here in Pike County," said Gerald McWorter, who was raised in Chicago. "We grew up hearing the stories about Pike County. Many of us have been to Pike County before, some when we were very small" (Husar 2004).

Phil Bradshaw led a candid discussion with all the attendees. First, the family members expressed their concern over the condition of the cemetery. They said that they really wanted to do something to preserve and restore it. Allen Kirkpatrick expressed concern that Juliet Walker, his sister, was not invited to participate in the project. I explained that Chris Fennell met Walker in her office at the University of Texas to try to convince her about the utility of archaeology and our desire to have her participate in the project. I told the group that we tried.

Gerald McWorter expressed his concern about the issue of harmony when describing the history of the place to news reporters. He explained that the story that their family matriarch, Thelma Elise McWorter Kirkpatrick Wheaton (1907–2001), instilled in him and his cousins was that New Philadelphia was about freedom. Freedom should be the focus of the story of Frank McWorter. Terry Martin expressed his agreement with the theme of freedom, and he also explained that a newspaper account should not be seen as fact. Many times reporters do not check their story with their subjects, and reporters lose even more control of the article once it reaches the headline editor. The use of the word *harmony* was very contentious throughout the first year of the archaeology program, and Juliet Walker protested any newspaper articles that used it. The *Boston Globe* headline "Artifacts Show Harmony" reflects the sentiment of the New Philadelphia Association, and their opinion became quickly associated with our research program. No one on the archaeology program ever used the word when speaking to any newspaper reporter.

The archaeology team was very curious about the multiracial community and how it existed from the frontier days into the early twentieth century. Some type of hierarchy probably existed based on skin color, even though the McWorters accumulated a significant amount of wealth. I am thinking about possible parallels with a project at Manassas National Battlefield Park for which I served as a principal investigator. In that case an African American farmer, James Robinson, became the third wealthiest farmer in the county before and after the American Civil War in a predominantly white community. Most of his wealth was in land. His house, however, was smaller than those of the surrounding farm families. We believe that Robinson intentionally maintained a smaller house as a way to avoid the ostentatious display of wealth (E. K. Martin et al. 1997).

Gerald McWorter spoke for the family:

Frankly, we want the story to not turn out that Frank was a "good ole boy" from Pike County, and we all loved him, and it was wonderful. . . . This was a hell of a struggle and he had to emerge over a lot. . . . If we bring New Philadelphia back and we bring Frank back, it has to be in the spirit of freedom. It's got to be in the spirit of beating back this glorification of slavery and the Confederacy as if they weren't traitors and terrorists . . . to use contemporary language. (Minutes of the Barry Apple Festival Visit 2004)

Gerald later explained that Thelma, the matriarch of the family, instilled the family history in them:

I will tell you a story about Thelma, how I think this preservation of family history began. She went to Fisk University and at Fisk University people said black people don't document and know their history. She said that's not true, I do know my history. She came back here and got a bunch of documents and took them back to Fisk. That's really the core set of documents that the family has always referred to. (Minutes of the Barry Apple Festival Visit 2004)

Turning to the archaeology project, Gerald explained:

The New Philadelphia dig is a wonderful opportunity for us to dig back into the past and raise it up and actually talk about what courage it took to live in New Philadelphia. . . . How many families have an opportunity at a National Science Foundation grant to add another little piece to the overall clipboard? . . . We have to figure out a way of not acting like we're writing the Pat Boone version of New Philadelphia, you know—happy, white socks and white bucks kind of version—of American history. (Minutes of the Barry Apple Festival Visit 2004)

Gerald expressed his delight with the New Philadelphia archaeology website we developed at the University of Maryland and the University of Illinois. "I want to express my appreciation for the research that's gone on so far as well as the web. The posting of the information is a wonderful thing that we are all indebted to you for and look forward to more" (Minutes of the Barry Apple Festival Visit 2004).

I felt that the McWorter family members who attended this meeting were pleased with the initial contact with the New Philadelphia Association and the archaeology team. The NPA served as good hosts and the McWorters who attended the meeting pledged that they wanted to cooperate and move the project forward. They were very eager to help restore the cemetery. Gerald McWorter reaffirmed that he appreciated the transparency of the archaeology project. "The archaeological and oral history work," wrote the *Quincy Herald Whig*, "ties into the vision of [Allen] Kirkpatrick's late mother Thelma, who worked to preserve her family's history. She shared stories about her father Arthur [McWorter], the grandfather of the cousins and the grandson of Free Frank" (Husar 2004).

At the end of the meeting at the Baptist church one McWorter family member said, "We have covered a tremendous amount of ground" (Husar 2004). Terry Martin encouraged the family to visit the site again during the 2005 season, and plans began for a family reunion, part of which was to be held at the archaeology site. Phil Bradshaw offered to show the family his pig houses and offered Wayne Riley's services to roast a hog. "Let's get a picture of everyone," he said at the end of the meeting (Minutes of the Barry Apple Festival Visit 2004). Everyone mingled and stood together in the church pews: McWorter descendents, members of the New Philadelphia Association, and members of the archaeology research team. Despite some differences, we stood united to work together to help bring this project to fruition.

COMMEMORATING FRANK MCWORTER AND NEW PHILADELPHIA

In February 2005 Governor Rod Blagojevich named a portion of Interstate 72, which runs through Pike County, after "Free Frank" McWorter. Sandra McWorter and several members of the New Philadelphia Association and Terry Martin of the Illinois State Museum attended the ceremony. Blagojevich announced the designation during a celebration of African American History Month held at the Abraham Lincoln Presidential Library in Springfield. "Today, in the home state of Abraham Lincoln, one of the most notable figures in the fight for racial equality, we honor the countless contributions made by African-Americans throughout our state's rich history," he said. "This month is dedicated to remembering and celebrating their extraordinary achievements, including that of 'Free Frank' McWorter, a brave pioneer of his time" (Husar 2005c).

With Illinois being such a large state, and with so many contributions made by African Americans, "to have this one chosen was really a feather in our hat," Phil Bradshaw said, referring to the efforts of the New Philadelphia Association. "We think it's great the governor has taken an interest. We're very pleased he chose to name the highway in this manner. We think it's a historic site that goes along very well with the Mark Twain, the Abraham Lincoln 'Looking for Lincoln' project, and the Mormon activities that go on in Western Illinois" (Husar 2005c). Sandra McWorter represented the family and attended the festivities, arriving via bus and train. Delighted that she attended the ceremony and represented the family, the governor flew her back to Chicago in his jet.

Several months later the Federal Highway Administration placed signs on a thirty-five-mile stretch of highway in Pike County designating a stretch of Interstate 72 the "Free Frank McWorter Historic Memorial Highway"; additional signs found their way along exit 20 of the Interstate and along Highway 106 directing tourists to New Philadelphia. Unfortunately at New Philadelphia there is space for only two cars overlooking an open field, and little interpretation is found at the site. Most of the land is still privately owned, and efforts are under way to protect the site from future residential or commercial development.

At the beginning of the second field season, on June 2, 2005, Terry Martin and I accompanied several members of the New Philadelphia Association to attend the hearing for the nomination of the town site to the National Register of Historic Places. The National Register is the nation's list of buildings, sites, and districts that are considered worthy of recognition and preservation. The designation provides some protection to properties. For instance, federally funded, licensed, permitted, or assisted projects (such as a state highway, sewerage plant, or bank construction) must be reviewed for their effect on historic resources. Designation also allows owners of income-producing properties (industrial, commercial, and rental residential) to take advantage of tax benefits for rehabilitation. Owner-occupied residential properties listed in the National Register also qualify for a rehabilitation tax incentive program. National Register properties may qualify for matching grant programs in Illinois; in particular, properties that are owned by nonprofit organizations or public entities qualify for the Illinois Heritage Grant Program. This is a matching grant program (1:1) for restoration and rehabilitation projects. Each year the program must be newly funded, and therefore is subject to change or cancellation. There are also other federal grant programs that owners of National Register properties can apply to.

Michelle Huttes, a graduate student at the University of Illinois at Springfield, wrote the nomination as partial fulfillment for her master's degree in history. The project had overwhelming support from the state's political heavyweights. Governor Blagojevich wrote in support of the nomination, "By including this site on the National Register, we strive to raise the visibility of New Philadelphia and make it part of our national public memory" (letter, April 4, 2005). U.S. Senator Richard Durbin declared, "Recent efforts to uncover the history [of New Philadelphia] will go a long way towards enriching our heritage" (letter, March 28, 2005). Senator Barack Obama noted, "Archaeological work conducted at the site will provide important information for many areas of our nation's history that [have] previously been marginalized" (letter, June 1, 2005). Other politicians did not respond to Michelle's request for a letter of support. However, we all felt good going into the hearing because of the strong support from the state and federal officials.

We were last on the docket. Michelle gave a ten-minute PowerPoint presentation to the Illinois Historic Sites Advisory Council to support her nomination. Then Carol McCartney, a local historian and columnist who lives in Pike County, presented a short plea for support of the project. Next Sandra McWorter spoke to the board; she explained her ancestral connection to the place and stated that the town is an important part of our national history. There was little deliberation before the nomination passed unanimously. Michelle was excited because her graduate work made a significant contribution to the project and she finished her requirements for her graduate degree. We all celebrated over lunch in a local restaurant, then headed back to the field school, where Chris Fennell and our graduate students, Chris Valvano, Carrie Christman, and Charlotte King, continued to supervise the NSF-REU students. Next, and the last step, the keeper of the National Register in the National Park Service approved the nomination on August 11, 2005.

My sense from talking to the local residents outside of the New Philadelphia Association is that they felt no connection to the New Philadelphia project because the history of the place has always focused on one person and one family. It is difficult to deny the feats of Frank McWorter, his wife, and the rest of his family as they settled in this uncharted territory in the 1830s and battled racism in a state with some of the nation's toughest Black Codes. However, including the entire town on the National Register allows for more local residents to feel part of the bigger project. The McWorter family's support for the nomination also sent a clear message to the Pike County community that the family was interested in knowing more about the entire town: the black and white residents, carpenters, laborers, and farmers. The descendants' support of the nomination encouraged an inclusive search and discovery of the area's history.

THE SECOND FIELD SEASON
The Elusive Anomaly

Michael Hargrave worked for three days with the field school students at the beginning of the 2005 season; they identified several geophysical anomalies that we all thought worthy of testing. The geophysical survey indicated that an anomaly existed toward the middle of the western end of block 3, lot 5, close to Broad Street. Terry Martin and his NSF-REU crew began work to identify and explore the anomaly. The historical research shows that the first land transaction of this lot occurred in 1854. This date seemed a bit late, since this was a prime piece of real estate in the early town. It is on Broad Street and close to the main road stretching out across the township. The census records and the tax assessments indicate that Arden Cobb owned this land in the 1860s. Cobb had improvements on lots 3 and 4, although none are indicated on lot 5.

The walkover survey also produced a large quantity of domestic artifacts in the area, and we thought that there was a reasonable chance of finding a domestic site. Up to this point Hargrave's geophysical survey results were flawless, and we successfully ground-truthed some of the anomalies he identified. An examination of the 1939 aerial photograph of New Philadelphia shows no visible landscape features on this lot. Since no improvements appear on the 1867 tax assessment, and because we located a large concentration of artifacts on the surface, we thought that there was a chance that the anomaly could be associated with an earlier occupation or activity. Therefore we decided to ground-truth the anomaly.

The summer of 2005 was one of the driest on record and it was difficult to core the area before testing. Some of the old-timers who came around for an occasional visit told me that the weather was almost as bad as the drought in the 1930s. Coring could not easily penetrate deep into the soil anywhere in the town site. Therefore we proceeded with systematic testing with 5-by-5-foot units in the area of the anomaly in lot 5 (Figure 19).

The summer's efforts on this lot were disappointing. The team found a post mold that tapered toward the bottom, perhaps the remains of a fence post driven into the ground. On the last day they found the remains of an ash scatter with a few metal fragment inclusions and a few rocks. At this point we did not know the size of the feature, and we covered the units at the end of the field season with this mystery not yet solved. Could we have missed the anomaly, or was the ash layer the anomaly, or was the ground so hard and dry that the geophysical survey data were not as clear as the previous season? After comparing the geophysical work over three seasons Hargrave believed it was latter. We went back the following spring and systematically cored in the unexcavated area near the ash pit. We did not have any positive results, so we decided not to pursue this feature during the following field season. The failed test is part of any archaeological project. We use the available archaeological and geophysical data and make the best decisions based

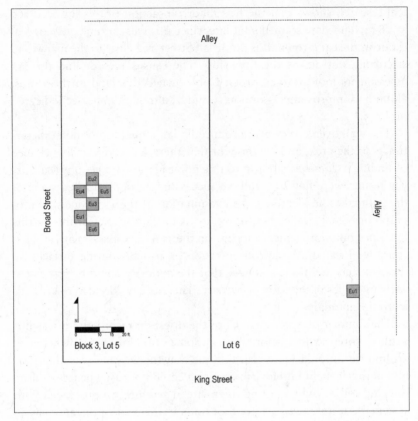

FIGURE 19. The systematic placement of six excavation units in search of an elusive anomaly in block 3, lot 5. Drawing by Christopher Valvano.

on this information. Many professional archaeologists will tell you that negative information is still information. At this point we are certain that the activities on lot 5 during the nineteenth century left a light footprint in the archaeological record and help provide a clearer picture of the settlement of the town.

"The Negro Schoolhouse"

The 1867 tax records indicate that no improvements existed on block 9, lot 4, although oral histories indicate that the "Negro schoolhouse" was located there until about 1872. This building may be the earliest school associated with New Philadelphia. When George and

M. Kimbrews acquired the lot and the schoolhouse in 1884 they parti-
tioned the house, creating a duplex, with each brother living in one section. They held the land until 1909; by the 1920s the building stood in
poor repair. We know that a second schoolhouse, which was racially
integrated, stood just outside the north edge of the town and was built
in 1874 on land donated by the McWorters.

Finding the early schoolhouse would be an important part of interpreting the town to future visitors. Education is an important foundation of any society, but especially to this community, since African
Americans were denied the right to an education while in bondage. The
topic of education is an important part of the struggle for freedom and
the fight for justice that we want to make public with our work in New
Philadelphia. If we could find the early schoolhouse it could be an important interpretive symbol of the New Philadelphia landscape.

Archaeologists identified a large concentration of artifacts on the western edge of this lot during the 2002–3 walkover survey. A heavy concentration of nails in the southwest corner suggests the presence of a former
building. The 1939 aerial photograph shows a structure in the southwest
corner of the lot, and the geophysical survey identified two anomalies
in the southwest corner and the center of the lot. Based on this information the archaeology team decided to ground-truth these two anomalies with the hope of finding the early schoolhouse.

Excavations led by Chris Valvano with his team of NSF-REU students
found the remains of a stone pier that would have supported the building.
The base of the pier rests on the subsoil and measures 1.5 feet north–south
(Figure 20). The team searched for other stone piers, but to no avail. I
think they were lucky to find even this one pier because there has been
significant erosion on this part of the site and plowing went deeper into
the subsoil, erasing many subterranean archaeological features. A stone
pier that may have been deep enough to escape the plow's impact could
no longer avoid being hit after significant erosion and was subsequently
moved by the farmer. The identified stone pier is likely to be associated
with the Kimbrew residence and may have previously served as a support beneath the "Negro schoolhouse." Archaeologists found slate pen-
cils in adjacent lots, another clue related to the presence of literacy and
education in the town.

In 2008 a geophysical survey and excavations focused on the southern half of block 8, lots 1 and 2 in search of the schoolhouse. From 1858
through the end of the nineteenth century deed transactions note a portion

FIGURE 20. A stone pier that served as part of the foundation for a building, possibly the "Negro schoolhouse." Photograph by Christopher Valvano.

measuring 30 feet (E-W) by 21 feet (N-S) in the southwest corner of block 8, lot 1 as the "schoolhouse lot." By 1902 it is no longer mentioned in the deeds. The archaeology team tested a few anomalies. Flat glass, brick fragments, and cut nails were found in the area, suggesting that a nineteenth-century structure once stood there (Fennell 2008). Or it could have been a place where an outbuilding once stood. No evidence of a foundation existed, and perhaps that is why the deeds always noted that area as the "schoolhouse lot." So far, our best archaeological evidence for the schoolhouse coincides with the oral history. It may be the building that the Kimbrews purchased: block 9, lot 4.

Squire and Louisa McWorter's Home

In the second summer of excavations Chris Fennell instructed the University of Illinois field school, which participated in the excavations. Some of the Illinois students worked with NSF-REU students, and the rest broke up into two teams, one working on block 13, lot 3, and the other on block 13, lot 4. This work became very significant because this area is one of the very few where we know that a McWorter family member lived.

Squire McWorter acquired the deed to block 13, lots 3 and 4 in 1854. He immediately built a sizable two-story house, the biggest in New Philadelphia proper. The archaeology shows that it had a cellar and a fieldstone foundation. Squire died in 1855 and his wife, Louisa, continued to live in the house until her death in 1883. The 1850 Federal Census classifies Squire and Louisa as mulatto with five children. A twenty-two-year-old white woman named Mary A. (with no last name), who was born in England, lived in their household. Her daughter, also named Mary, is listed as mulatto, three years old, and born in Canada; her second daughter, Lucy, is noted as five months old, classified as mulatto, and born in Illinois.

Mary A. does not have a different surname, so she is probably a McWorter and the wife of young Frank, the son of Free Frank. Young Frank was enslaved and escaped to Canada in 1826 and freed when Frank Sr. exchanged his saltpeter operations for young Frank's freedom, which allowed him to be reunited with his family (Walker 1983a:62). According to Walker (71), young Frank made the trip to Illinois from Kentucky with the family in 1830. If he did marry Mary A. and fathered young Mary in Canada in 1847, perhaps he was involved in the Underground Railroad and returned to Canada on at least one occasion, when he met Mary A. In the 1850 census young Mary is their child. To make matters a bit confusing, the 1850 census lists young Frank in the same household with Frank and Lucy. Perhaps young Frank happened to be at his parents' house the day of the census and the census enumerator assumed he lived with them. Or maybe he was ill and his parents were caring for him. Young Frank died a year later.

In the 1855 state census Squire is classified as black, with eleven household members, and livestock valued at $165. He died after this census and Louisa became the head of the household. Yet they are not listed as living in New Philadelphia in the 1860 Federal Census; instead they are listed as "Free Inhabitants in the 3rd Ward of Quincy City." Louisa "McQuarter" is listed in "Keziah" Clark's household along with her son Squire (thirteen years old) and son George W. (eleven). We can speculate at this time that these two matriarchs, Louisa and Keziah, may have participated in Underground Railroad activities since Quincy has strong Underground Railroad connections. Five years later, and maybe earlier than that, according to the Illinois state census, Louisa was back in New Philadelphia and head of the household, along with daughter Lucy, son George, and Kezia (Casiah) and Thomas Clark, who were Louisa's mother and brother. This time Louisa is classified as black, with a total of four members in the household and livestock valued at $300.

In 1870 Louisa (forty-five years old) was classified as mulatto, with her children Lucy and George. Willie Jones, a six-year-old mulatto boy from Illinois, also resided in the household. We do not know their relationship to this boy, but he was probably an orphan whom Louisa took in. Casiah (Keziah) Clark, who owned block 9, lot 5, lived in Louisa's house. She is noted as seventy years old and mulatto. Her thirty-year-old son, Thomas, interestingly, is classified as white and also living in the household. The perception of whiteness by Euro-Americans changed significantly through the nineteenth and into the twentieth century; for instance, the Irish were not considered white until the end of the nineteenth century. The fluidity of racial categorizations is also shown in the fact that people throughout the New Philadelphia region changed color on various censuses.

In 1880 Louisa was still noted as the head of the household, with her son George (age twenty-eight) and daughter Lucy J. (age thirty-four). They are all described as mulatto. Kessiah (Casiah) Clark (seventy-six) is still part of the household, along with Charles Jones (listed as Willie in the 1870 census), a fifteen-year-old mulatto boy. In this document he is listed as an abandoned child and a laborer from Illinois.

The earliest tax assessments in 1867 indicate that Louisa McWorter owned lots 1–8 in block 13, valued at $16 with $150 of improvements, which includes the two-story house and associated outbuildings. The value of the lots and improvements increased substantially in the following year, to $40 and $200, respectively. After Louisa died in 1883 the deed was transferred to her son George, who then transferred the property in 1883 to Lucy Jane McKinney, Louisa's daughter (listed as Lucy J. in the 1880 Federal Census). Lucy and her family lived in the house until the early twentieth century.

Virgil Burdick owned the house by 1930 and rented it. According to Larry Burdick's late twentieth-century account of the town, the house had a full basement and a large single-story structure attached to the rear that served as the kitchen. A barn and a well also existed on the property. The house burned on December 7, 1937 (Burdick 1992: n.p.), and there is no signature of any structures on the surface of the lot in a 1939 aerial photograph.

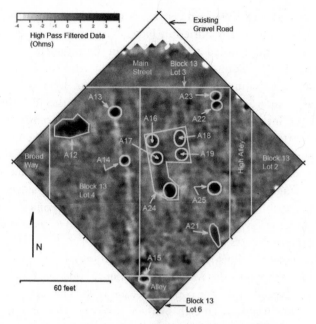

FIGURE 21. Anomalies located in the geophysical survey in block 13, lots 3 and 4. Squire and Louisa McWorter owned these lots, on which they constructed a two-story house with a basement. The land also contained a barn and other outbuildings. Map by Michael Hargrave. Overlay by Christopher Fennell.

During the walkover survey the archaeology team found a large concentration of artifacts in lots 3 and 4 of block 13. Most of these are domestic artifacts, although there is a heavy concentration of cut nails, suggesting the presence of a domestic structure in the vicinity. The geophysical survey identified many anomalies throughout that area, and the archaeology team, consisting of University of Illinois undergraduates working with graduate students Phil Millhouse and Eva Pajuelo, concentrated on one anomaly in lot 4 and one in lot 3 (Figure 21).

One of our biggest surprises was the finding in lot 3 of a Union uniform button. It may be associated with one of two people who lived on the lot. Young Squire, son of Louisa and Squire, served in the 38th Regiment, Company G, in the United States Colored Infantry. He entered as a private and left as a corporal. The information about his service is on the Ancestry.com website on Civil War veterans. Thomas Clark, son of Casiah (Keziah) Clark and living in Louisa McWorter's household, according to the 1870 federal census, is classified as a thirty-year-old white farmer. Thomas is buried in New Philadelphia's African American cemetery and is noted as Tom Clark in the cemetery records. According to the Pike County cemetery records, he also served in the Civil War. Other individuals from New Philadelphia who served in the Civil War include Simeon Clark, who also served in the 38th Regiment, U.S. Colored Infantry, in Company F. The Pike County cemetery records refer to Martin Kimbro (Kimbrew) as an "old soldier" when he died in 1907 at the age of seventy, so he may have served in the Civil War as well. While it is difficult to tie the artifact to a specific person, the connection to the Civil War is significant, linking New Philadelphia residents to the event that legally ended slavery in the United States. It contributes to the story of race, the Civil War, and the quest for freedom (*Cemetery Records of Pike County, Illinois* 1979).

At the end of the field season the archaeology team found several foundations related to the McWorter residence, one five feet deep and the other only as deep as one course of stonework. The team also placed two soil cores in an area north of the McWorter foundations (in the vicinity of anomalies A18 and A19) to about seven feet below the plow zone. At about 3.5 feet the core sample contained charcoal and ash, the remains of the burned barn. After the structure burned, the Burdicks placed a large amount of fill over the remains. The soil probably came from an artificial pond located about five hundred feet to the east of block 13.

In lot 4 the team defined the northern foundation wall for the McWorter cellar that ran in an east-west direction. The team also placed excavation units on the southern boundary of the same anomaly. At the base of the plow zone is a fieldstone foundation that runs in an east-west direction. The foundation was impacted by plowing; gaps appear in places along the wall, and some of the fieldstones are scattered and adjacent to the foundation.

The archaeology on block 13 was much more difficult than we had anticipated. We believed that we would find the signature of the burned house, such as timbers and charcoal, but we had no idea that most of the remains would be under almost four feet of fill. However, by the end of the season we were all pleased that the University of Illinois team located the remains of parts of the complex once owned by Squire and Louisa McWorter. The physical remains are nice evidence of the McWorter family's being part of the town site.

I considered this field season to be the highlight of the field project. With the combined field schools operating, we got a lot of work done and revealed more of the site. We now had a better idea of the filling and erosion that had occurred to the town, and we were able to confirm some of the anomalies on the site. The site was officially placed on the National Register of Historic Places at the end of the summer. Key places and artifacts were found to help support the stories of education and freedom. We also anticipated the McWorter family reunion, which planned to hold one of its events at the archaeology site at the end of the field season.

CHAPTER 8

Family Reunion and Division

In January 2005 *Smithsonian Magazine* ran an article on the archaeology project and mentioned how the notion of harmony had been miscast in the media. However, the New Philadelphia Association still supported the idea of a harmonious past, and through the summers of 2004 and 2005 newspapers increasingly picked up on this issue. Unfortunately the archaeology team was being saddled with the idea that harmony existed in the town. It was a perfect foil that created controversy between some of the descendants and the NPA, both groups with different views of the past. I felt as though we were caught in the middle on this issue. Controversy sells newspapers, and I suspect that differences will continue to highlight some media stories. Dana Mackenzie, the journalist for *Smithsonian Magazine,* stated Walker's view:

> The "premise that New Philadelphia was a town where blacks and whites lived in racial harmony . . . is just not historical reality, any more than to claim that slaves lived happily on plantations," argued Juliet Walker. . . .
> Shackel denies any attempt to idealize the past. "While the archaeology will probably not be able to show harmony or disharmony, it can illustrate the way of life for groups of people living in a biracial community," he says. "Archaeology is a way to provide a story of a people who have not been traditionally recorded in history. Our goal is to tell the story of New Philadelphia from the bottom up and provide an inclusive story of the town."
> Despite their disagreements, both Walker and Shackel would like to see New Philadelphia commemorated by more than a roadside plaque. Walker envisions rebuilding the town. Shackel, who has the support of the New

Philadelphia Association . . . hopes to turn the site into a state or national park. (Mackenzie 2005)

The *Smithsonian Magazine* article highlights professional differences. However, it does end on a positive note and it set a tone for subsequent news coverage. It emphasized that although there are differences, the various interest groups are working toward a common goal: placing the town site in the public memory of the nation. Perhaps reconciliation was on the horizon.

It surprised me that several people wrote to the magazine in response to Mackenzie's piece on the project. A letter to the editor that the magazine decided not to publish reached me several days after the issue arrived at newsstands. The author wrote about her father, who grew up near New Philadelphia. He had given her a copy of *Free Frank,* and she still treasures the book. She always tells her children that they can do anything if they want it badly enough, and she uses the Frank McWorter story as an example. She said that after reading the book she and her husband decided to look for the cemetery and the town:

> We got a little lost on all of the dirt roads and stopped where we thought it must be, only to be approached by a somewhat unfriendly farmer. We told him we were looking for New Philadelphia, and he replied, "Oh you mean that n———er town. It was over there." I was horrified by the farmer's language and attitude, and even a little scared, for reasons I can't articulate other than no one in my family ever used that term. (Margaret Watson Rutledge, letter to the editor, January 14, 2005)

The letter highlights the racism that still exists in the area and is another reason that it pained me that the NPA insisted on keeping the myth of harmony on their website.

In the spring of 2005 many members of the McWorter family planned that part of their family reunion would be held at New Philadelphia, with the cooperation of the NPA and the archaeology program. The family scheduled their event for the end of June 2005 in Springfield, Illinois, with the idea of making a trip to the archaeology site and visiting the family cemetery. In April Juliet Walker released an announcement to the local county press stating her plans to film a documentary on Free Frank's life and New Philadelphia. During an interview with the *Quincy Herald Whig,* Walker made it clear that she wanted to maintain her differences with the archaeology program, the NPA, and family members who supported the archaeology project. She claimed, "The documentary is going to generate national attention, not only because of the significance of [Frank McWorter's] life, but also the controversy that will be generated on how attempts were made to rewrite the black historical experience." Filming was to begin in the spring of 2005 and wrap up by the end of the year, with the possibility of a Pike County premiere during Black History Month in February 2006 (Husar 2005b). As of this writing, in 2010, I have not heard of the film premiering in Pike County.

Walker told the *Quincy Herald Whig,* "My mother, Thelma Elise Kirkpatrick Wheaton, was the caretaker of the history of Free Frank, a slave who purchased the freedom of 16 members of his family and became the first African-American town founder in America. . . . It was her last wish that I tell the story of his life to the world. She also wanted me to recreate the town of New Philadelphia, and I have committed every breath I have to complete her dream." The reporter noted, "The project brings Walker back to Pike County this summer in a step toward fulfilling her mother's dream" (Husar 2005b).

During the field school we had weekly lectures by prominent scholars who discussed their research with the students and the local community. On Thursday evening, June 23, 2005, Gerald McWorter spoke to the archaeology field school (thirty students and staff), interested community members (about thirty-five people), and about a dozen McWorter family members and relatives. He packed the lodge's main room; some people had to stand along the back wall. After all of the controversy in the newspapers about the meaning of New Philadelphia, people came to hear a positive voice from a member of the legendary McWorter family. Gerald spoke with confidence and had complete control of his audience. We hung onto his words. He explained, "As a person who came of age in the 1960s, my historical legacy was awakened. The freedom road chose me as much as I chose it." He added, "Frank is remembered because he gave his life for freedom, freedom of his family, and as a successful entrepreneur and a leader in a nineteenth century integrated community." The *Quincy Herald Whig* reported that the interest in the project "created a 'family' of the sort favored by [Gerald] McWorter's late aunt Thelma, the genealogist and hub of his own family. 'Her definition of family was not blood relation. Her definition was blood, marriage, really close friends and anybody who would insist on being included,' [Gerald] McWorter said" (Husar 2005a).

Other McWorter descendants expressed their excitement about his talk and the research project. Shirley McWorter Moss exclaimed, "Knowing the dig is taking place, all of the things taking place to find out about Free Frank and honor Free Frank, it was overwhelming" (Husar 2005a).

The following day, Friday, June 24, 2005, Juliet Walker scheduled a press conference in front of the library in downtown Barry. At noon she unveiled her architectural model and plans for rebuilding New Philadelphia, even though she does not own nor does she have permission to build on the original site of New Philadelphia. The three local county newspapers attended the conference. She claimed that work would begin in 2007 and would cost from $500,000 to $1,000,000 (Pat Likes, personal communication). The St. Louis and Springfield daily newspapers mentioned the upcoming family reunion and Walker's plans to rebuild New Philadelphia. Walker acknowledged that she could not rebuild the town on the original site. However, she announced that she was in the process of negotiating the purchase of another parcel of land in Pike County. She also claimed that she did not see that it was important to build the town on the original site: "Why is it important where the town is? You don't need the site. There is nothing on that site. The town could be restored anywhere because nothing's left" (Browning 2005). Even though the archaeology team has made all of our research available by posting it on our websites, with oral histories and census and tax data showing people and houses in the town into the twentieth century, Walker still maintained that the town was gone after 1869. I was also interviewed, and the same article concluded with me saying, "We don't pretend that we're the final source, but we are all very dedicated to building a history of the town" (Browning 2005).

Although the archaeology project is beginning to uncover the footprints of the town, it would be virtually impossible to accurately rebuild New Philadelphia. We will probably never know the size and height of many of the buildings we are uncovering, since what usually remains are the pit cellars. We also do not know with certainty which houses were of log construction and which were of frame construction. It would be inappropriate to make these assumptions and create an inaccurate image of the town.

THE DAY OF THE REUNION

The NPA arranged for part of the McWorter family reunion to be held at the archaeology site on Saturday, June 25. The bus arrived at 11:30 in the morning, as the temperatures soared into the mid 90s—a typical midwestern summer afternoon.

The McWorter family handed out a news release stating the purpose of their gathering at New Philadelphia. The document, signed by Shirley McWorter Moss, Allen Kirkpatrick, Sandra McWorter, Gerald McWorter, Patricia McWorter, and Lonie McWorter Vond Wilson, stated:

We have gathered at this time for several reasons:

1) We are connecting members of the family who have independently been doing genealogical research, and who have not known each other in the past. New research is redefining the lineage of the McWorter family.

2) We have been honored to have Gov. Blagojevich dedicate a stretch of Interstate 72 in Illinois to Frank McWorter, so we are pleased to gather to affirm our ancestral family founder.

3) We are very interested in the National Science Foundation sponsored archaeological project to study the material remains of the town of New Philadelphia founded by Frank McWorter in 1836.

4) Finally, we are interested in cooperating with the New Philadelphia Association in building a lasting monument to keep the memory of Frank McWorter as part of the local history of Pike County, Illinois.

We are a diverse and geographically dispersed family. . . . We have many family initiatives regarding family history and historical restoration projects. . . . Our goal is to encourage all family members, and interested parties in Illinois and throughout the country to contribute their ideas so that in the near future we can gather as a family and come to final plans.

Our family is united around the goal of preserving the memory and legacy of freedom started by Frank and Lucy McWorter. We encourage everyone willing to join and contribute to this effort. (Moss et al. 2005).

The archaeology crew guided the family around the site, and members of the NPA transported other family members to the cemetery. Archaeologists had several cellar features exposed and were in the process of excavating a well. Washing the artifacts near the main gathering area drew the most attention, and some of the younger family members helped with the cleaning.

The NPA always puts on a great spread, and this was no exception. Barbequed chicken and pork and homemade desserts were the highlight. The governor sent a representative to this gathering. As the field events began to wind down, the archaeology team, the NPA, and many McWorter family members went to the Baptist church in Barry to meet as a group for a second time. At the meeting the family expressed their amazement at how much attention their family and the town of New Philadelphia was receiving in the press. They were delighted that the National Science Foundation supported the project, and they thought that the prestige of the town was heightened when the *Smithsonian Magazine* covered it in January 2005. Even more important, the town was in the process of being added to the National Register of Historic Places. At the meeting the NPA pledged to work with the family to move ahead and help support them to restore the cemetery.

Gerald McWorter, the spokesperson for the family at this event, also made the commitment to work with the NPA toward preserving the history of the town and the restoration of the cemetery. I believe that the family members who came to the site felt that there was considerable momentum in the project and that by working cooperatively they could help promote the heroic story of Frank and Lucy McWorter's quest for freedom.

AFTER THE REUNION

The *Rockford Register* reported my evening talk about the New Philadelphia archaeology program at the Illinois State Museum before eighty local citizens, about a month after the McWorter family reunion. I repeated my belief that it is important to look at the New Philadelphia project in an inclusive way. I questioned, "Is New Philadelphia about one man, Frank McWorter? . . . Is it about the African-American community and its ability to survive 100 years in a racist society? Is it about freedom? Is it about race relations in a biracial town? Or is it about the other people that are not recorded in the historical records? My answer is: I think it's all of the above" (Chambers 2005). I spoke about how archaeology can contribute to promoting social justice, and I stated a three-point plan. First, we need to critically analyze and expose racism in the past and present and dismantle the structures of oppression when we can. Second, we should explore diversity in the past and promote it in the present. Third, it is important to create a color-conscious past rather than a color-blind past (Husar 2005d).

After the talk the NPA began planning a ceremony and celebration with the McWorter family for the end of September to celebrate the placing of the town on the National Register of Historic Places, the same weekend as the Barry Apple Festival. Many McWorter family members came for the ceremony. Janet Davies, host of *190 North,* a news show produced by Chicago television station ABC7, filmed the event. She interviewed community members and local descendants for a short four-minute segment that aired in February 2006. Phil Bradshaw hosted the ceremony and the cameras rolled. Michelle Huttes, the author of the nomination, gave a short presentation, followed by a few words by me and Terry Martin. We all stressed that placing the site on the National Register is an important step in placing New Philadelphia in the national public memory. New Philadelphia was featured on the 2005 Illinois Archaeology Awareness Month poster, and Terry handed out copies to attending dignitaries. Gerald McWorter spoke about his family history and said that it should always be important to emphasize the concept of freedom when remembering New Philadelphia. When he finished, Senator Deanna Demuzio, the local state senator, took the stage. She pledged to do whatever she could to help preserve the land where New Philadelphia once stood. After Demuzio finished her speech Bradshaw asked Juliet Walker to say a few words. She held up two books, both of them *Free Frank,* and she spoke about studying with John Hope Franklin, one of the most celebrated historians of our time. She emphasized the importance of her research and thanked the NPA for their hard work. After the ceremony we left for the Apple Festival parade, and Davies remained, interviewing Walker.

Archaeology magazine featured the New Philadelphia archaeology project in the September/October 2005 issue. Chris Fennell worked diligently with writer Jennifer Pinkowski to help coordinate her efforts to interview McWorter family members who had arrived for the family reunion. In the issue is a wonderful picture of field school student Hannah Mills, a descendant of New Philadelphia's Johnson family, doing archaeology. There is another great photograph of Sandra McWorter in her overalls at a sifting screen, looking for artifacts. Pinkowski mentioned that Sandra's views and relationship to the excavations are very different from that of her first cousin, Juliet Walker. Even though New Philadelphia was then on the National Register of Historic Places because of the archaeology, Walker believed that "the town's importance begins and ends with Free Frank. 'What makes New Philadelphia interesting was that it was founded by a black person before the Civil War." Feeling that her work as a black scholar has been hijacked, she protested, "I have been working on this for decades. From my perspective, it's an exploitation of a slave laborer, and a descendant of his" (Pinkowski 2005:46, 47). In the article Chris Fennell responded by highlighting the importance of multivocality: "This is a town with a very complex heritage, so it makes it hard to say that any one person has a claim on it" (47).

Gerald McWorter offered the view of some of the other family members: "I understand [Walker's] passion about protecting the integrity of our family history. She is not pleased with the archaeological research, but many of us are. . . . We have the material remains of our ancestors that we didn't have before. I'm grateful to the archaeologists for that" (Pinkowski 2005:47). He later told the *Rockford Register Star*, "I'm really excited about [the archaeology project]. I welcome it and I embrace it. That's why we're here. I try to lend moral support" (Chambers 2007b).

In late 2005 Walker began to make positive acknowledgments of the National Science Foundation grant and later the National Register of Historic Places nomination for the town site. "It is indeed gratifying that my book has precipitated a series of activities that honor the life and contributions to this nation's history made by my great-great-grandfather," she said (Husar 2005b). Her website (www.newphiladelphiaillinois.org/about-origin.shtml) claims that her work was instrumental in the awarding of the NSF grant and includes a banner highlighting the addition of the town site to the National Register of Historic Places. While acknowledging the successes of the archaeology project, she still stated opposition to the program: "As a historian, I have significant concerns about how Free Frank is being presented by the New Philadelphia Association, the people connected with the dig," she said (Husar 2005b).

THE TRADITIONAL MCWORTER HOMESITE

Pleased with the publicity and the great success of the archaeological excavations, including placing the town on the National Register of Historic Places, we thought that the next important step was to collect enough data to nominate the site as a National Historic Landmark. Although we had gathered significant information about the town site, there is a strip of land about ten acres in size immediately to the north of New Philadelphia and adjacent to the northeastern half of the site that we had not yet explored. It holds the site of the traditional McWorter homesite and the New Philadelphia schoolhouse. Only a cellar hole is visible at the homesite, and a few architectural remains are scattered in a field where the school once stood. Adjacent and to the northwest of the town is another parcel of land that the McWorters once owned. We thought we should survey both properties to determine the chronology and relationship of the property to the development of New Philadelphia.

Solomon McWorter once owned this plot of land. The area holds what we are now calling the McWorter traditional homesite. Today it contains part of a fieldstone foundation and a cellar and a cistern, which is surrounded by a cluster of trees. There is a family tradition that the former house on the site was built by Frank McWorter (Walker 1983c: n20); other family stories indicate that it was the house built by his son Solomon (Simpson 1981:40).

Solomon was born enslaved in 1815, and in 1835 Frank purchased his freedom. The 1872 Pike County Atlas described Solomon as "now living on, and is the owner of, the old homestead, in Hadley Township, where his father first settled" (*Atlas Map of Pike County* 1872:54). In 1863 he married Frances F. Coleman, who was born in Missouri in 1843. By 1872 they had four children, one son and three daughters. The Atlas notes, "There are few men in Pike County who are succeeding better than he. Solomon's education is rather limited, but he is a man of good natural abilities, and very industrious, and prospering well. He is now owner of five hundred acres of first-class land, well stocked with cattle, hogs, horses, and mules. He is a man of good moral habits, and is highly respected by his neighbors" (54).

Helen McWorter Simpson, granddaughter of Solomon, described going back to the family home in Hadley Township: "We finally reached the farm in the early evening just as the shadows were falling. Here at last was the family home. This was the house that my grandfather, Solomon McWorter, had built as soon as he could when the growing family had become too large for the log cabin in which my father, the oldest child, had been born" (1981:40). In Simpson's account, Solomon established a new McWorter residence in about 1864 or 1865, soon after his 1863 marriage and the birth of his first child in 1864 (see Walker 1983a:168). The 1860 map of Pike County shows the McWorter house just north and a bit west of New Philadelphia's Broad Street. The 1872 Pike County Atlas no longer has a structure in this location, but one can be found further to the east, in about the same place where the cellar is located. My hunch is that the feature that we are calling the traditional McWorter homesite is probably the remains of the 1864–65 house built by Solomon and Frances. An archaeological survey would help clarify this issue.

We decided to perform the survey in the spring of 2006. However, Roger Woods, the owner of the land, asked that we do it before he planted his spring crops, during the first week of April. The field was loaded with corn stalks from the previous year and the ground visibility ranged from 10 to 15 percent. We asked Woods to disk the soil several weeks before we arrived. This work would turn the soil and make the ground more visible, thereby increasing our chances of finding artifacts.

Unfortunately for the archaeologists, February had some snow and early March had torrential rains. Major storms hit the area before we arrived and a tornado touched down in the capital city, Springfield. The plans did not go as smoothly as I had hoped.

I had my plane ticket to fly into Springfield during the third weekend in March. This was the only time in the month that the *Farmer's Almanac* did not predict "chilly" temperatures and "snow in the north and rain in the south." March 16–20 were listed as sunny and mild. We had to get the survey in before the April planting. Both Terry Martin and Chris Fennell thought it was a risky scheme. They didn't have much faith in the *Almanac*. Many of the local Pike County residents also thought we were crazy coming to the area during the third week of March since the weather is so unpredictable at that time of year.

Placing our faith in the *Farmer's Almanac* one more time, I landed in Springfield with Charlotte King on Thursday and we drove out to the site. When we were close to New Philadelphia we saw Roger Woods in the distance disking the field. I breathed a sigh of relief. He was working the soil even though it was still moist from a very wet spring. Terry and Chris met us at the site and we surveyed in several areas to give us a baseline for our walkover survey of the traditional homesite.

The following day Terry came out with a few volunteers and we began walking the northeast field. The most visible features associated with the traditional McWorter homesite are the remains of the cellar and a nearby cistern, which are surrounded by a cluster of trees in the middle of the field. At the far eastern portion of the field the New Philadelphia schoolhouse has all but vanished from the landscape. By the end of the first day our hunch turned out to be correct. After quick analysis by Charlotte King of the several hundred artifacts collected around the cellar, it became clear that the site dates no earlier than the Civil War era. The McWorter traditional homesite is the home that Solomon built in about 1864 after he moved out of the original McWorter cabin (Figure 22).

At the end of the day we asked ourselves, Where could the original McWorter homesite be located? The 1860s map placed the homestead to the north and a bit west of Broad Street. This area was on a different parcel of land, so we had to ask another landowner for permission to do a survey. Natalie Armistead, always eager to help, placed the call while Terry and I took core samples in the area of several anomalies in New Philadelphia proper in preparation for the summer field season. In the meantime Chris and several volunteers identified and collected artifacts

FIGURE 22. The pedestrian survey of the McWorter traditional homesite. Photograph by Paul A. Shackel.

from around the traditional homesite. We received an initial okay from one of the landowners, and Terry and I decided to wait for the crew to finish collecting artifacts in the field before we made our way across the road to begin the survey. Just before lunch a car came up the gravel road; a woman jumped out and approached us while we cored a potential feature. She explained that although she wanted to give us permission, several family members owned the land, and not all of them agreed to allow us to survey the land. She did not say what sticking points had arisen in their family conversation. We were denied access to the property, and the mystery of the exact location of the original McWorter homesite still remains unsolved. I have a hunch it is adjacent to the northeast corner of the original town site.

THE NEW PHILADELPHIA CEMETERY

At the request of Sandra McWorter, Michael Hargrave performed a geophysical survey of the New Philadelphia cemetery during the same weekend as our survey of the traditional homesite. To get to the cemetery you need to follow a gravel road and a wooded path, down a valley, through a creek, and up another hill. Four-wheel drive is a requirement, unless you want to hike to the place. The earliest known burial in the cemetery is that of Francis McWorter, son of Frank and Lucy, and dates to 1851, and the most recent burial is James Washington's in 1950. The cemetery was deeded to the county in 1885 (*Cemetery Records of Pike County, Illinois* 1979; Matteson 1964:33; Simpson 1981:9).

In 1964 Grace Matteson described her experience locating the New Philadelphia cemetery:

> We rode right up to the cemetery gate. The cemetery, which was no doubt once a pretty place, with shade trees here and there, is overgrown now with brambles, briars, and covered with an accumulation of dead leaves, so that it was difficult to find the graves.
>
> Most of the headstones had fallen to the ground, and some had been broken, with pieces scattered a few feet apart. Most of the inscriptions were still decipherable—after they had been cleaned off. . . .
>
> With the men doing the heavy lifting and digging, quite a number of stones were unearthed; one of them being the marker for a woman nearly 106 years old. This was Judy Armstead, born in 1800, who died in 1906. The name of "Armstead" had not appeared in the history of Philadelphia.
>
> The markers for "Free Frank" and "Free Lucy" were uncovered [and we] copied all of the inscriptions, which were decipherable, as follows:

Christena Watts, "wife of Otis Watts," b. April 23, 1892, d. Feb 16, 1916

Myrtyle G., "their daughter," b. Dec. 7, 1914, d. Sept. 8, 1915

Louisa Walker, "wife of John W. Wright," b. Feb 11, 1846, d. Jan 1, 1873 (or 1878)

Lettie Walker, "daughter of J. & L.," d. May 23, 1862, aged 16y.

Sarah McWorter, "She was the mother of six children. All are dead but Commodore and Hiley," d. Mar. 22, 1891, aged 77y.

Francis McWorter, d. June 21, 1851, Aged 46 y, 9 m.

Moses Wagner, b. Aug 22, 1815, d. Mar. 9, 1880, aged 64 y, 6 m, 17 d.

Commodore McWorter, d. Mar. 15, 1855, aged 32 y, 11 m, 12 d.

Squire McWorter, d. Dec. 18, 1855, aged 38 y, 3 m

Franke McWorter, d. Sept. 7, 1854, aged 77 y, 27 d

Lucy McWorter, "wife of F. McWorter," born in 1771, d. Aug. 23, 1870

Solomon McWorter, d. Jan. 7, 1879, aged 63 y, 11 m, 3 d.

Judy Armstead, b. May 13, 1800, d. Mar. 12, 1906, aged 105 y, 10m

FIGURE 23. Civil War markers were placed on graves at the turn of the century.
Photograph by Paul A. Shackel.

Stones did not mark the grave locations of Lucy McWorter (b. 1888, d. 1913), Aphelia McWorter (Walker) (d. 1915), Oregon Walker (d. 1906), Mary (McWorter) Washington (d. 1922), Ruby Zenobia Washington (d. 1916), and Wilber E. Washington (d. 1910). There are two commemorative Civil War metal stars placed on two graves believed to be for Tom Clark (Civil War) and Martin Kimbo ([Kimbrew], d. 1907, age seventy) (*Cemetery Records of Pike County, Illinois* 1979:149). Matteson (1964:26–27) wrote that James Washington, who died on May 1, 1950, was the last person buried in the cemetery. He does not have a grave marker, nor is his burial recorded in the cemetery records (Figure 23).

Hargrave used a gradiometer to record magnetic readings, as well as a resistance meter to detect subsurface disturbances (Hargrave 2006b:1). The following year Chris used a combination of a global positioning device and a total station to record ground depressions to overlay the results with the geophysical survey and possibly find other unmarked graves. According to the *Cemetery Records of Pike County* (1979) there are twenty-four individuals buried in the New Philadelphia

FIGURE 24. Artifacts remaining at a gravesite in the New Philadelphia cemetery. Photograph by Paul A. Shackel.

cemetery. The electrical resistance survey indicates the presence of twenty-two graves. Perhaps in a few cases a shaft may have been used for more than one individual, or, as is typical in most cemeteries with unmarked graves, newer graves could have cut into the unmarked or forgotten graves. Depressions measuring about six feet long and several feet wide are scattered within the fenced area and follow an east-west direction.

Charlotte worked closely with Chris recording the surface artifacts that appeared to have been left on some of the graves. To the common eye it looks like a few people may have had a party in the area. Broken pieces of glass of different colors and designs are located on grave depressions and in other places close to headstones. Some animal bones are also present in the vicinity of a few graves (Figure 24). Charlotte identified the artifacts on the surface without removing them from their original context. Our thought is that these objects, dating to the late nineteenth and early twentieth centuries, were intentionally left at the site for spiritual and ceremonial reasons, so we wanted to honor those practices by keeping the artifacts in place.

Many cultures leave grave goods or memorials at gravesites. The items left in the New Philadelphia cemetery appear to follow a pattern seen at other cemeteries with strong African American traditions. A large proportion of the enslaved Africans came to the United States from the Kongo region of West Africa, and African American burial ground traditions tend to have some of the same elements found in the BaKongo culture. King (2010) has since researched the meaning and spatial distribution of the artifacts. All of the glass and ceramic artifacts found in the cemetery were broken. The ritual of breaking ceramic or glass vessels that once belonged to the deceased often symbolizes the release of the spirit. Milk-glass fragments found may also represent the symbolic color of the spirit world in the BaKongo cosmology. A glass piece with a sunburst design represents the setting sun, a symbol of death, or the rising sun, a representation of rebirth (Morrow 2002:105–7; King 2007, 2010; M. R. Little 1998:23).

There are also large freshwater mussel shells in the cemetery. In the BaKongo culture shells represent immortality and the cycling of lives. About a dozen different animal bones were found, and Terry Martin has identified some of them as lamb. Leaving food on a grave has the symbolic value of providing nourishment in the afterlife, and this tradition was also popular among the BaKongo (King 2010; Vlach 1990).

In the New Philadelphia cemetery there are several connections to African traditional practices that lasted into the early twentieth century (King 2010). The McWorter descendants are carefully planning the restoration of the cemetery, including the stabilization of some of the headstones and placing a general memorial in or near the cemetery to commemorate all of those buried, marked and unmarked, who contributed to the history of New Philadelphia. The family wants to create a place where all people can come and contemplate the past, present, and future. Pike County has since appointed a board, which includes local citizens and descendants, with responsibility for overseeing the cemetery.

CHAPTER 9

Three Generations of Building and One Hundred Years of Living in New Philadelphia

The third field season began much like the first. Terry Martin zipped back and forth to the Springfield airport, picking up students. In the three years of our fieldwork students came from as far as Puerto Rico and as close as Barry, Illinois. Chris Fennell surveyed in a grid for Michael Hargrave's geophysical work and we prepared for our orientation meeting with the students. We already knew that McWorter family members planned to visit the site toward the end of June.

This field season furnished significant information that confirmed that New Philadelphia had at least three generations of building and that people lived in the town for almost one hundred years. It was a dynamic place, with families building, remodeling, and adding extensions to their houses and tearing down older buildings and temporary log cabins. Archaeological evidence helped to support the oral histories and documentary records about the long time depth of the place.

FIRST GENERATION OF BUILDING AND ABANDONMENT

The walkover survey identified a large quantity of artifacts in the eastern portion of block 4. A concentration of cut nails on the surface suggests that a building, and possibly buildings, once stood in the immediate area (Gwaltney 2004). Close to the intersection of the blacktop road and Broad Street, in lot 1, a filled-in well is still visible on the surface. At present it is difficult to ascertain its age, although it was probably used into the twentieth century. Michael Hargrave performed a geophysical survey of this area and identified several anomalies.

Spaulding Burdick acquired the southern half of lot 1 in 1846 and D. A. Kittle purchased the northern half of the lot in 1848, both from Frank McWorter. The 1850 Federal Census lists Spaulding Burdick as a sixty-three-year-old shoemaker from Rhode Island. His household included Ann (twenty-two years old) from Massachusetts and John (fourteen) and Benj. (nine), both of whom were born in New York. The census enumerators listed the members of the household as white. Burdick owned the property into the 1860s.

D. A. Kittle is listed in the 1850 Federal Census as a twenty-nine-year-old merchant living with his wife, Sophia, who is the same age. Both originated from Ohio, although in the 1880 census, while living in Iowa, David listed Virginia as his birthplace. The family is classified as white. Kittle had sold his lot by 1854 to James and Elizabeth Taylor, both from Delaware. Benjamin, James's brother, is taxed on the land in 1855. However, John and Augusta Sider owned the property from 1858 to 1869. John was born in Kentucky and his wife in Ohio. John came to Pike County by 1850 and is listed as a laborer. He farmed a small plot of land adjacent to the town. John died in 1863 and left the homestead to his wife, which she retained until three weeks before she remarried in 1869 (T. Martin and Martin 2010).

The Hadley Township tax records show the north and southern half of block 4, lot 1 had no improvements from at least 1867 (the date of the earliest known tax records from Hadley Township) until 1883. In 1883 A. B. Johnson had a total of $150 in improvements; however, the tax assessment combines Johnson's improvements on lots 1, 2, and 3, making it difficult to determine which lots were improved. John Kellum subsequently owned the lot. Grace Matteson's 1964 collection of oral histories indicate that Kellum tended "a sort of grocery" on this block at the turn of the twentieth century. In the nineteenth century a grocery typically sold goods and alcohol; however, because we have not found Kellum's account book we are uncertain at this point about what he sold. The small structure valued at $150 in the 1883 tax records may have been the store operated by John Kellum before he moved to another nearby community (Matteson 1964: postscript 3). No structures are noticeable on this lot in the 1939 aerial photograph.

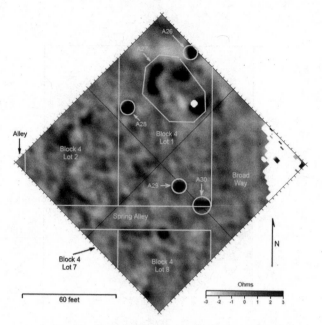

FIGURE 25. Geophysical survey locating several anomalies (A28, A29, A30) in block 4, lot 1. Map by Michael Hargrave. Overlay by Christopher Fennell.

The Burdicks

In the summer of 2005 the archaeology team, supervised by Chris Valvano of Michigan State University, placed eight 5 feet by 5 feet excavation units in a lot owned by the Burdicks. The placement of these units corresponded with the anomalies identified by Michael Hargrave in his 2005 geophysical survey. The students uncovered the outline of two features below the plow zone. When compared to the surrounding soil, the features are defined by their content of plaster, mortar, and brick as well as some glass, ceramics, and iron fragments. We labeled these features 7 and 13 (Figures 25 and 26).

Feature 7 is rectangular in shape and measures about 10.0 feet east-west by 3.5 feet north-south. Archaeologists did not have a chance to bisect this feature before the end of the 2005 field season, although several ceramic sherds dating to the 1830s–1840s on the top of the feature indicate that it is probably associated with the early settlement of the town, and possibly the Burdick family. We had to wait until the following summer (2006) before we could explore this feature.

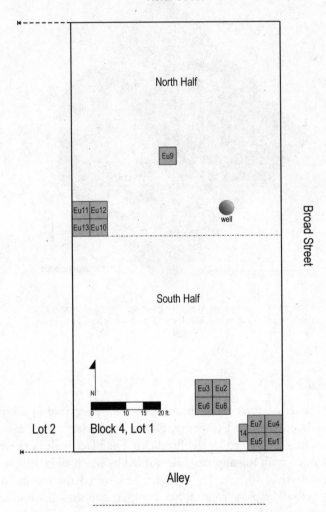

North Street

North Half

Eu9

well

Broad Street

South Half

N

0   10   15   20 ft.

Lot 2   Block 4, Lot 1

Eu11 Eu12
Eu13 Eu10

Eu3 Eu2
Eu6 Eu8

14 Eu7 Eu4
    Eu5 Eu1

Alley

FIGURE 26. Location of excavation units in the northern and southern halves of block 4, lot 1. Drawing by Christopher Valvano.

In 2006 Valvano and his team bisected the feature lengthwise, excavating the southern section, which measures about 10.5 feet by 1.75 feet. The feature fill contains a large quantity of brick and stone rubble. It is about 1.3 feet deep (below the plow zone), and the bottom is consistently flat throughout its entire length (Figures 27 and 28).

FIGURE 27. A pit cellar, feature 7, in the southern half of block 4, lot 1 (included in excavation units 1, 4, 5, 7, and 14 in the area of A30) in the process of being bisected and excavated. Photograph by Paul A. Shackel.

After removing the soil and artifacts it became clear that the feature once served as a pit cellar. Based on pattern designs and makers' marks on ceramics, we concluded that the feature contains artifacts that date from the 1830s and a few that date from the 1840s. Very few refined samples of earthenware, such as plates and teacups, came from the feature, and only a few stoneware vessels for food storage are present. A tumbler base and a medicine bottle with the words "... WAND' MIXT [URE]" embossed on its side also came from the feature. A possible mend with a sherd from the same vessel found in feature 13 (which has a substantially larger sample size of artifacts and dates to at least 1845, based on a transfer print design on a ceramic sherd) provides additional lines of evidence that the pit cellar and feature 13 were filled about the same time, in the 1840s. The fill also includes an abundant amount of domestic pig bones and some rat bones (Hsieh and Martin 2006). Rats are opportunists and scavenge food remains left by humans. Originally coming overseas with the early voyagers to the

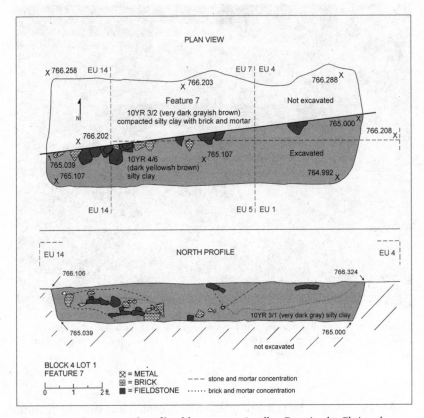

PLAN VIEW

FIGURE 28. Plan view and profile of feature 7, a pit cellar. Drawing by Christopher Valvano.

Americas, their remains can be found in almost any historic archaeological assemblage. The presence of Old World rat bones helps to paint the scene of an open refuse pit where rodents scavenged. Different bird species are also present and include domestic chickens, which were probably raised on site, adjacent to the house, and prairie chicken, which would have been wild. The delicate remains of buffalo fish bones and the hard-shelled freshwater mussel helps us imagine trips to nearby Kaiser Creek and the Illinois River to fish and gather food (Hsieh and Martin 2006). An early twentieth-century newspaper account describes a scene likely very similar to such nineteenth-century activities: "Mr. and Mrs. McWorter returned from the Illinois river Sunday, where they went Saturday to fish. . . . Quite a crowd is expected at the fish fry at Philadelphia Thursday" (*Barry Record*, August 16, 1906:8).

FIGURE 29. A well in the southern half of block 4, lot 1 (included in excavation units 2, 3, 6, and 8 in the area of A29) that has been bisected and excavated. Photograph by Paul A. Shackel.

The pit cellar was constructed perhaps as late as 1846, the year Burdick purchased the lot. The large quantity of rubble in the feature indicates that it was filled with surrounding soil and debris soon after the cabin was dismantled and removed. A small amount of raspberry seeds from this feature is evidence that it served as a receptacle for chamber pot refuse for a short time.

About ten feet northeast of the pit cellar the archaeology team uncovered feature 13. The feature has a circular shape and measures about 9 feet north-south and 8 feet east-west. Valvano's team bisected the feature, and after several weeks of excavations we realized that its original function was a well. At about two feet below the plow zone the excavators began to find large quantities of fieldstone and mortar. The team excavated feature 13 to a depth of 4.2 feet below the plow zone and it retained its circular shape (Figure 29).

The majority of the ceramic vessels from the well of feature 13 are refined earthenware. The redware include a portion of a pie plate, and there are only a few stoneware storage vessels. Transfer prints are the most popular decoration on the plates. There are also some shell-edged and

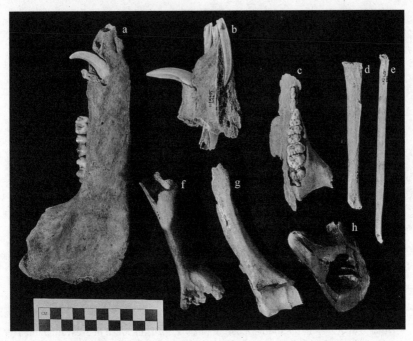

FIGURE 30. A sample of faunal remains from feature 13: (a) pig mandible, (b) pig mandible, (c) juvenile pig maxilla, (d) turkey bone (tibiotarsus), (e) Canada goose bone (radius), (f) pig humerus, (g) burned sheep humerus, (h) cow humerus, saw-cut and burned. Photograph by Terrance Martin.

hand-painted ceramics. Glass comprises less than 3 percent of the entire assemblage. The datable ceramic materials from this well were manufactured in the 1830s and 1840s, and a marble pattern on a plate (by John Wedgewood, 1845–60; see P. Williams 1978:643) provides a TPQ (*terminus post quem,* "the date after which") date of 1845 for the feature fill. That means it was filled some time after 1845. The pit cellar ceramic assemblage is rather small, with a slightly earlier date (the majority of artifacts tend to be from the 1830s, although a few date to the 1840s); the well assemblage is much larger, with materials dating to the 1830s and 1840s. Two ceramic pieces from the same vessel of redware are from the well and the pit cellar, suggesting that they were filled about the same time (Bailey 2006).

Domestic pig and cattle each account for about 40 percent of the biomass in this faunal assemblage, and other domestic and wild species are part of the assemblage (T. Martin and Martin 2010; Figure 30). This finding is important because many archaeologists in the region attribute the high frequency of pig biomass supplemented by small wild game such as squirrel and rabbit to a southern cultural preference, a pattern known as the Upland South tradition (McCorvie 1987:108–9). I believe that the Burdick family assemblage challenges us to think differently about these foodways patterns; other variables need to be considered, such as access to local and regional markets and the ease of raising livestock in a small commercial town. New Philadelphia is in the west-central portion of the state, where northern and southern traditions meet. It seems that pork dominated the local cultural traditions, and upon arriving in New Philadelphia Burdick adopted this tradition.

An in-depth study of the 1840 and 1850 Agricultural Census of Hadley Township shows that New York farmers raised equal numbers of swine and beef cattle, whereas the average Kentucky farmer raised three times (in 1840) to six and a half times (in 1850) as many swine as cattle (C. Martin and Martin 2010). Pork, though not necessarily a favorite in the northern cuisine, had some advantages. For instance, salting or pickling can easily preserve pork, but it is more difficult to preserve beef; preserved meat would have been helpful during the early settlement of the town (T. J. Martin and Brand 2002:8). So having a high percentage of pork biomass, equal to the cattle biomass, should not be surprising in this region.

The mortar pieces found in the well of feature 13 are rather large, some three to four inches thick and some over a foot long. The architectural debris is related to the cabin that sat over the pit cellar (feature 7), located only ten feet away, and was disposed of in the well when the structure was dismantled. The large pieces of mortar served as chinking, or infill material between the logs in the cabin. It became clear that we had found evidence of one of the early and usually temporary log cabins in New Philadelphia. We were astonished when Valvano found a piece of mortar that measures about 1.5 feet long with an impressed nine-inch corncob. The corn had been eaten and the cob was used as filler for the chinking (Figure 31). Typically small stones are used for chinking in order to give the mortar some stability and help the mixture last a bit longer.

Chapman (1880) describes a typical log dwelling in Pike County. He explains that logs were cut to equal size and joined together with notches cut into the ends. Gaps between the logs were then daubed and occasionally repaired, a process done to keep the dwelling weather-tight. Log cabins were typically one story, sometimes built as high as eight feet. An end chimney was made of stone or clay. A window about two feet wide was cut into one wall and covered with glass or greased paper. The one-room dwelling served as a "kitchen, dining-room, sitting-room, bed-room, and parlor" (342).

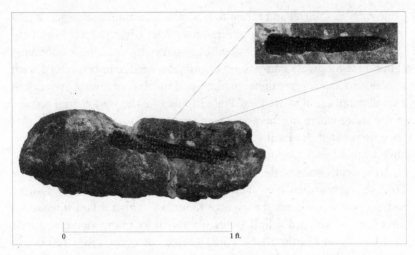

FIGURE 31. Corncob impression in mortar from feature 13. This material was used for the chinking of a log cabin that once stood over the pit cellar (feature 7) in block 4, lot 1. Photograph by Christopher Valvano.

Generally the archaeological evidence suggests that the Burdick cabin did not last long, maybe a few years. Architectural elements from the cabin, such as window glass, mortar, and cut nails, were pushed into the nearby well. This part of the archaeological record provides an indication of the first generation of building, in the form of a log house, in New Philadelphia. Log houses are rare on the landscape today because they were often seen as initial and temporary dwellings instead of permanent dwellings needing to be preserved over time. If a family did not like the location for some reason, they could easily dismantle the structure or move on, since they were minimally invested (Mazrim 2007:78). Log houses were relatively quick and easy to erect and were often constructed with great skill. This rapid construction and deconstruction seems to have been the case with this particular New Philadelphia cabin. Having been built at some point in the 1840s, the cabin was gone within twenty years; the earliest known tax records, those from 1867, do not show any improvements on the southern half of block 4, lot 1. The cabin had disappeared from the landscape, and the pit cellar and well were filled.

The Kittles, Taylors, and Siders

We obtained a series of soil core samples in the area of cored anomaly A28 identified by Hargrave in the geophysical survey. Solid resistance

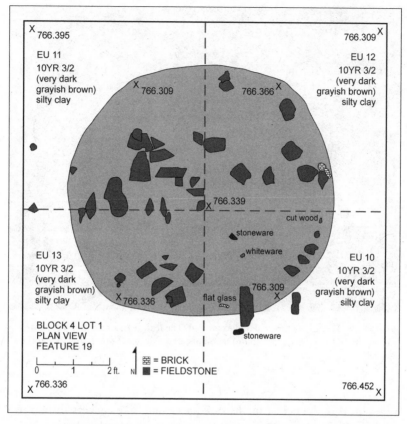

FIGURE 32. Plan view of feature 19 prior to excavation (included in excavation units 10, 11, 12, and 13 in the area of A28). Drawing by Christopher Valvano.

to the core probe was encountered at a number of places, and we recovered brick and mortar fragments in a few samples. Based on these positive results Valvano's archaeology team placed four excavation units (10, 11, 12, and 13; see Figure 26) in this area to further investigate the anomaly and retrieve some information about another New Philadelphia family.

Beneath the plow zone the team found a scatter of fieldstones creating a seven-foot circular shape, with stones scattered inside the feature. Each stone is about one foot wide or slightly larger (Figures 32 and 33). The plow must have hit and dislodged these stones, since they do not form an identifiable pattern. We labeled it feature 19, and the students began excavating the southern half of it. After removing some soil it became

FIGURE 33. Feature 19 bisected and excavated. The feature measures 6.0 feet across (east–west) and 5.0 feet (north–south) if completely excavated. Photograph by Paul A. Shackel.

apparent that the fieldstone feature has square-like corners. It had five courses of stone and exists to a depth of 2.8 feet below the plow zone. On the surface it measures 5.0 feet north-south and 6.0 feet east-west (if extending the northern boundary to the unexcavated areas). No mortar was used to bind the stones; it was dry-laid.

There are significantly more glass containers in feature 19 when compared to the southern half of the lot (features 7 and 13), and almost all of the glass containers date to about the 1850s. The ceramic assemblage also dates to the same era. The majority of ceramics are refined earthenware. Fragments of stoneware and redware vessels are also present, but to a much lesser degree; the amount of glass vessels is proportionately higher. Many of these are food containers. The decorations on the plates and cups include blue, black, red, and purple transfer prints. There is a much smaller number of plates that are hand-painted and shell-edged when compared to the Burdick assemblage. However, a glass flask with clasping hands and the word "Union" written on the uppermost part of the bottle was inspired by the Civil War and helps provide a

9 in.

front   back

FIGURE 34. "Union" bottle dating to the 1860s. Photograph by Christopher Valvano.

date for this feature to the early 1860s (McCorvie 1987:92; Figure 34). Therefore the fill in this feature is probably related to the Sider family. It is interesting to speculate on the political conversations that were stimulated by the "Union" bottle, especially since John came from Kentucky and Augusta came from Ohio. Soon after John's death the property appears to have been abandoned, and the feature filled, including the "Union" bottle.

The feature contains a very large number of cow remains compared to the other assemblages found throughout the town site. Domestic pig is also present, but to a lesser degree. The majority of the cow bones have saw, chop, or knife marks, most of them on vertebrae or rib bones. Some studies (Schulz and Gust 1983:48) indicate that these would be prime cuts of beef. Sawed cow bones associated with the Sider family suggest that they purchased their meat from a market (T. J. Martin and Brand 2002:7) or that a butcher traveled to the community to cut the meat for the family, a common practice in the nineteenth century (Whittaker 1999:53). The presence of pig cranial fragments suggests that the heads were boiled down to make headcheese, and the lack of cow skull fragments suggests that they were discarded with the butchering remains (Price 1985:48–49). Other mammal remains include opossum, eastern cottontail or domestic rabbit, fox squirrel and other squirrel species, Old World rat, and sheep or goat. The only identified bird species was domestic chicken, making up the majority of all the bird bones found within the feature. The high proportion of cow is indicative of a northern diet (Hsieh and Martin 2006; T. Martin and Martin 2010).

A large cluster of raspberry and ground cherry seeds, typical of remains of a privy or the deposition of chamber pots, is located at the bottom 0.1 foot of the feature, and a layer of clay caps the seed deposits (E. S. Smith 2006). We struggled with two scenarios for the original function of the stone-lined feature. D. A. Kittle could have constructed it soon after he purchased the property from Frank McWorter in 1848. Kittle is listed in the 1850 Federal Census records as a merchant and, like many other contemporary merchants, he would have bought and sold perishable goods. He may have invested in his business by constructing a short-term cool storage area for perishable items. If so, feature 19 represents the remains of a storage area that was built in about 1848 at the farthest location from the intersection of North and Broad Streets. The structure probably no longer served its original function by about the late 1850s or early 1860s. The feature was open for a while, and the thousands of raspberry seeds are a product of chamber pot disposal from the Sider family. It continued to be filled with domestic refuse, such as ceramics, bones, and glass. Some of the upper stones of the feature were eventually filled into the feature. The earliest known tax assessment in 1867 shows no improvements on the northern half of this lot. Therefore the original function of this feature no longer existed by the 1860s. Improvements on the lot do not appear until 1878.

A second possible scenario is that the feature originally served as a privy. While only 0.1 foot of the bottommost fill contains raspberry and ground cherry seeds, a clear signature of a privy, the feature may have been cleaned a few times during the occupation on the lot. A clay cap over the seeds indicates that the feature was intentionally sealed and used for trash disposal after its primary function no longer existed.

We discussed these scenarios with historical archaeologists familiar with the local context and era, and there was no consensus as to whether the original function of the feature was as a cool storage vault or a privy. However, we all agreed that the assemblage found within the feature is an important part of interpreting the late 1850s and early 1860s lifeways within the town. The glass and ceramics vessel analysis and the faunal assemblages are lines of evidence to understanding the transformation from frontier town to rural community (see more in-depth analysis in chapter 11).

THE SECOND GENERATION OF BUILDING AND ABANDONMENT

Sarah McWorter's Homesite

Christopher S. Luce purchased block 8, lot 2 from Frank McWorter in 1840. He was a Baptist preacher and shoemaker born in Maine; his wife, Sally, was born in New Hampshire. In 1850 he had two sons; the older is listed as fifteen and a farmer born in Maine, and the younger, Moses, is listed as eight and born in Illinois, most probably in New Philadelphia. All of the family members are listed as white. Frank McWorter contracted Luce to build a church and seminary in New Philadelphia. Luce failed to live up to his side of the deal, and Frank McWorter sued him (Walker 1983a:136–43).

After 1857 the lot was sold about a dozen times. Sarah McWorter, also known as Sally, was Frank and Lucy's daughter and was born in slavery in Kentucky. Her freedom was purchased by Free Frank in 1843 (Walker 1983a:148). Sarah purchased the property in 1860 and conveyed some form of interest in the property to A. B. Cobb in 1860. However, Sarah remained responsible for tax payments on the property through the 1860s; the 1867 tax assessment lists her as the owner and responsible for paying the taxes on lot 2, and Cobb as the owner and Sarah McWorter responsible for paying taxes on lot 1. The following year Cobb is listed as paying the taxes on lots 1 and 2, and Sarah Mc-Worter is also listed as being assessed for block 8, lot 2, although there were no values assessed for the lot. Why was Sarah listed in the tax records through 1868, even though Cobb owned the land? This situation made me wonder if Sarah McWorter could have been on the property until 1869, when Cobb was the sole person listed on the tax records as owner and the only person being assessed. Arden Cobb, listed as a physician from New York, owned the property by 1870. Sarah was accounted for in the 1860 and 1870 Federal Census as living

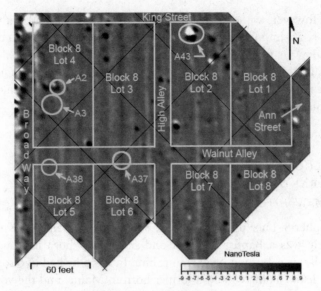

FIGURE 35. Resistivity survey indicating the location of anomaly A43 in block 8, lot 2. Survey by Michael Hargrave. Grid overlay by Christopher Fennell.

with Free Lucy on the McWorter farm, but perhaps between these times she could have actively inhabited the structure on block 8, lot 2. Perhaps the archaeology might lead us to some other clues.

The built environment is difficult to assess using the tax records. For instance, when Sarah McWorter was taxed on the property it was assessed for $8 in 1867. One year later there are improvements on the lot valued at about $100, a figure that remains relatively constant through most of the nineteenth century. The geophysical survey performed in 2006 indicates an anomaly (A43) on the north-central edge of block 2 (Figure 35).

A total of nine excavation units helped to define a large pit cellar that measures about 18.6 feet by 16.0 feet. Feature 14 is slightly darker than the surrounding soil and contains small pieces of plaster with imprints of lathing from interior walls. The plaster fragments helped to define the boundaries of the feature. The lathing and interior plaster walls indicate a more substantial commitment to creating a more permanent structure with more refined qualities, such as whitewashed plaster walls (Figure 36). The feature is the largest pit cellar found in New Philadelphia. Robert Mazrim (2007:84) explains, "Cellar sizes increased significantly during the close of the frontier period in Illinois, probably in

FIGURE 36. Top of feature 14 in block 8, lot 2. Photograph by Paul A. Shackel.

response to more permanent architecture, and the more frequent construction of large frame buildings."

Emily Helton, a former NSF-REU student and, during this season, crew chief for the project, led the archaeology team. They bisected the feature, removing the fill from the northern half. The bottom of the feature is a bit more than 2.5 feet below the bottom of the plow zone. There is a ramp that slopes into the cellar. The floor of the cellar is not even. There are several circular barrel depressions measuring 1.5 feet to 2.5 feet across and about 0.5 foot deep. Several smaller post holes running in a diagonal from the northwest to the southeast measure about 0.5 foot in diameter and are about 0.1 foot deep; these held timbers to stabilize the floor of the building (Figure 37). The cellar walls on the north and west edge of the feature are generally vertical.

Containers make up the majority of the glass assemblage; these are mostly canning jars and mostly date to the 1860s, although a "Consolidated Fruit Jar Co." bottle that dates from 1871 is from the top portion of the feature. The lower deposits dating to the 1860s have a higher proportion of ceramics with designs (hand-painted and transfer prints),

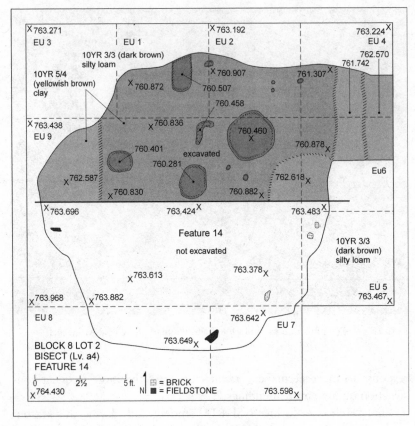

FIGURE 37. Drawing of feature 14 with the northern half excavated. Notice the post holes and barrel depressions. Drawing by Christopher Valvano.

while the upper levels that date to the early 1870s have a higher proportion of plain white ceramics (Eppler and Helton 2006; Figure 38).

A Mason jar with a patent date of 1858 (manufactured from 1860 to 1875) and a glass flask dating to the 1850s is also present. An anthropomorphic design on a terracotta pipe, also known as a Turk's head pipe, is part of this assemblage. Architectural-related materials recovered include cut nails, window glass, and plaster. Large quantities of faunal remains exist throughout the feature fill, although the majority of faunal remains are below the rubble fill. Domestic pig dominates the faunal assemblage, although there is a large amount of chicken bones. At the bottom of the feature archaeologists recovered several pig jaw bones (Livingston and Martin 2006).

FIGURE 38. Ceramic vessel assemblage from feature 14. The lower levels (a3 and a4) were deposited in the 1860s, and levels a1 and a2 were deposited in the early 1870s. Photograph by Christopher Valvano.

The many different transfer printed ceramic wares are tea wares, plates, and bowls. The most prevalent decorations are red floral patterns, which were common from about 1829 to 1843 (Samford 1997:20–21). Other transfer prints date to the 1840s and 1850s.

The team excavated through fieldstone foundation rubble and architectural debris in the top portion of the cellar. The lower half had a higher density of soil and artifacts. This archaeological formation indicates that the filling of the feature did not occur in one episode. It appears that the house was dismantled by 1867 since the tax records show $3 of improvements on the lot. By 1868 a house was built somewhere else on the property. The open cellar served as a trash receptacle, probably for Sarah McWorter, and maybe later by the Cobb family. The fieldstone foundation and chimney remained around the cellar hole for several years, and the cellar was used as a trash dump. The faunal remains in the lowest portion of the feature show considerable gnawing by rodents. There is also a considerable number of Old World rat bones in this lower deposit. After the accumulation of some trash and an infestation of rodents the fieldstone foundation was pushed into the cellar hole and any unwanted architectural debris was placed in the feature. The upper part of the fill contains the most recent diagnostic artifacts, including the Mason jar and the "Consolidated Fruit Jar Co." bottle (J. Jacoby 2006; Livingston and Martin 2006; T. Martin and Martin 2010).

THE THIRD GENERATION OF BUILDING AND ABANDONMENT
Investing in Twentieth-Century New Philadelphia

The archaeology in block 3, lot 7 challenges the long-held belief that the town died after the railroad bypassed it in 1869. The property shows a long tradition of speculation, as many people bought and sold this lot and lived on it for a short time. Spaulding Burdick and Adam Hadsell owned the parcel in the 1850s. Adam Hadsell is listed in the 1850 Federal Census as a farmer born in Massachusetts; his wife, Electa, and three children were born in New York. His oldest son is listed as a farmer. They are all listed as white.

The Hadley Township tax assessments indicate that Alexander Clark had $57 worth of improvements on this lot in 1867. The value of these improvements increased to $350 in 1875, but decreased to $250 in the 1878 and 1883 assessments. By 1888 Squire and George McWorter (sons of Louisa and Squire) owned the land, with improvements assessed at $75 for lots 7 and 8. By the early twentieth century Fred and Nancy Venicombe owned the property. Oral history from Larry Burdick (1992) indicates that the Venicombes built a house on the lot around the turn of the century.

The geophysical survey by Michael Hargrave revealed anomaly A1, and we decided to excavate in the area in 2006 (Figure 39). The anomaly was relatively long and narrow and ran in an east-west direction. Terry Martin led this excavation team, which identified a dense limestone and brick rubble layer under the sod (feature 15). This feature is probably a product of farmers taking stones from the plowed field and tossing them in the area not being planted. Artifacts in and around the rubble include

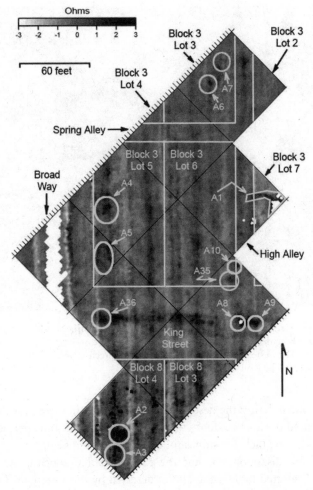

FIGURE 39. Electrical resistance map showing the location of anomaly A1 in the eastern and central portion of block 3, lot 7. Map by Michael Hargrave. Grid overlay by Christopher Fennell.

nails, glass, ceramics, brick, mortar, nails, metal, and coal. This area has by far the largest quantity of wire nails found at New Philadelphia. Wire nails were first widely manufactured in the 1890s and continue to be manufactured today. Along with several other diagnostic artifacts, such as glassware and toys (including a metal train locomotive, an ivory elephant with a compass, and doll parts), we have a good idea that this archaeological context on the top layers of soil dates to after 1890, and probably closer to the 1930s. The assemblage is related to a twentieth-century

FIGURE 40. Fieldstone foundation in block 3, lot 7. The northeast and northwest corners have been detected. The northern wall runs in an east–west direction and is 15 feet long. The western wall runs in a north–south direction and is at least 20 feet long. Photograph by Paul A. Shackel.

occupation, and after the destruction of a building in the 1930s the Venicombes used the area to dump their trash. During this time period it also served as a receptacle for stones found in the plowed field.

We were disappointed that the rubble scatter appeared to be the anomaly detected by Hargrave. Not deterred by this outcome, Terry encouraged his crew to continue digging. Their perseverance paid off. His team discovered a fieldstone foundation under the rubble layer. Several more excavation units found the general dimension of the foundation, which measures 15 feet east-west and at least 20 feet north-south (Figure 40). The foundation is 1.5 feet wide, and all three walls are level throughout. The eastern section of the foundation is deeper and served as a storage cellar.

There is a layer of small bits of plaster found in and around the foundation, which represent the remains of the building's plaster walls. The deposits create a nice division of the soils, clearly separating the different artifacts found below it and above it. The deposits below the plaster date from before the destruction of the building, and the soil and artifacts above the plaster date from after its destruction. The soil below the plaster layer contains many artifacts that are whole or nearly whole. They are deposits that were well protected from the trampling of feet and agriculture disturbances, unlike the deposits above the plaster. These protected artifacts include a cathedral-style decorated pepper sauce bottle (late nineteenth century) and an ironstone plate produced by the Peoria Pottery Company from 1888 to 1890. Cut nails rather than wire nails are present in the lower deposits. Cut nails were generally manufactured between about the 1790s and the 1890s (Colon 2006).

The two distinct layers of artifacts separated by the plaster hint that there were two distinct household occupations and two distinct construction episodes on these foundations. The presence of cut nails along with artifacts dating to the 1880s and 1890s inside the foundation indicates that a wood building was destroyed in about the 1880s. The lack of artifacts dating from much earlier indicates that the building was constructed after the Civil War era. When the house was destroyed in about the 1880s the former cellar served as a dumping area for a short time. In about 1900 Fred and Nancy Venicombe rebuilt a house on the same foundations. They did not dig out the basement, and the floor of their house protected the archaeological deposits. When the second house was torn down in the 1920s the area once again became a dump for residents and farmers. The Venicombes lived to the east of these foundations in the 1930s.

The sealed 1880s context has several types of artifacts that provide information about late nineteenth-century life in New Philadelphia. For instance, several patent medicine bottles are in this assemblage. Patent medicine bottles are usually amber, aquamarine, or light green in color. The color helps to protect the content from sunlight. They usually had square or rectangular shoulders and a cork closure (Ketchum 1975:76–92; Munsey 1970:65). The medicines served as popular cure-all self-medicating remedies, especially when doctors were not available (Colon 2006). These concoctions usually had high alcohol content and potentially other harmful ingredients. In the early twentieth century, along with the professionalization of medicine, progressives lobbied for the Pure Food and Drug Act (1906). One of the consequences of the Act was the mandate that the ingredients be labeled on the bottle. Subsequently the use of patent medicines decreased sharply beginning in the twentieth century. Finding patent medicine bottles in nineteenth-century archaeological contexts is common throughout the United States, including in Illinois (Phillippe 1990: 221). While New Philadelphia had a resident doctor for a short time, the use of patent medicines served as an alternative to professional medicine.

The archaeological record at this homesite is also very important to the story of New Philadelphia. It shows that while some people left town after 1869, others saw the place as home and invested in the town by rebuilding. It is clear that although only about a half-dozen households remained in the town by 1900 they were not waiting for the town to disappear. The Venicombe family invested time and resources to stay in New Philadelphia, with the intention of making it their home for several decades. They were among the last residents in the town.

Blacksmith Shop

Blacksmithing is one of the last entrepreneurial activities that survived in New Philadelphia into the early twentieth century. Oral histories indicate that Squire McWorter, grandson of the town's founder and son of Louisa and Squire, operated a blacksmithing business in the northern part of town, close to the main road in block 3, lot 1. A notice of his estate sale in 1915 lists a fair amount of blacksmith tools (McWorter 1915). Many people owned the land prior to McWorter's blacksmith operations, and the tax records from the 1867 through the 1880s show small improvements to the land. Squire and George McWorter are listed for tax assessments on the property in 1883 and 1888.

Alexander Clark, son of Kassiah (Casiah), paid taxes on block 3, lot 1 from 1867 through 1872, even though our research through the land deeds in the county courthouse does not show him listed as owning the property. He is known to be one of the town's early blacksmiths. Alexander owned lots 1 and 2 in block 15; however, the archaeological survey did not find any remains in the area that would be typical of a blacksmith shop. James Davis's (1998) work on frontier Illinois provides a good model for looking at the settlement of New Philadelphia. Davis shows that crafts like blacksmithing are usually located on the eastern side of towns, where smoke and bad odors carried by the west-to-east prevailing winds would have minimal impact on the town. The blacksmith shop located on block 3, lot 1 is situated on the northern and eastern edge of the settled portion of the town. I believe there is a good chance that the area may have been the site of the earlier blacksmith shop owned by Clark and subsequently by McWorter.

Alexander Clark is listed in the 1860 Federal Census as a blacksmith with a household of six people, who are classified as mulatto. He is included in the 1865 state census as a black individual with a household of six people. William Clark is listed in the 1870 Federal Census as a blacksmith with a household of eight people; all are classified as mulatto. Based on these records it is likely that blacksmithing occurred on this property from at least the 1860s, and maybe even earlier. It is a tradition that passed from the Clark to the McWorter family.

One of Michael Hargrave's first duties in the spring of 2006 was to perform a geophysical survey of the locale remembered to be the site of the town's blacksmith shop. Natalie Armistead had walked the area and found scrap pieces of metal and broken iron implements, including ladles and hooks, on the surface. The ground surface is about fifteen to twenty feet lower than the lands adjacent to Broad and Main Streets. During heavy rains small streams of water inundate the area, and the land stays soggy for several days to several weeks. However, because of the drought in 2005 and 2006 and the drier than usual conditions, Hargrave was able to conduct a geophysical survey of the area. Even though we had some rain in June and the soil retained some moisture, it was not soggy.

Block 3, lot 1 has a strong magnetic reading, and Hargrave and Fennell labeled it anomaly A42 (Figure 41). The archaeology team placed four excavation units in the area of anomaly A42 and recovered some domestic artifacts, although there is a high concentration of metal artifacts, charcoal, and slag throughout the area. It seems that A42 is a waste pile that is most often associated with blacksmith shops. The artifacts show that the smith was involved in coopering (barrel straps), farrier work (horse shoes, nails, and bridal equipment), and wagon repair (wagon parts). Like many rural craftsmen he functioned as a jack-of-all-trades. It is likely that blacksmithing activities occurred throughout the life of the town. The discovery of modern wire nails and threaded pipes indicates that the smith worked into the early 1900s (Maranville, Martin, and Sandels 2006).

The waste pile is often adjacent to blacksmith shops. However, the crew did not find foundation stones. Burdick (1992) remembers a pole building in the area we excavated. A pole building would have a faint archaeological signature and would be difficult to identify. The blacksmith shop probably sat closer to the road, with the waste pile behind the building. If this is the case, signatures of the blacksmith shop's foundations were likely partially covered or destroyed when the state graded the road about twenty years ago.

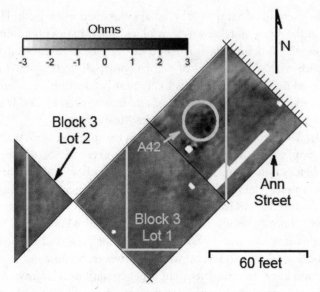

FIGURE 41. Magnetometer survey indicates the presence of a large quantity of metal in the area known to have been the site of a blacksmith shop in block 3, lot 1. Survey by Michael Hargrave. Grid overlay by Christopher Fennell.

CONCLUDING THOUGHTS

It became clear at the end of the third field season that many important undisturbed archaeological features are still present in the fields that now encompass New Philadelphia. It is also very clear that New Philadelphia was a place where businesses survived even after the railroad bypassed the town. People bought and sold land, built houses, let them decay, and tore them down. There were open cellars where trash was deposited and rats infested the town on occasion, much like any other rural community. However, people continued to see the place as a viable place to live into the twentieth century. A blacksmith shop remained until the early twentieth century, and several houses were built after the railroad bypassed the town. The physical existence of the place is much more complicated than previously thought. The organic nature of the town makes it difficult to develop ideas on how to represent the place, now a fallow field, to the American public.

CHAPTER 10

A Case for Landmark Status

At the beginning of the third season in 2006 Terry Martin encouraged Vergil Noble, a National Park Service archaeologist, to visit the site. Noble coordinates and oversees National Historic Landmark nominations from the Midwest region. The NHL program has over 2,400 designated places, extraordinary places that have meaning for all Americans. We wanted to nominate New Philadelphia as a NHL because it provides archaeological information about the development and lifeways of a multicultural rural community. The high integrity of the archaeological record allows us to understand the community and the interactions among residents. It shows how people lived together in a multiracial community within a highly racialized society. By studying many households of different backgrounds, the archaeology of New Philadelphia allows us to challenge the ways that historical archaeologists study race within communities (King 2008).

If we were to obtain landmark status for the New Philadelphia town site it would lay the groundwork for creating a state or national park, although it takes congressional action to create a national park. About one in eight NHLs is a national park. If we could demonstrate that this site is worthy of being a NHL, our chances of saving and preserving the site would increase. Therefore we needed to develop the groundwork to explain the town's national significance.

CHANGING ARCHAEOLOGICAL PERCEPTIONS

What makes New Philadelphia so interesting to me is that it existed as a multiracial rural community for about one hundred years. During the course of several field seasons the archaeology team identified and excavated features that belonged to people of Euro-American and African American descent. How groups interacted with each other and whether they tried to distinguish themselves from each other using material markers is intriguing. We expected to find dietary (T. Martin and Martin 2010) and consumer (Shackel 2010) differences between households from different regions; we might also be able to identify differences between households of various racial categorizations. It's not the different categories of race that would create different consumer behavior, but how people were treated and how they reacted to this treatment because of their classification that would lead to consuming different products and using different material markers to create distinct groups (Mullins 1999). Therefore we anticipated finding that the different settlers of different backgrounds participated in a consumer society in different ways. How and why they participated in consumer culture was one of the initial project questions.

Identity studies in the form of ethnicity, race, class, and gender drive much of historical archaeology scholarship today. The search for identity in the past is complicated because the definitions of groups are malleable and ever changing. At times identity can be somewhat elusive in the archaeological record. In the case of New Philadelphia, much like many other places, the development of historical context helps to get at the meaning of the relationship between identity and material culture.

Dell Upton (1996) explains that defining group identity through material signatures can become problematic if we see groups as never changing through time and space. Sian Jones (1997:100) reminds us that "there is rarely a one-to-one relationship between representations of ethnicity and the entire range of cultural practices and social conditions associated with a particular group." Definitions of ethnicity by groups are constantly being renegotiated as people change, groups interact, and ideas and material culture are exchanged. Issues of domination and resistance can come into play, and issues of class should also be considered when examining the material culture.

Barbara Voss (2005:427–28) points out that there are many archaeological studies of Overseas Chinese communities that identify Asian cultural markers. The emphasis has been on acculturation and creating a visible opposition between Eastern traditions and Westernization. While celebrating diversity and multiethnic heritage is important for our national values, we need to be careful about creating oppositions and developing heritage for any ethnic group with the idea that the archaeological assemblages are a product of a static community with a fixed identity. In fact efforts to identify differences in the material culture used in everyday behavior to define group boundaries have often proven challenging. For instance, Voss explains that while many archaeologists have created oppositions to highlight differences between Overseas Chinese and Western cultures, there are also many cultural remains that are similar to other non-Chinese sites. She notes that Sherri Gust's work shows how the faunal assemblages varied between Overseas Chinese households. Gust (1993:208) observed that the butchering marks found in the remains of some of the households consisted of a "standard Euroamerican style" of food preparation. R. Scott Baxter and Rebecca Allen (2002:292–96) show that the San Jose Chinese community had many economic ties to American manufacturers and distributors, thus potentially blurring any forms of easily identifiable cultural markers.

Group identity and boundaries are usually seen as being reinforced through the use of symbols. A significant amount of scholarship related to African American archaeology has been about the persistence of tradition. These studies have identified artifacts that have some association or memory with Africa, such as cowrie shells, blue beads, and gaming pieces. The experience of slavery and searching for power and identity has also dominated the literature (Fennell 2007; Leone et al. 2005; Orser 1998; Singleton 1995).

The historical archaeology work at New Philadelphia explores the everyday material culture of settlers of different racial and regional backgrounds and different genders. The search for identity through the everyday material culture is elusive if context is not developed. How people are defined, constrained, or enabled because of their social identity makes for a complicated scenario at New Philadelphia.

CONSUMING IDENTITY

Communities like New Philadelphia were vital for the growth and development of the agricultural life in the region. From the 1850s and into the 1930s the town had a mix of immigrants, mostly from the North and the Upland South. Those of midwestern and northern origins are the largest groups throughout the century (King 2006). In Hadley Township, where New Philadelphia is situated, the majority of its residents were born in Illinois. Ohio was the second largest contributor of people to the area from 1850 through 1880. Pennsylvania was the third largest supplier of immigrants until 1870 and 1880, when Missouri took its place (Seligman 2007).

An analysis of ceramics and glass vessels from six features associated with five households provides some answers about the development of identity in this rural community. Artifacts from three features are associated with households from the North and date to the 1840s (the Burdicks, Euro-Americans from New England, features 7 and 13) and 1850s (the Siders, Euro-Americans from Kentucky and Ohio, feature 19). Three additional features are associated with households from the Upland South and Illinois and date to the 1850s (the Clarks, African Americans from Kentucky, feature 1), 1860s (Sarah McWorter, African American from Kentucky, feature 14), and 1880s (Squire and George McWorter, African American from Illinois, parents born in Kentucky, block 3, lot 7).

A summary of the ceramic and glass vessels from features associated with different households provides a small data set for comparison (Tables A.1–A.4). However, if we view the data in terms of the presence and absence of vessels, a few observations are clear. For instance, all households had a relatively high proportion of medicine bottles, an indication of self-medication, and each of the households participated in a consumer society. Glass and ceramic vessels are similar among the different households, indicating that they had similar access to markets and purchased fashionable contemporary wares.

The archaeological evidence of the steamboat *Bertrand* is telling of the types of consumer goods that would be found in a frontier situation in the 1860s. Bound from St. Louis to the mining towns of Montana via the Missouri River, it sank north of Omaha with its hull filled with tools, equipment, food, and clothing. In addition to the necessities, the cargo also included, "olive oil, and mustard from France, bottled tamarinds and a variety of canned fruits, several varieties of alcoholic bitters, powdered canned lemonade, and brandied cherries" (B. J. Little 2007:31). This evidence, as well as the recovered consumer goods from New Philadelphia, such as dishes and plates, should challenge some of the Hollywood-inspired stereotypes of the frontier as devoid of luxury consumer goods.

The types of material culture found in each of New Philadelphia's households varied slightly. Some households preferred using only small plates; this phenomenon may be indicative of a dining style whereby plates were removed from the table after each course. In all likelihood it seems that this form of dining, known as dining "à la Russe," or "à la practical" in the hybrid American style, was practiced by some of the households. Other households had only large plates, suggesting one-course meals. Those households with the large plates also had a relatively larger proportion of bowls, suggesting the serving of stews, another indication of one-course meals. The use of large plates conforms to a dining etiquette that shows a conscious selection of certain middle-class ideals (setting a proper table) and resistance to others (segmentation of the meal into many individual courses) (Lucas 1994). There is no strong relation between ethnic group or region of origin and the conformity to one of the dining styles.

All of the households had refined ceramics, but none of them had matched sets, even though mass marketing of consumer goods existed and material goods could be easily accessed in Pike County by the 1840s. These assemblages run counter to Victorian expectations for ceramic consumption and are similar to what Paul Mullins (1999:148) found at African American sites in Annapolis from about the same time period. It appears that the different households in New Philadelphia acquired their assemblages piecemeal in order to acquire a larger and more complete set. Each ceramic assemblage varied in color, decoration, and functional type, despite the community's access to larger markets and participation in the consumer society. Nevertheless households made a choice about what they purchased and how they used the goods. Barbara Little (1994, 1997) explains that households in a consumer society acquire fashionable goods, such as ceramics, as a cultural necessity. However, they may reject the meaning associated with these objects, such as the implied necessity for matched sets. By embracing the ideology of consumerism, these households embedded themselves in the market economy and reinforced their roles in that economy as objectified individuals empowered to sell their products and their labor (Palus and Shackel 2006).

In New Philadelphia the meaning of the tea ceremony is probably different from that found in urban areas. For instance, Diana Wall (1991:78) shows that in a mid-nineteenth-century context in New York City families belonging to the upper middle class and lower middle class used similar tableware and the dinner probably had the same social meaning in both contexts. However, the wealthier family had more expensive porcelain tea wares while the poorer family tended to have cheaper, undecorated ironstone tea wares. The New Philadelphia households drank tea, but used less expensive ceramics. At New Philadelphia, like many other rural communities, status was likely acquired by personal character and landholdings rather than through the display of material culture.

The ceramic and glass assemblages for five households vary somewhat, but there is no clear pattern of different uses between African American and Euro-American sites. There are also no clear differences between households from northern states and those from the Upland South and Illinois. What is clear is that all of these households have access to the marketplace. They are all buying the most fashionable goods, although not necessarily adhering to all of the rules in a consumer society, such as buying and using matched sets of dishes and tea wares.

Archaeology can counter our preconceived notions about communities. By the end of the 1840s the Illinois frontier was well established and had access to eastern markets and goods. The archaeological data from the late 1840s through the 1880s show some signs of material homogeneity between the sites. Some of the consumer goods suggest that the New Philadelphia community did not necessarily develop in bounded isolated ethnic groups, each group having its own cultural and material traits despite the widespread racial tensions in the area before and after the American Civil War.

This phenomenon appears to be true at other communities with African American representation. For instance, Linda Stine's (1990) work in the North Carolina Piedmont, an area that followed the Upland South tradition, provides a comparison of a farming community with a racial makeup similar to New Philadelphia's. Almost 30 percent of the population was classified as African American at the turn of the twentieth century. Differences between blacks and whites are difficult to discern in many forms of material culture. People of the same class, regardless of color, lived in similar types of homes. "For the most part area farmstead facades would not help an outsider predict a family's wealth, social status, or ethnic background" (45). Residents in the community could purchase the same types of goods on credit or using cash. Comparing the archaeological assemblage of a site inhabited by an African American family and another occupied by a white family, both from the same economic stratum, Stine found no significant difference between the types of artifacts. The only reflections of inequal-

ity on the landscape are the separate cemeteries and segregated schoolhouses (49).

Charles Cheek and Amy Friedlander (1990) discuss the archaeology of
African American alley dwellings in Washington, D.C., and compare them
to dwellings on the street inhabited by whites at the turn of the twentieth
century. They found no significant difference in the relative value of each
of the ceramics assemblages, nor a clear difference in the types of meats
consumed by these households. They expected to see a greater amount of
bowls in the African American assemblage, which has been the case on
plantation sites, but both assemblages are about the same (52–53). However, a few differences between the assemblages do exist; for instance, the
white households had a greater variety of glass tableware vessels, and
the African Americans had more pigs' feet in their diet. These distinctions
are explained as ethnic differences. However, a more developed context
should also factor in economic, class, and regional differences. For instance, other studies show a large quantity of pigs' feet found in an assemblage belonging to a wealthy Euro-American (Burk 1993). The pattern
is also common in the Upland South area (T. Martin and Martin 2010;
C. Martin and Martin 2010; McCorvie 1987). So ethnicity may not be the
only variable to reflect on; class and wealth should also be considered. In
New Castle County, Delaware, Wade Catts and Jay Custer (1990) examined an African American occupation from the late nineteenth and early
twentieth centuries. Compared to similar sites they found great variability
in the assemblages, showing that all members of the community participated fully in the consumer culture. In their study in South Carolina,
Melanie Cabak and Mary Inkrot (1997) also found that there is a low cor-
relation between ethnicity and material culture.

While archaeologists have a tradition of looking for distinct groups
when examining assemblages, there are only a few instances in which
ethnic markers are visible in the material culture. In New Philadelphia
the consumer goods seem homogenized between the different households; ethnicity and regional background did not play a role in creating
material differences. Although the faunal assemblages tend to be small,
some generalizations can be made (see chapter 9; T. Martin and Martin
2010). For instance, the expected dietary patterns do not hold true for
some of the earliest residents. The Burdicks from New England have a
relatively high proportion of both pig and cattle biomass in their assemblage; on the other hand, the Siders from Kentucky and Ohio have
a high percentage of cow bones in their diet. The other households

(Clark, Sarah McWorter, and Squire and George McWorter) tend to have a high percentage of pig biomass in their diet. The lesson from this scenario, I believe, is that archaeologists need to avoid developing quantitative patterns that rely on few variables. Most historical archaeologists have long ago given up any kind of easy reliance on one or two artifacts as racial markers. Regional background may be important, but when you begin to factor in race, ethnicity, class, and gender the scenario becomes more complex and it is more challenging to predict the past.

GAMING PIECES AND IDENTITY

The gaming pieces found at New Philadelphia may be associated with the game known as mancala. Mancala refers to a large family of games based on distributing seeds, pebbles, pieces of ceramics and glass, or shells into holes or cups. Until now these gaming pieces have been identified only at African American sites, mostly near the quarters of enslaved people.

Mathematicians who study games often call the mancala family "sowing games." Mancala, derived from the Arabic word *manqala*, meaning "to move," is also called adi, adji, awale, awele, awari, ayo, ayo-ayo, gepeta, ourin, ourri, oware, wari, warra, or warri. The game developed about four thousand years ago in the Middle East and is also played widely in Africa. The boards, number of playing pieces, number of players, and rules of play vary greatly. The playing board may have two, three, or four rows of cups or holes, and each row may contain anywhere from five to thirty-six holes. Some games require ten playing pieces (usually seeds) per cup, while others require only four. The winner either has to accumulate the most playing pieces or get rid of all of his or her pieces (Culin 1894). African people often played with pebbles or cowry shells, using hollows scooped into the earth or pecked into stone. They brought versions of the mancala game with them to the Caribbean and the United States during the seventeenth and eighteenth centuries (Galke 2000; National Park Service 2005a; Patten 1992; Samford 1994). Susan Kern (2005) infers that several counting pieces found near slave quarters at Shadwell, the boyhood home of Thomas Jefferson, could have been used as mancala pieces. They were small pieces of worked and polished shell and ceramic that often served as markers for games.

Ethnographic information from the early twentieth century indicates the long tradition of the game. Felix von Luschan (1919) mentioned

FIGURE 42. A sample of gaming pieces found on African American and Euro-American sites in New Philadelphia. Photograph by Christopher Valvano.

warra being played in the southern states and communities with large African American populations. Melville Herskovitz (1932) wrote about wari being played in several different Caribbean islands. He mentioned that men mostly played the game, although there were no specific sanctions against women participating.

The typical mancala pieces found archaeologically are small, usually diamond-shaped objects fashioned out of broken ceramic and glass sherds. These sherds are smoothed and worn around the edges from years of play (National Park Service 2005b). The pieces at New Philadelphia are mostly whiteware or yellowware, the former being the most common. All have a color on them, most being a remnant of the ceramic glaze, while a few had color applied to the earthen body. Some of the pieces are worn glass sherds. All of the pieces are between a half and three-quarters of an inch in size. Because mancala pieces were only being found at African American sites it is easy to see why some would think that these gaming pieces would be a good cultural marker for archaeologists (Figure 42). However, in New Philadelphia the gaming pieces are found at free African American as well as Euro-American sites, thereby complicating the story of who played the game. Apparently the game crosses racial boundaries, indicating that ethnic markers can become meaningless when dealing with a multiracial community. Having people of European descent playing the game also opens up new possibilities, showing a level of interaction that existed in the town that is not necessarily found in the documentary records.

BUTTONS, IDENTITY, AND WOMEN'S LABOR

There is a plethora of clothing-related items found at two sites where African American women were heads of households. Eric Klingelhofer (1985:14) noticed that African American sites tend to have a higher proportion of buttons, and therefore these items are a signature of black sites. Other archaeologists (e.g., Wilke 2000) identified items related to clothing, such as buttons, buckles, and beads, as objects of adornment. They signify agency and the creation of group boundaries. However, when examined in the context of wealth and class, these items can tell another story about the economic and social life of women in a rural nineteenth-century community. I provide two scenarios to expand the possibilities of interpreting these items from New Philadelphia.

First is an analogy of the little-known activity of junking, the collecting of unwanted materials for reuse or recycling that developed in the mid-nineteenth century (Praetzellis and Praetzellis 1990). For some, junking developed into a full-time occupation, while others junked to supplement their income. Sometimes youth participated in these activities to provide additional resources to the family. Junking could include the collection of glass, sold by the hundreds of pounds, or gathering old clothes and rags, paper, iron, and tin (Borchert 1982:96). Clothes could be resold, and rags could be sold to brokers, who then sold them to paper mills to make rag paper. Rags could also be shredded and rewoven into "shoddy cloth," which is inferior to the original wool product and much cheaper (LaRoche and McGowen 2001:70; Praetzellis and Praetzellis 1990).

There is a large cache of buttons from feature 1, which is associated with Casiah Clark, and feature 14, which is probably associated with Sarah McWorter's ownership (Figure 43). The material provides for an interesting scenario about life in rural Illinois. B. J. Little and Kasner (2001:62) show that junking was a major part of the nineteenth-century economy, and the high number of buttons found near dwellings may indicate the production of rags. It served as an economic sideline for a household. The same scenario should be considered for the two

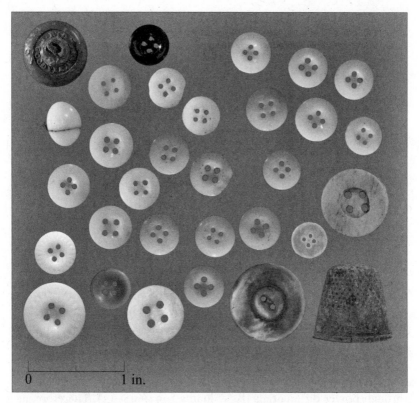

FIGURE 43. A sample of buttons found at Sarah McWorter's homestead. Photograph by Christopher Valvano.

New Philadelphia families where women served as the head of their household. While the rural economy existed mainly on barter and trade, the intricacies of this system are not well documented, nor is the process of junking (Praetzellis and Praetzellis 1990).

In another scenario Elizabeth Jordan (2005:217–32), using material culture and context from a former washing place in Cape Town, South Africa, demonstrates that items like buttons, buckles, and beads should be considered byproducts of women's labor. Accounts of washerwomen helped her develop her case study, although similar scenarios are possible when women took in laundry from neighbors. The washing process includes soaking the clothes, beating them, rubbing soap in them, and beating them again. Through the process buttons and other clothing items were broken or fell off the garment. Items left in pockets would also be lost. Washing could be done at almost any stage of life; widows often turned to this occupation to supplement their income. Carter Woodson (1930), using examples from the United States, explains that the washing served as an important activity to help African American families survive. These scenarios should help us think about the complexity of the archaeological record and consider the many variables, such as race, class, and gender, that need to be considered when developing a context for any archaeological assemblage.

BLACK AND WHITE IDENTITY

The search for identity has a long tradition in archaeology (Trigger 2006). V. Gordon Childe and many of his contemporaries working in the earlier part of the twentieth century used culture markers to identify population movements. Today, as then, ethnic interpretations of archaeology are playing a role in contemporary conflicts, such as the Serbs' and Albanians' claim over the territory of Kosovo (Hakenbeck 2004:1).

Historical archaeological studies of ethnicity are often related to consumption and the marketplace. However, it is difficult to correlate material culture with the categories of ethnicity and race (B. J. Little and Kasner 2001:63). These categories are not natural, but are created through power differentials (B. Williams 1992:608–12). Therefore, accessing race and ethnicity purely on the basis of material culture can be problematic. Material objects cannot be simple ethnic markers, although they can reflect ethnic significance, if you know the meaning and the cues (Orser 2004).

Hall (1996:443) argues that identity is produced within specific historical and social conditions; he describes the implications of looking for ethnicity based on skin color:

> The end of the essential Black subject is something which people are increasingly debating, but they may not have fully reckoned with its political consequences. What is at issue here is the recognition of the extraordinary diversity of subjective positions, social experiences and cultural identities which compose the category "black"; that is, the recognition that "black" is essentially a politically and culturally *constructed* category, which cannot be grounded in a set of fixed trans-cultural or transcendental racial categories and which has no guarantees in nature. (443)

In other words, cultural markers are always changing and meanings shifting depending on sociopolitical contexts. Ethnic identities are not a given, and their fluidity can affect archaeological interpretations. Ethnic groups are not static, nor are they neatly defined and segmented into predetermined groups. Instead they should be understood as the result of social and political processes of categorization (Vermeersch 2004:23).

Paul Mullins's (1999) work in Annapolis, Maryland, uncovered everyday consumer goods among African American households and provides an important way to think about finding expected ethnic and racial differences in the archaeological record. Mullins builds a case to show that African Americans participated in consumerism as a strategy to confront racism. Consumerism has a symbolic appeal; it is empowering, and it allows people to participate in a type of consumer civil citizenship. This purchasing power was important to African Americans because they were excluded from American social and economic life. Mullins emphasizes that we should avoid any monolithic characterizations of blacks, especially when constricted by genteel whites (173). In a similar way, all of the households at New Philadelphia participated in a consumer culture, and the homogenization of material may be a way of showing that they all participated equally in a consumer civil citizenship.

When examining New Philadelphia's historical narrative we can observe how African American identity was created. One of the first county histories of the area reaffirms the subordinated position, or the "otherness" of African Americans. Chapman (1880:217) wrote that in the early 1830s a black man was chased out of town because he wanted to marry a white woman. Jess Thompson (1967:151) writes, "The first white man in Hadley Township was a colored man." In this case the McWorter family is seen as "others" and "outsiders" to the region when compared to the other settlers because of their skin color.

The story of Ansel Vond is an example of changing identity, an identity that was controlled by others. Vond was a head of household and lived on a farm adjacent to and north of New Philadelphia. He first appears in the 1860 Federal Census, where he is classified as black; his wife, Lucy Ann, is listed as mulatto. In 1870 they are both classified as white. In the 1880 census their color changes again, and they are listed as mulatto. Clearly each census taker saw the Vond family differently. The census recordings reflect the changing need for whites to create otherness when describing people of color. An 1862 newspaper account in the *Pike County Democrat* described the growing anti-African American sentiment, the fear of white men potentially losing their jobs, and their opposition to a war to "liberate the niggers" (Waggoner

1999:67, 79). By the end of the Civil War most Illinoisans accepted the outcome of the war, and in 1865 the state voided all of its past Black Codes. At the end of the Civil War New Philadelphia's population hit its peak and thereafter steadily declined. Perhaps the Vonds, who had become well established in the community, were no longer seen as a threat and were able to "pass." However, by the 1880s, on the eve of Jim Crow, racism and prejudice was on the rise again, and the white census taker made sure to create distinctions based on color. At the turn of the century sundown towns developed around New Philadelphia (Loewen 2005). Oral histories also indicate that the Ku Klux Klan was active from the 1920s into the 1960s.

Sometimes there are strong relationships between ethnic identity and material culture, and items such as clothing, food, and other everyday materials signal meaning and identity. Goods can create, enforce, and reinforce behavior. They create and maintain social boundaries and communicate a whole set of clues that elicit appropriate behaviors (Bourdieu 1977). Goods may have different meanings in different social circumstances as their messages are continually changed and renegotiated. Goods can be used to justify and support different subgroups in society, and they can mask, contradict, or exaggerate social relations (Douglas and Isherwood 1979; Hodder 1982; D. Miller 1987; D. Miller and Tilley 1984; Rapoport 1990).

Archaeologists have recognized that cultural uniformity of material goods between groups may be an expression of within-group cohesion and competition (Hodder 1979:447, 1982:7). As a multiracial town founded in the 1830s, New Philadelphia shows that although we can identify people by race according to the historical records, identifying groups through their material culture is difficult. Despite residents' different ethnic backgrounds, places of origin, genders, and occupations, there do not appear to be any discernable differences between the sites in terms of consumer material culture. The boundaries sometimes found in material culture when comparing households of different backgrounds seem to be blurred. Access to market goods appears to be similar among the different households, and all of the households rejected the Victorian ideal of matched sets. Gaming pieces traditionally associated with African Americans are found in both white and black households. These findings suggest the possibility that people from different ethnic groups spent leisure time together, either in the form of play or gambling. They challenge our perceptions of having a game associated with one ethnic group, and they allow us to challenge some of the Africanisms often assumed by many historical archaeologists.

While identity is very fluid and always changing, households of very different backgrounds used material culture to create some form of group identity at the level of consumer goods. The sameness of the assemblages and the rejection of Victorian ideals contributed to what may be a type of group cohesion between people of different backgrounds. Differences did exist in landholding and livestock, personal wealth, access to government and law, and general stature in the community, among other areas. The examination of material culture at New Philadelphia helps to provide a scenario of how goods were used to shape and create a community in a racist society.

LANDMARK STATUS

On October 29, 2008, Charlotte King presented a background of the archaeology project and the research on identity to the National Historic Landmark board, which met in Washington, D.C. Charlotte also did a fantastic job of gathering letters of support from citizens and professionals in Illinois, as well as congressmen, senators, and local politicians. The chair of the committee was most impressed with her persistence in getting a letter of support from Barack Obama while he was crossing the nation during his presidential campaign. Chris Fennell and I attended the meeting to support Charlotte in answering questions. Several members of the New Philadelphia Association, including Phil Bradshaw and Carol McCartney, gave short testimonies in support of the nomination. Patricia McWorter also presented a statement on behalf of some of her family members:

> My name is Patricia McWorter, a great-great-granddaughter of Frank and Lucy McWorter, and I rise to speak for and represent my family. We are so very pleased to be here helping the nation embrace its true self, something we have always known in our family, but now you will be enabling us to share and develop this story as part of the official history of the country. We thank you for this long overdue public recognition.
>
> First and foremost I want to say that the importance of Frank and Lucy's accomplishments, specifically the founding and development of the abolitionist town of New Philadelphia, is about our family and all of the town's descendents, but it is also about Illinois and the entire United States. It's a message we can send to the world.
>
> This story takes us back to the time of the birth of Frank and Lucy McWorter as slaves in the eighteenth century at the time of the founding of this

country [1771 and 1777]. There have been some African Americans who have had their voices heard from the slave experience. Frederick Douglass, Harriet Tubman, Phyllis Wheatley, and Nat Turner, but there are so many, many more coming to the fore. The McWorter—New Philadelphia legacy is one of those voices.

Now, over 150 years since the death of Frank McWorter we stand here today reflecting on the meaning of his life and the town of New Philadelphia. Everyone is clear that the political struggle against slavery brings up the name of President Abraham Lincoln. Everyone is also clear that the moral and cultural struggle over slavery brings up the name of Mark Twain. Lincoln lived and worked in Springfield, and Mark Twain did the same across the river in Hannibal, Missouri. But where is the voice of the African American? We are fortunate to be able to call the name of Frank McWorter, who gives us the chance to learn from the agency of an African American.

1. Frank McWorter demonstrates the possibility of change based on what we can only call the birth of the American spirit for freedom. Born one year after the U.S. won its national liberation from England, this slave worked under slavery, bought his pregnant wife first so that his fifth child would be born free, and in the end buying 16 family members including himself.

2. The town of New Philadelphia was an example of abolitionism at work, the sharing of a community by whites and Blacks, both as neighbors and as members of the same family. This was their lifestyle less than 20 miles from slavery. These were proud and noble people who were living up to the American dream in spite of what shape America was in at that time.

Our future is in the past. New Philadelphia is a key to the future of this country.

The McWorters and the town of New Philadelphia were about freedom:

1. They assisted slaves running to freedom—"Get to that New Philadelphia and one of those McWorter boys will give you a horse, a pair of shoes and guide you to Canada and freedom."—So goes our family oral history.

2. Grandchildren fought in the Civil War as part of the Union Army, Infantry 38th Regiment, United States Colored Infantry [Squire McWorter, 1846—1915].

But most important of all is that they lived free in Illinois and are a beacon light for all to see that the American possibility is a great challenge for all of us to live up to. We are strengthened by the memory of New Philadelphia.

One can read the testimony in the Pike County History of 1880 to see that the story has always been part of the local Illinois history. Now is the time for this to officially become part of the national narrative, part of our collective story. Frank McWorter and New Philadelphia are about what a Black man accomplished, what an abolitionist town accomplished, and what hard work and sacrifice for family, for freedom for all, can lead to even under the most adverse of conditions. Isn't this the message we need to send today, to ourselves and the entire world, that this is what this country strives to be about when we are at our best?

As a family we are committed to working with the New Philadelphia Association and the governmental organizations from the federal, state, county and local levels to make this a site of national heritage that we can all learn from and be proud of for years to come.

Thank you.

There were a few tears in the eyes of some of the committee members. They were moved by the story of Frank and Lucy McWorter and their family, and impressed with the sincere delivery of the founder's great-great-granddaughter. There were a few questions about the archaeology, and one of the panelists wanted some assurance that the entire site would not be totally excavated so that the archaeology would be well preserved. The National Historic Landmarks Committee recommended designation and it received unanimous approval. The secretary of the interior designated it in January 2009.

CHAPTER 11

Some Thoughts, but Not
the Final Word

New Philadelphia is about entrepreneurial success and freedom. However, when dealing with many different stakeholders, it is sometimes difficult to establish a coherent message for the place. Trying to change the way people remember the history of any place does not come quickly, nor does it come easily. Whether internally coherent or contradictory to the dominant view, memories validate the individual's version of the past, sometimes by being selective about what is being presented to the public. The same historical and material representation may have divergent meanings to different audiences, and there can be competing interests that struggle to create a specific memory of a place (Glassberg 1996:9–10; Lowenthal 1985). Understanding how and why some groups have different perspectives on an event or a place is important for critically evaluating and understanding the development and meaning of a place like New Philadelphia.

MEMORY AND REPRESENTATION

The collective memory of New Philadelphia does not rely solely on professional historical scholarship; it also takes into account the local and descendant communities and institutions. The act of politicians supporting road signage on the federal highway helps raise the visibility of the place, which helps this version of history become part of the national collective memory. However, different group agendas and perspectives cause the collective memory of the place to be continuously in flux. The tensions between and within groups who struggle for control over the collective public memory are ongoing because the political stakes are high.

The question about representation continues to play a significant role in the debate about how to present New Philadelphia to the public. After almost a decade of research, the question is *What is the next step?* Many McWorter family members see our archaeology project as a way to promote and preserve the stories of their family and this very important town. At least one family member feels that we are not accurately representing the most important story of the place, that of the founder of the town. The desires of the local and descendant communities for preserving the site are truly varied.

Juliet Walker has stated to the media that New Philadelphia existed as a frontier town in the 1850s until its demise as a town in 1870 (Husar 2005b). Yet the documentary and archaeological records make it very clear that the town did not disappear in 1870. There was a steady exodus from the town after the railroad was routed around it in 1869, and the town continued to contract for the next several decades. Family ties, social networks, and established livelihoods kept some families around for several more generations. A portion of the town was reverted to agriculture in 1885, but continued occupation is indicated by the fact that the community supported a blacksmith shop and a grocery into the early twentieth century. Geographer Ronald Grim (1977:12) defines a town as "a nucleation of houses representing two or more households or extended families and in which a livelihood is gained from service activities as well as from agriculture." These circumstances are certainly the case for New Philadelphia into the twentieth century. About a half-dozen households remained in the town into the 1920s. The remaining households in the twentieth century owned blocks (made up of eight lots) rather than single lots. Agriculture and husbandry occurred in greater intensity within the town's boundaries. However, people still called the place New Philadelphia, and the new schoolhouse built in the 1870s became the social center for community activities into the 1940s and 1950s.

In 1990 Juliet Walker told the *Pike County Express* that she wants to restore part of New Philadelphia: "We'd like to build something with the vitality of New Salem. It wouldn't be that extensive, but we would at least like to restore the businesses and some of the key buildings." The *Pike County Express* reported that she believes that eight to nine acres would be necessary to develop the site property (Coulson 1990). Using New Salem as a model for rebuilding, as Walker suggested, would be questionable to many in the various historic preservation fields.

New Salem, located about twenty-five miles north of Springfield, Illinois, is where Abraham Lincoln lived from 1831 to 1837, prior to moving to Springfield. It was abandoned by 1839, and in 1847 a traveler called the place desolate. Many people remembered New Salem as a rough place, although its past became romanticized in the late nineteenth century. It soon became part of the larger narrative of American progress (Taylor and Johnson 2004b:181). New Salem became the place where Lincoln overcame the hardships of the American frontier. It is now seen by many as a national shrine, a site of America's "civil religion," a site that is responsible for the myth of trajectories from Lincoln's log cabin to the White House (Bruner 1994:399).

In 1906 William Randolph Hearst helped to convey the ownership of the former town to the Old Salem Chautauqua Association. Reconstruction of some of the buildings occurred about a decade later, but with very little archaeological or architectural evidence. Archaeological excavations by the Lincoln League located the remains of two foundations. Beyond these general building dimensions, no other evidence existed regarding the above-ground characteristics of the buildings. Questions remained about the buildings' walls (log or hewn), placement of doors and windows, types of floor, and types of roof. In 1918 these details did not seem to bother those involved in the reconstruction. The old settlers were dying off, and the Lincoln League rushed to build these structures as a way to memorialize them before they were gone (Taylor and Johnson 2004b: 188–95). The reconstruction "sprang from a deep longing for places, objects, and images that would serve as 'vehicles of sacred contact' to a vanishing pioneer past" (195). However, much of the reconstruction relied on guesswork to determine the approximate shape and size of each structure. Even though some crude archaeological techniques were employed, the placement of some buildings was incorrect (Mazrim 2007:41; Taylor and Johnson 2004a:262).

In 1919 the site was donated to the State of Illinois. By 1932 the state had razed the first generation of reconstructed buildings, and a second building phase began (Bruner 1994:407). The state excavated eleven or twelve buildings in the early 1930s for the next phase of reconstruction by the Civil Conservation Corps (CCC) and an additional eight or nine sites in the mid- to late 1930s. The goal of the archaeology was to provide an approximate dimension for the reconstruction of the buildings, but it could not provide information about the above-ground characteristics of the building (Taylor and Johnson 2004a:263–65).

For those reconstructing New Salem, *authentic* meant associating the new buildings with a known villager. However, several families occupied many of these places over the course of the town's existence. Nevertheless each structure is labeled with only one family name, depending on who Joseph Booton, the architect in charge, and others thought were the most prominent families to live in a particular house. Today each building displays stories about only one of the settlers who occupied it (Taylor and Johnson 2004a:267). Edward Bruner (1994:405) warns us, "The consequence is to fix history, to solidify it, and to simplify it."

After reconstructing several buildings, a civil engineering company from Springfield could not correlate the existing rebuilt structures with the lots of the original town plan. Adjustments to lot lines became necessary to make the survey conform to the existing landscape. In fact a 1995 archaeological survey indicates that part of the main street is incorrectly located, and therefore several buildings are mistakenly associated with the wrong families (Taylor and Johnson 2004a:271). Four of the twenty-two reconstructed buildings are located in places that are *not* based on archaeological remains.

The goal of the CCC reconstruction was to re-create the appearance of the town and its history and enable visitors to immerse themselves in the experience of visualizing the past (Taylor and Johnson 2004b:174–78). All of the reconstructed buildings are finely crafted, and Booton reasoned that the people of New Salem were " 'exceedingly energetic' people who used 'simple methods' to erect 'neat and tidy' houses 'according to the best standards' during a rather advanced stage in frontier development" (quoted in Taylor and Johnson 2004a:268). None of the buildings appeared hastily built, and all of the structures had hewn logs instead of rounded logs. The recreated settlement has an aura of refinement—for a frontier town. However, later oral histories describe crude buildings and rounded log construction (Bruner 1994:402; Taylor and Johnson 2004a:268). The New Salem that is standing and visited by hundreds of thousands of tourists each year reflects the historic preservation and interpretation philosophy of the 1930s. Rebuilding took precedence over any thought for historical accuracy.

Edward Bruner (1994:401–2) points out many other compromises to the authenticity of New Salem:

Gutters are constructed on the log cabins to channel the rainwater. In the past the animals would have roamed free, but now they are fenced in so that animal waste is not scattered throughout the village and so that visitors are protected. There are fences, made to look as if they were original, that are designed to direct the flow of tourist traffic. Unobtrusive restrooms have been built with drinking fountains on the side, a convenience not found in the 1830s. Along the path, benches have been erected so that the visitors may sit and rest. The road is now paved so that when it rains the tourists do not have to walk in the mud. The schoolhouse in the 1830s was located 1.5 miles away from the village, but it has been reconstructed inside the compound for the convenience of the visitors. The carding mill is supposedly operated entirely by animal power, by oxen moving in a circle, but it has a hidden motor. The Rutledge Tavern and the first Berry-Lincoln Store have electric heaters placed so that they cannot be seen by the tourists. The caulking between the logs on the sides of the cabins is now made of cement, but in the 1830s cement had not yet been invented.

Security gates, an access ramp, and perfectly mowed fields are other instances that challenge the authenticity of the place. Bruner (1994:404) sums it up nicely with his assessment: "New Salem is an idealized community that leaves out the conflict, tension, and dirt of the 1830s. New Salem is . . . presented as an idyllic, peaceful, harmonious village."

Because of many of the mishaps in previous reconstructions, such as at New Salem, the preservation community strongly objects to any form of reconstruction without clear documentation that would make the reconstruction 100 percent accurate. For this reason there are few recent reconstructions found on the American landscape. *The Secretary of the Interior's Standards for the Treatment of Historic Properties* (n.d.) outlines the criteria for reconstructing buildings on federal property:

1. Reconstruction will be used to depict vanished or non-surviving portions of a property when documentary and physical evidence is available to permit accurate reconstruction with minimal conjecture, and such reconstruction is essential to the public understanding of the property.

2. Reconstruction of a landscape, building, structure, or object in its historic location will be preceded by a thorough archeological investigation to identify and evaluate those features and artifacts, which are essential to an accurate reconstruction. If such resources must be disturbed, mitigation measures will be undertaken.

3. Reconstruction will include measures to preserve any remaining historic materials, features, and spatial relationships.

4. Reconstruction will be based on the accurate duplication of historic features and elements substantiated by documentary or physical evidence rather than on conjectural designs or the availability of different features

from other historic properties. A reconstructed property will re-create the appearance of the non-surviving historic property in materials, design, color, and texture.

5. A reconstruction will be clearly identified as a contemporary re-creation.

6. Designs that were never executed historically will not be constructed.

These criteria, numbers 4 and 6 above, make it clear that any reconstruction of buildings at New Philadelphia will only be conjectural (4) since no photographs exist and the archaeological record has revealed only subsurface features, such as cellars and cisterns. Because of their ephemeral nature, foundations associated with the earliest structures do not exist. It is not clear that any reconstruction could accurately duplicate the true nature of the original buildings (6).

The *Management Policies* of the National Park Service (2006:72) also has standards for reconstruction of missing structures:

> No matter how well conceived or executed, reconstructions are contemporary interpretations of the past rather than authentic survivals from it. The National Park Service will not reconstruct a missing structure unless: 1) there is no alternative that would accomplish the park's interpretive mission; 2) *sufficient data exist to enable its accurate reconstruction based on the duplication of historic features substantiated by documentary or physical evidence rather than on conjectural designs or features from other structures;* 3) reconstruction will occur in the original location; 4) the disturbance or loss of significant archeological resources is minimized and mitigated by data recovery; and 4) reconstruction is approved by the Director. (emphasis added)

The policy also states, "A structure will not be reconstructed to appear damaged or ruined. *Generalized representations of typical structures will not be attempted*" (72, emphasis added). It is clear from *The Secretary of the Interior's Standards* and the National Park Service's *Management Policies* that reconstructions should not occur if there are not enough data to accurately and faithfully rebuild a structure. So, although private citizens and organizations can easily reconstruct places without any repercussions, if the New Philadelphia Association plans to donate the property to the state or the federal government it should be aware of the rules that guide the built environment. Any form of rebuilding could damage the integrity of the site and jeopardize the significance of the place.

Interpreting the landscape of New Philadelphia is a very difficult task, especially when there is no physical or architectural evidence of what exactly existed above the ground in the town. A few memory maps exist, such as the Burdick map (Figure 6), but they are not detailed. Further-more a major question for interpreting the landscape of New Philadel-phia is which time period should be represented. The archaeological record shows us that some of the houses that were built in the 1840s were gone from the landscape by the 1850s. Some houses existed through the 1870s, and some were built in the 1880s and around 1900. Rebuilding a town like New Salem, or even New Philadelphia, often means that only one time period and only one history is interpreted, at the expense of other histories and other time periods. The question is, *Should you pro-mote one history at the expense of other histories?* Since the 1970s preser-vationists, museum professionals, historians, and archaeologists have not supported the idea of reconstruction. Time-freezing a place (reconstruct-ing it to a specific time period) has significant political ramifications when you consider who might be left out of the story. Our goal at New Philadel-phia from the beginning was to be as inclusive as possible and to tell all of the stories of the town, from the 1830s through the 1930s. Any attempt to reconstruct a town at New Philadelphia would be contrary to the recom-mendation of *The Secretary of the Interior's Standards* and the National Park Service's *Management Policies,* and it could also jeopardize the site's consideration as nationally significant.

My suggestion is that an interpretive center be built that explains the history and development of New Philadelphia and the contributions of the McWorter family. House foundations could be outlined, and perhaps ghost structures placed in the area where houses were once located in or-der to give a sense of the height, bulk, and closeness of the town (Figures 44 and 45). This type of representation admits that we have only partial knowledge of what the buildings may have looked like and that the in-formation we do have is based on below-ground evidence. The streets should be outlined and interpretive signs should be placed throughout the town site explaining the activities at each house lot, incorporating our ar-chaeological findings. Visitors should get the sense that New Philadelphia once stood as a small bustling rural community where building, rebuild-ing, demolition, and decay were part of the landscape. The story of free-dom and the eventual abandonment of the town are also a major part of the story. It was a multiracial community that survived for almost a cen-tury, and any interpretation of the place needs to acknowledge the entire town over its entire existence.

Places on the American landscape mark who we are as a community and a nation. What we save and what we commemorate are expressions

FIGURE 44. An example of a ghost structure, in St. Mary's City, Maryland.
Photograph by Paul A. Shackel.

of what we see as important in our lives today. The research project at New Philadelphia has the ability to remember new histories and provide insights that may not be agreeable to all of the stakeholders. However, we have all seen and experienced places that try to freeze time in the built environment, and the consequences are devastating to the cultural resources. At a place that has become familiar to me, Harpers Ferry National Historical Park, the decision in the 1950s to recreate the town's Civil War era meant that late nineteenth- and early twentieth-century buildings and histories were considered unimportant. The National Park Service literally erased them from the landscape with bulldozers. Today we see that decision was a big mistake. Unfortunately the park has lost many of its props telling the story of labor, class, and everyday life of the post–Civil War era (Moyer and Shackel 2008). Even today, in the twenty-first century, a place like Manassas National Battlefield Park is busy trying to reconstruct the Civil War landscape at the expense of the postemancipation story of a free African American family. Buildings continue to be modified and removed that are not directly associated with the battle (E. K. Martin et al. 1997). I can only imagine that in the future cultural resource managers and historians will regret the severe

FIGURE 45. An example of a ghost structure, in Jefferson Patterson Park and Museum, St. Leonard, Maryland. Photograph by Paul A. Shackel.

modification of the park's landscape and their difficulty in telling an inclusive story of the park.

The year we began excavating at New Philadelphia, the Free Frank New Philadelphia Historic Preservation Foundation, a 501(c)3 organization, was formed with the goal of recreating the town, to be called the Free Frank New Philadelphia Historic Frontier Town. The Foundation's (2006b) website announced, "This project will be an interactive painstaking rebuilding of the architectural features of the buildings and the social life in New Philadelphia at its height in the 1850s."

The Free Frank New Philadelphia Historic Preservation Foundation website (2006c) clearly states that its mission is to celebrate the achievements of Frank McWorter and African American entrepreneurship and to rebuild New Philadelphia. The site suggests that the recreated town should also have historical actors: "There will be men, women and children dressed in clothing from the frontier period working, playing and living in a daily routine that will be reminiscent of life in Free Frank's New Philadelphia" (2006b). The site quotes from Walker's (1983a:132–33) book and describes some of the craft activities that may have taken place in New Philadelphia: "The wheelwright made and repaired wheels, carriages and wagons. . . . Farmers with their ox or horse-drawn wagons used the services of both the wheelwright and the blacksmith, who in addition to repairing axles, also shoed horses and [repaired] farm tools" (2006b). Then, in the fashion of many outdoor museums that interpret nineteenth-century daily life, the website explains, "At the interactive frontier museum visitors will help the shoemaker make shoes, the cabinet-maker make cabinets, and help sort mail [at] the post office and attend frontier school. The visitors will assist the farmer planting and participate in the hand making of clothes. The visitors will learn how to churn butter and grind corn for baking and cooking food. There will be a restaurant that serves authentic frontier food. Visitors will listen to and learn how to play music of the time and help the merchant in the general store" (2006b).

The Free Frank New Philadelphia Historic Preservation Foundation website also discusses the development of a general store "where you can purchase souvenirs to remind you of your visit to the restored historic frontier town. Or you can wait until you return home and purchase them online at our secured website." It boasts of a line of "frontier clothing for women, girls, men and boys that you can order online or purchase while on your visit to Free Frank's New Philadelphia." There is the opportunity "to enjoy the same foods that Free Frank, his family and the New Philadelphians enjoyed. The delicious food will be available to take home with you or you will be able to order it online and have it delivered to your home." You can also purchase period furniture and holiday ornaments (2006a).

There are many versions of nineteenth-century living history museums scattered across the United States that are apolitical and avoid the tough histories of the past. At the National Park Service Discovery 2000 conference, the historian John Hope Franklin, one of America's most celebrated historians, explained in his keynote address that the difficult histories are important and need to be made part of the official memory of any place:

> The places that commemorate sad history are not places in which we wallow, or wallow in remorse, but instead places in which we may be moved to a new resolve, to be better citizens. . . . Explaining history from a variety of angles makes it not only more interesting, but more true. When it is more true, more people come to feel that they have a part in it. That is where patriotism and loyalty intersect with truth. (National Park Service 2000)

Creating a new living history museum has the potential to tell more than a story about wheelwrights, blacksmiths, and cabinetmakers. The development of a living history museum is the perfect opportunity to discuss issues of race, freedom, and entrepreneurship in the larger context of the Illinois frontier, as well as the local context of New Philadelphia. What was it like for an African American craftsman to practice his trade in a predominantly white township, and a multiracial community? What kind of interactions did the shoemaker have with the white and black communities? How did the 1853 Illinois legislation that prohibited the immigration of blacks into the state affect the growth and development of New Philadelphia? How did this legislation impact the family ties of the African Americans already established in the area? How were several African American families able to settle in this community soon after the passing of this legislation? How did women support the growth and development of the town? How did the women heads of households manage to survive in a new rural community? How did the development of sundown towns affect the white and black residents of New Philadelphia?

When looking at any heritage site we not only need to interpret the dominant culture, but we also need to understand that other histories exist and are important to the place's history. There are several elements that will help any multiethnic site be more inclusive and help address some of the tough histories that John Hope Franklin tells us need to be part of the national public memory.

Opening up a heritage site to different viewpoints makes the relationship of archaeology to heritage tourism much more complicated. We must navigate the different interests as scholars and professionals, and the interests of many other stakeholders (Glassberg 1998:5). This point is made explicit in Timothy Breen's (1989) study of East Hampton, Long Island, where he demonstrates how a community actively created its own history. He shows how individuals and groups actively made decisions about what history to create about their past and how these decisions were influenced by economic development choices. The creation of collective memories on the personal and local levels is not necessarily exclusive from larger issues. Our recent work in New Philadelphia provides an example of some of the benefits and pitfalls of working on a project with many stakeholders that support different views of the past. Yet although discussions about the place have sometimes been tense, we all agree on the importance of the site.

"WE'RE ALL PART OF THE SAME HERITAGE"

Janet Davies is the host and executive producer of *190 North,* an entertainment and lifestyle program on ABC TV Chicago. It is a top-rated program in its time slot, and Davies has been nominated for forty-nine regional Emmys and has won a Silver Dome Award from the Illinois Broadcasters Association. Davies visited us at the Illinois State Museum as we were processing artifacts at the end of the second field season. The crew recorded several hours of interviews for a four-minute segment that aired in the fall of 2005. Her ratings received a bump with the New Philadelphia clip. "Our ratings jumped an unbelievable 8 points with this story! That's jaw-dropping, " it was reported on the New Philadelphia blog. The results encouraged her to come back during the next field season and shoot some footage of the fieldwork.

On June 16–17, 2006, descendants and the media packed New Philadelphia. Many from the local community and family descendants came to participate in a "Day of Discovery" organized by Claire Fuller Martin and Sandra McWorter. Many descendants of the more than 200 families who once resided at New Philadelphia and the surrounding region attended this event, shared genealogical and historical research and photographs, and toured the archaeological excavations. Davies and her crew filmed descendants and the activities, and reporters from the *Los Angeles Times,* the *Rockford Register Star,* and the *Quincy Herald Whig* interviewed archaeologists and the students. Davies's new and expanded half-hour segment on New Philadelphia, "Rediscovering a Black Pioneer's Dream," appeared in October 2006. The show was nominated for an Emmy. It gave a voice to the descendants, many of whom showed support for the overall project.

On July 14, 2006, the project appeared on the front page of the *Los Angeles Times* with the headline "A Land of Racial Harmony?" At first it seemed as though the reporter had dug up an old controversy and an old title, but, as they say, there is no such thing as bad press. The reporter quoted Sandra McWorter supporting the research project: "We want to do everything we can to unearth the truth and celebrate our past. We want to know what really happened" (Huffstutter 2006). Gerald McWorter chimed in on the issue of racial harmony:

There's no evidence to say folks didn't get along. Why would whites buy land in and move to New Philadelphia, if they had a problem supporting and living with freed slaves? . . . Was it utopia? Probably not," said Gerald, director of Africana studies at the University of Toledo, Ohio. "Was it filled with conflict? No." [Juliet] Walker disagreed. "There were blacks on the frontier. There were whites on the frontier. To say these people were happily living side by side is like saying that slaves were happy on the plantation.(Huffstutter 2006)

Walker told another reporter, "You know that Free Frank and his friends were involved in the Underground Railroad. The slaves were secreted to Free Frank's house. Free Frank never lived in the town. So if the town was such a place of racial harmony, why is it that the fugitive slaves were hidden away from the whites in the township and then taken to Canada as opposed to, 'Here is the town! Live here in racial harmony'" (quoted in Chambers 2007a:4D).

There is, I believe, the possibility that the residents of New Philadelphia may have participated in the Underground Railroad, or at least supported its activities. In fact there are family stories by white families mentioned earlier that suggest that the surrounding community was involved in the Underground Railroad. There are also instances where former enslaved and free African Americans came to live in the surrounding areas of New Philadelphia, so it must have been seen as being at least tolerant of racial differences. For instance, in a similar story of freedom, John Walker was born enslaved in Virginia and purchased his freedom in 1834. In 1861 he purchased a farm adjacent to New Philadelphia and moved there with his wife and children. In another case, Thomas H. Thomas purchased his and his wife Sophia's freedom prior to coming to Pike County in 1857 and settled southwest of Philadelphia. Ansel Vond came to Pike County and settled adjacent to and north of New Philadelphia in 1858. James Washington is another African American who settled close to New Philadelphia after the Civil War (Matteson 1964:29; *Atlas Map of Pike County* 1872). They were coming to the New Philadelphia area, only twenty-three miles from the border of a slave state. As we do additional oral histories there is always the chance of finding out that other families may also have participated in the Underground Railroad. More research is still needed. With all of these pieces coming together Gerald McWorter exclaimed in the *Rockford Register Star* web feature story, "So we're talking about this being a hell of a freedom story" (quoted in Chambers 2007b).

Unlike the many other newspaper articles on the project, P. J. Huffstutter of the *Los Angeles Times* took another angle to the story. She described Karen Wall's efforts to uncover McWorter family history. Wall is the paternal grandmother of a McWorter descendant who got in touch with Sandra McWorter through the Internet. Huffstutter reported, "Wall, who is white, was welcomed by the McWorters even though she is connected to the town only by marriage. 'These are our people. This is our homecoming,' [Sandra] McWorter said. 'We're all part of the same heritage and we all want the same thing—to preserve New Philadelphia' " (Huffstutter 2006).

SANCTIFIED SITES

Often there is no single interpretation for the historical landscapes and monuments of America. They have different meanings for different people, and it is the struggle for control over meaning that makes the historical places dynamic and interesting. While creating a particular memory of an event helps to make it part of society's official history, the act of marking off and preserving land or creating monuments sanctifies the memory. The New Philadelphia Association and the many descendants associated with the town are working toward that goal. Kenneth Foote (1997) remarks that there must be some type of public ceremony that describes why an object is important and why the site should be remembered. These places or monuments then serve to remind future generations "of a virtue or sacrifice or to warn them of events to be avoided" (8).

Sanctified sites and memorials have a distinctive appearance in the landscape.

> First, they are often clearly bounded from the surrounding environment and marked with great specificity as to what happened where. Second, sanctified sites are usually carefully maintained for long periods of time—decades, generations, and centuries. Third, sanctification typically involves a change of ownership, often a transfer from private to public stewardship. Fourth, sanctified sites frequently attract continued ritual commemoration, such as annual memorial services or pilgrimage. Fifth, sanctified sites often attract additional and sometimes even unrelated monuments and memorials through a process of accretion. That is, once sanctified, these sites seem to act as foci for other commemorative efforts. (Foote 1997:9)

While the New Philadelphia Association is working to purchase the town site, the site is clearly marked with an interpretive sign and the landowners have erected cabins over foundations and maintain the fields. The goal of the New Philadelphia Association is to eventually hand over the property to a state or federal caretaker to make it a park to interpret the important moral lesson about the tragedies of the past and the hope for the future. They are continually trying to raise money to purchase and preserve the town site. Most recently the Archaeological Conservancy has purchased and protected over nine acres of the area most densely occupied around Broad and Main Streets. The McWorter family reunion at the site in 2005 was one important ritual that helped sanction the New Philadelphia town site. Michelle Huttes's nomination of the site for the National Register of Historic Places in 2005 was another significant event that helped sanctify the place. The town site is now considered nationally significant because of the potential of the archaeological record. Charlotte King's nomination of the site as a National Historic Landmark, one of the highest designations awarded by the federal government, was approved by the Secretary of the Interior in 2009. The nomination was accepted because of the importance of the archaeology at the site to answer important questions about race and the struggle for freedom on the western frontier.

During a recent trip to the World Archaeology Conference I came across the poem "We Saw a Vision," inscribed in the Garden of Remembrance in Dublin. It is reproduced on the dedication page of this book. It is striking how people of different backgrounds who have been oppressed for generations have similar values: freedom and hope for the future as well as a call to remember the struggle. While the many stakeholders unite to preserve New Philadelphia, I hope that its core values of hope and freedom become the centerpiece for remembering and valuing this historic place.

Appendix

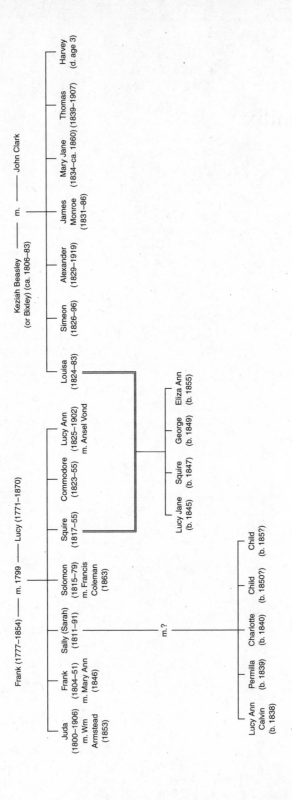

Frank (1777–1854) —— m. 1799 —— Lucy (1771–1870)

Keziah Beasley
(or Bixley) (ca. 1806–83) —— m. —— John Clark

Juda
(1800–1906)
m. Wm
Armstead
(1853)

Frank
(1804–51)
m. Mary Ann
(1846)

Sally (Sarah)
(1811–91)

Solomon
(1815–79)
m. Francis
Coleman
(1863)

Squire
(1817–55)

Commodore
(1823–55)

Lucy Ann
(1825–1902)
m. Ansel Vond

Louisa
(1824–83)

Simeon
(1826–96)

Alexander
(1829–1919)

James
Monroe
(1831–86)

Mary Jane
(1834–ca. 1860)

Thomas
(1839–1907)

Harvey
(d. age 3)

m.?

Lucy Jane
(b. 1845)

Squire
(b. 1847)

George
(b. 1849)

Eliza Ann
(b. 1855)

Lucy Ann
Calvin
(b. 1838)

Permilla
(b. 1839)

Charlotte
(b. 1840)

Child
(b. 1850?)

Child
(b. 1857?)

TABLE A.1   CERAMIC VESSELS FROM TWO HOUSEHOLDS FROM THE NORTHEAST

Functional Category	Form	Burdick Household Feature 7		Burdick Household Feature 13		Kittle Household Feature 19	
		N	%	N	%	N	%
Tableware	Plate 10"	0	0	0	0	0	0
	Plate 9"	0	0	3	15	5	22.7
	Plate 8"	0	0	1	5	0	0
	Plate 7"	0	0	0	0	0	0
	Plate 6"	1	14.3	3	15	0	0
	Plate 5"	1	14.3	0	0	0	0
	Plate 4"	0	0	2	10	4	18.2
	Plate (unidentified)	5	71.4	11	55	13	59
	Total Plates	7	100	20	100	22	99.9
	Platter	0	0	0	0	0	0
	Flatware	1	25	3	75	1	14.3
	Tureen	0	0	0	0	0	0
	Pitcher	0	0	0	0	0	0
	Bowl	1	25	0	0	2	28.6
	Holloware	2	50	1	25	4	57.1
	Subtotal	4	100	4	100	7	100
Tea wares	Cup	0	0	0	0	1	100
	Saucer	0	0	3	100	0	0
	Subtotal	*0*	*0*	*3*	*100*	*1*	*100*
Storage/Preparation	Crock	3	100	5	55.6	1	50
	Bowl	0	0	2	22.2	1	50
	Jug	0	0	0	0	0	0
	Bottle	0	0	0	0	0	0
	Other holloware	0	0	2	22.2	0	0
	Subtotal	*3*	*100*	*9*	*100*	*2*	*100*
Other/Unidentified							
	Flower pot	0		0		0	
	Chamber pot	0		0		0	

Functional Category	Form	Clark Household		S. McWorter Household		S. & G. McWorter Household	
		Feature 1		Feature 14		Block 3, Lot 7	
		N	%	N	%	N	%
Tableware	Plate 10"	0	0	5	35.7	1	10
	Plate 9"	0	0	5	35.7	2	20
	Plate 8"	0	0	0	0	0	0
	Plate 7"	1	11.1	0	0	0	0
	Plate 6"	1	11.1	0	0	0	0
	Plate 5"	0	0	0	0	0	0
	Plate 4"	0	0	0	0	0	0
	Plate (unidentified)	7	77.8	4	28.6	7	70
	Total Plates	9	100	14	100	10	100
	Platter	0	0	0	0	0	0
	Flatware	1	100	0	0	0	0
	Tureen	0	0	0	0	0	0
	Pitcher	0	0	0	0	0	0
	Bowl	0	0	6	60	1	50
	Holloware	0	0	4	40	1	50
	Subtotal	1	100	10	100	2	100
Tea wares	Cup	3	42.9	3	37.5	2	50
	Saucer	4	57.1	5	62.5	2	50
	Subtotal	7	100	8	100	4	100
Storage/Preparation	Crock	6	75	5	55.6	5	55.6
	Bowl	1	12.5	0	0	2	22.2
	Jug	0	0	1	11.1	1	11.1
	Bottle	0	0	0	0	0	0
	Other holloware	1	12.5	3	33.3	1	11.1
	Subtotal	8	100	9	100	9	100
Other/Unidentified	Flower pot	0		0		0	
	Chamber pot	0		0		0	

TABLE A.3   GLASS VESSELS FROM TWO HOUSEHOLDS FROM THE NORTHEAST

| | Burdick Household | | Burdick Household | | Kittle Household | |
| | Feature 7 | | Feature 13 | | Feature 19 | |
Vessel Type/Container	N	%	N	%	N	%
Liquor/whiskey	0	0	0	0	0	0
Beer bottles	0	0	0	0	0	0
Wine bottles	0	0	0	0	0	0
Nonalcoholic	0	0	0	0	0	0
Beverages	0	0	0	0	0	0
Other bottles	0	0	0	0	1	10
Food (bottle or jar)	0	0	0	0	1	10
Medicinal	1	50	0	0	7	70
Chemical	0	0	0	0	0	0
Toiletry	0	0	0	0	0	0
Tumbler	1	50	0	0	1	10
Personal	0	0	0	0	0	0
Other	0	0	1	100	0	0
Total	2	100	1	100	10	100

TABLE A.4   GLASS VESSELS FROM THREE HOUSEHOLDS FROM THE UPLAND
SOUTH AND ILLINOIS

Vessel Type/Container	Clark Household Feature 1		S. McWorter Household Feature 14		S. & G. McWorter Household Block 3, Lot 7	
	N	%	N	%	N	%
Liquor/whiskey	2	18.2	2	6.7	1	5.6
Beer bottles	0	0	1	3.3	0	0
Wine bottles	0	0	0	0	0	0
Nonalcoholic	0	0	0	0	0	0
Beverages	0	0	0	0	0	0
Other bottles	3	27.3	5	16.7	1	5.6
Food (bottle or jar)	0	0	6	20	4	22.2
Medicinal	5	45.5	11	36.7	8	44.4
Chemical	0	0	0	0	0	0
Toiletry	0	0	0	0	0	0
Tumbler	1	9.1	3	10	1	5.6
Personal	0	0	0	0	0	0
Other	0	0	2	6.7	3	16.7
Total	11	100	30	100	18	100.1

References

African American Registry. 2005. Black Settlement Offers Rich History. www
.aaregistry.com/african_american_history/347/Black_settlements_offer_rich
_history. Accessed June 17, 2007.

Allan, Theodore W. 1994. *The Invention of the White Race.* Vol. 1. London:
Verso.

Angle, Paul M. 1967. The Illinois Black Laws. *Chicago History* 8(3):65–75.

Armstrong, Douglas V., and LouAnn Wurst. 2003. Clay Faces in an Abolitionist Church: The Wesleyan Methodist Church in Syracuse, New York. *Historical Archaeology* 37(2):19–37.

Atlas Map of Pike County, Illinois. 1872. Compiled, drawn, and published
from personal examinations and surveys. Davenport, IA: Andreas Lyter.

Bailey, Megan. 2006. Minimum Vessel Analysis for Features 7, 13, and 19,
Block 4. In *New Philadelphia Archaeology: Race, Community and the Illi-
nois Frontier,* edited by Paul A. Shackel. www.heritage.umd.edu/chrsweb/
New%20Philadelphia/2006report/3C.pdf. Accessed, March 16, 2010.

Bauchat, Caitlin L., and Emily Helton. 2006. Minimum Vessel Analysis for
Feature 1, Block 9, Lot 5. In *New Philadelphia Archaeology: Race, Community and the Illinois Frontier,* edited by Paul A. Shackel. www.heritage.umd
.edu/chrsweb/New%20Philadelphia/2006report/3F.pdf. Accessed March
16, 2010.

Baxter, R. S., and R. Allen. 2002. Archaeological Investigations of Life within
the Woolen Mills Chinatown, San Jose. In *The Chinese in America: A History from Gold Mountain to the New Millennium,* edited by Susie Lan Cas-
sel. Walnut Creek, CA: AltaMira Press.

Blagojevich, Rod. 2005. Letter of support for the National Register nomination
for New Philadelphia. 4 April On file, National Register of Historic Places,
National Park Service, Washington, DC.

Blakey, Michael L. 1987. Skull Doctors: Intrinsic Social and Political Bias in the History of American Physical Anthropology. With Special Reference to the Work of Alec Hrdlicka. *Critique of Anthropology* 7(2):7–35.

Boas, Franz. 1911. *The Mind of the Primitive Man*. New York: Macmillan.

———. 1912. *Changes in Bodily Form of Descendants of Immigrants*. New York: Columbia University Press.

Borchert, James. 1982. *Alley Life in Washington: Family, Community, Religion, and Folklife in the City, 1850–1970*. Chicago: University of Illinois Press.

Bourdieu, Pierre. 1977. *Outline of a Theory of Practice*. New York: Cambridge University Press.

Bowser, Gillian. 2000. *National Park Service Community Study Report*. www .nps.gov/community/community_report.htm. Accessed March 1, 2006.

Breen, Timothy H. 1989. *Imagining the Past: East Hampton Histories*. Reading, MA: Addison-Wesley.

Breen, T. H., and Stephen Innes. 1980. *"Myne Owne Ground": Race and Freedom on Virginia's Eastern Shore, 1640–1676*. New York: Oxford University Press.

Browning, Tamara. 2005. Historic Revival of Town Planned. *State Journal Register* (Springfield, IL). June 27. www.sj-r.com/sections/news. Accessed June 27, 2005.

Bruner, Edward M. 1994. Abraham Lincoln as Authentic Reproduction: A Critique of Postmodernism. *American Anthropologist* 96(2):397–415.

Buck, Solon Justice. 1917. *Illinois in 1818*. Springfield: Illinois Centennial Commission.

Burdick, Larry. 1992. New Philadelphia: Where I Lived. Typescript, on file Pike County Historical Society, Pittsfield, IL.

Burk, Brett J. 1993. Pigs' Feet in a Politician's Privy. In *Interdisciplinary Investigations of Domestic Life in Government Block B: Perspectives on Harpers Ferry's Armory and Commercial District*, edited by Paul A. Shackel. Occasional Report No. 6. Washington, DC: National Park Service, National Capital Region.

Burlend, Rebecca. 1936. *A True Picture of Emigration*. Edited by Milo Milton Quaife. Chicago: Lakeside Press.

Cabak, Melanie A., and Mary Inkrot. 1997. *Old Farm: New Farm. An Archaeology of Rural Modernization in the Aiken Plateau, 1875–1950*. Savannah River Archaeological Research Papers 9, South Carolina Institute of Archaeology and Anthropology, University of South Carolina, Columbia.

Carter, Ron. 2004. Interview. July 8. www.heritage.umd.edu/CHRSWeb/New %20Philadelphia/oralhistories.htm#Carter. Accessed February 13, 2007.

Catts, Wade P., and Jay F. Custer. 1990. *Tenant Farmers, Stone Masons, and Black Laborers: Final Archaeological Investigations of the Thomas Williams Site, Glasgow, New Castle County, Delaware*. Department of Transportation Archeological Series 82, Newark, DE.

Cemetery Records of Pike County, Illinois. 1979. Vol. 4. Pittsfield, IL: Pike County Historical Society.

Cha-Jua Sundiata Keita. 2000. *America's First Black Town, Brooklyn, Illinois, 1830–1915*. Urbana: University of Illinois Press.

Chambers, Aaron. 2005. Explorers Look at Frontier Life in Biracial Town. *Rockford (IL) Register Star,* July 16. www.rrstar.com. Accessed July 10, 2007.

———. 2007a. Former Slave Founded Town That Vanished. *Rockford (IL) Register Star,* February 18, 1, 2D-4D.

———. 2007b. New Philadelphia: A Town Like No Other. *Rockford (IL) Register Star.* www.rrstar.com/flash/newphilly/index.html. Accessed June 20, 2007.

Chapman, Charles C. 1880. *History of Pike County, Illinois.* Chicago: C. C. Chapman.

Cheek, Charles D., and Amy Friedlander. 1990. Potter and Pig's Feet: Space, Ethnicity, and Neighborhood in Washington, D.C., 1880–1940. *Historical Archaeology* 24(1):34–60.

Colon, Maria Alejandra Nieves. 2006. Minimum Vessel Analysis for Block 3, Lot 7. In *New Philadelphia Archaeology: Race, Community and the Illinois Frontier,* edited by Paul A. Shackel. www.heritage.umd.edu/chrsweb/New%20Philadelphia/2006report/3B.pdf. Accessed March 16, 2010.

Conzen, Michael P., and Kay J. Carr, editors. 1988. *The Illinois & Michigan Canal National Heritage Corridor: A Guide to Its History and Sources.* De Kalb: Northern Illinois University Press.

Corgiat, Dean A. 2001. *Plant List of the New Philadelphia (McWorter) Cemetery.* Springfield: Illinois Department of Natural Resources.

Coulson, Tom. 1990. Free Frank Foundation Hopes to Restore His Gravesite and Town. *Pike County (IL) Express.* 6 October. Newspaper clipping in the possession of Carol McCartney, Pittsfield, IL.

Culin, Stewart. 1894. Mancala, the National Game of Africa. *Report of the National Museum,* 597–611.

Currier, Joel. 2004. Author Disputes Claims about Frontier Town. *St. Louis Post-Dispatch,* July 30.

Curry, Leonard P. 1981. *The Free Blacks in Urban America, 1800–1850: The Shadow of the Dream.* Chicago: University of Chicago Press.

Davis, James E. 1998. *Frontier Illinois.* Bloomington: Indiana University Press.

Dell, Floyd. 1933. *Homecoming: An Autobiography.* New York: Farrar & Rinehart.

Dillon, Merton L. 1961. *Elijah P. Lovejoy: Abolitionist Editor.* Urbana: University of Illinois Press.

Douglas, Mary, and Baron Isherwood. 1979. *The World of Goods: Towards an Anthropology of Consumerism.* New York: Norton.

Duke, Ruby. 2004. Interview. June 9. www.heritage.umd.edu/CHRSWeb/New%20Philadelphia/oralhistories.htm#Ruby_Duke. Accessed March 16, 2010.

Durbin, Richard J. 2005. Letter of support for the National Register nomination for New Philadelphia. March 28. On file, National Register of Historic Places, National Park Service, Washington, DC.

Epperson, Terrance. 1999. Constructing Difference: The Social and Spatial Order of the Chesapeake Plantation. In *"I, Too, Am America": Archaeological Studies of African–American Life,* edited by Theresa A. Singleton. Charlottesville: University Press of Virginia.

Eppler, Kimberly S., and Emily Helton. 2006 Minimum Vessel Analysis for Block 8, Lot 4. In *New Philadelphia Archaeology: Race, Community and the Illinois Frontier*, edited by Paul A. Shackel. www.heritage.umd.edu/chrsweb/New%20Philadelphia/2006report/3E.pdf. Accessed March 16, 2010.

Fennell, Christopher. 2007. *Crossroads, Cosmologies, and Ethnogenesis in the New World*. Gainesville: University Press of Florida.

————. 2008. New Philadelphia Archaeology. www.anthro.uiuc.edu/faculty/cfennell/NP/reports.html. Accessed January 1, 2009.

————. 2010. Damaging Detours: Routes, Racism, and New Philadelphia. In *An Archaeology of the Heartland: Race and Memory in New Philadelphia*, edited by Christopher Fennel, Terrance Martin, and Paul A. Shackel. Special edition of *Historical Archaeology* 44(1):138–54.

Ferguson, Leland. 1992. *Uncommon Ground: Archaeology and Early African America, 1600–1800*. Washington, DC: Smithsonian Institution Press.

Ferkenhoff, Eric. 2004. Artifacts Hint at Racial Harmony: Illinois Site Once Was Integrated Settlement. *Boston Globe*, July 24.

Fields, Walter. 2004. No Tears for Reagan. BlackAmericaToday.com. June 8. www.blackamericatoday.com/article.cfm?ArticleID=629. Accessed December 6, 2007.

Foner, Eric. 2002. *Who Owns History? Rethinking the Past in a Changing World*. New York: Hill and Wang.

Foote, Kenneth E. 1997. *Shadowed Ground: America's Landscapes of Violence and Tragedy*. Austin: University of Texas Press.

Foster, Mary Jo. 2004. Interview. June 9. www.heritage.umd.edu/CHRSWeb/New%20Philadelphia/oralhistories.htm#Mary_Jo_Foster. Accessed March 16, 2010.

Free Frank New Philadelphia Historic Preservation Foundation. 2006a. General Store. http://freefrank.org/general-store.shtml. Accessed March 16, 2010.

————. 2006b. Learn and Live History: Rebuilding New Philadelphia. http://freefrank.org/learn-live_rebuilding-new-p.shtml. Accessed March 16, 2010.

————. 2006c. Our Mission. http://freefrank.org/about-our-mission.shtml. Accessed March 16, 2010.

French, Scot. 2004. *The Rebellious Slave: Nat Turner in American Memory*. Boston: Houghton Mifflin.

Frost, Karolyn Smardz. 2007. *I've Got a Home in Glory Land: A Lost Tale of the Underground Railroad*. New York: Farrar, Straus and Giroux.

Galke, Laura J. 2000. "Free within Ourselves": African American Landscapes at Manassas Battlefield Park. In *Archaeological Perspectives on the Civil War*, edited by Clarence R. Geier and Stephen R. Potter. Gainesville: University Press of Florida.

Garden Plain, Kansas, 1884–1984. 1984. Centennial publication. Garden Plain, KS.

Gates, Henry Louis, Jr. 1994. *Colored People: A Memoir*. New York: Knopf.

General Assembly Records. 1837. A Bill entitled "An Act to change the name of Frank McWorter." Illinois State Archives Enrolled Laws No. 2031 HR No. 18, Box 48. On file, Illinois State Archives, Springfield.

Gertz, Elmer. 1963. The Black Laws of Illinois. *Journal of the Illinois State Historical Society* 56(3):454–73.

Glassberg, David. 1996. Public History and the Study of Memory. *Public Historian* 18(2):7–23.

———. 1998. Presenting History to the Public: The Study of Memory and the Uses of the Past. Understanding the Past. *CRM* 21(11):4–8.

Greenberg, Kenneth, editor. 2003. *Nat Turner: A Slave Rebellion in History and Memory.* New York: Oxford University Press.

Grim, Ronald E. 1977. The Absence of Towns in Seventeenth-Century Virginia: The Emergence of Service Centers in York County. Ph.D. dissertation, University of Maryland, College Park.

Grimshaw, William A. 1876. History of Pike County: A Centennial Address Delivered by Hon. William A. Grimshaw At Pittsfield, Pike County, Illinois July 4, 1876. Illinois State Historical Library, Springfield.

Gust, Sherri M. 1993. Animal Bones from Historic Chinese Sites: A Comparison of Sacramento, Woodland, Tucson, Ventura, and Lovelock. In *Hidden Heritage: Historical Archaeology of the Overseas Chinese,* edited by Priscilla Wegars. Amityville, NY: Baywood.

Gwaltney, Thomas. 2004. New Philadelphia Project Pedestrian Survey: Final Report and Catalog. Phase I Archeology at the Historic Town of New Philadelphia, Illinois. ArGIS Consultants, LLC, Bethesda, Maryland. www.heritage.umd.edu/CHRSWeb/New%20Philadelphia/NP_Final_Report_View.pdf. Accessed March 16, 2010.

Hakenbeck, Susanne. 2004. Reconsidering Ethnicity: An Introduction. *Archaeological Review from Cambridge* 19(2):1–6.

Hall, Jonathan M. 1996. *Ethnic Identity in Greek Antiquity.* New York: Cambridge University Press.

Handler, Richard, and Eric Gable. 1997. *The New History in an Old Museum: Creating the Past at Colonial Williamsburg.* Durham, NC: Duke University Press.

Handlin, Oscar, and Mary Handlin. 1950. Origins of the Southern Labor System. *William and Mary Quarterly,* no. 7: 199–222.

Hargrave, Michael L. 2006a. Geophysical Investigations at the New Philadelphia Site, Pike County, Illinois, 2004–2006. www.anthro.uiuc.edu/faculty/cfennell/NP/Geophys/geophysics.html. Accessed March 16, 2010.

———. 2006b. Geophysical Survey of the McWorter Cemetery, Pike County, Illinois. Submitted to Center for Heritage Resource Studies, University of Maryland, College Park.

Herskovits, Melville J. 1932. Wari in the New World. *Journal of the Royal Anthropological Institute of Great Britain and Ireland,* 62: 23–37.

Higbee, Judge Harry. 1907. Pike County: Its Past and Present: Held Thursday, August 29. Illinois State Historical Library, Springfield.

Hodder, Ian. 1979. Economic and Social Stress and Material Culture Patterning. *American Antiquity* 44(3): 446-54.

———. 1982. *Symbols in Action: Ethnoarchaeological Studies of Material Culture.* New York: Cambridge University Press.

Horton, James. 2000. Freedom Fighters: African Americans, Slavery, and the Coming Age of the Civil War. Paper presented at the National Park Service Symposium on Strengthening Interpretation of the Civil War Era. Washington, DC, May 9.

Hsieh, Athena, and Terrance Martin. 2006. Faunal Analysis for Features 7, 13, and 19. In *New Philadelphia Archaeology: Race, Community and the Illinois Frontier,* edited by Paul A. Shackel. www.heritage.umd.edu/chrsweb/New%20Philadelphia/2006report/3C.pdf. Accessed, March 16, 2010.

Huddleston, Connie M., and Carol J. Poplin. 2003. Comparing Pearlware Teacups to Shell Edge Plates: Examining Foodways Based on Ceramic Assemblages. Paper presented at the 36th Annual Conference on Historical and Underwater Archaeology, Providence, RI.

Huffstutter, P. J. 2006. Column One: A Land of Racial Harmony? *Los Angeles Times,* July 14. www.latimes.com/news/nationworld/nation/la-na-newphiladelphia14jul14,1,6149288.story?track=crosspromo&coll=la-headlines-nation&ctrack=1&cset=true. Accessed February 3, 2007.

Hughes, Grace. 2004 Interview. June 4. www.heritage.umd.edu/CHRSWeb/New%20Philadelphia/oralhistories.htm#Grace_and_Thomas_Hughes. Accessed March 16, 2010.

Husar, Deborah. 2004. Family Involvement Gives Life to History in New Philadelphia. *Quincy (IL) Herald Whig,* October 4. www.whig.com/314038114030564.php. Accessed February 15, 2007.

———. 2005a. Free Frank Leaves Descendents a Legacy of Freedom. *Quincy (IL) Herald Whig,* June 24. www.whig.com/289267086285617.php. Accessed February 15, 2007.

———. 2005b. Free Frank Descendant Plans to Film Documentary. *Quincy (IL) Herald Whig,* April 17. On line. www.whig.com/311717367623343.php. Accessed February 15, 2007.

———. 2005c. Portion of I-72 Named After "Free Frank" McWhorter. *Quincy (IL) Herald Whig,* February 25. www.whig.com/306857586910710.php. Accessed February 15, 2007.

———. 2005d. Research Answers, Raises Questions. *Quincy (IL) Herald Whig,* July 16. www.whig.com/299296212686383.php. Accessed February 15, 2007.

Hutton, Frankie. 1983. Economic Considerations in the American Colonization Society's Early Effort to Emigrate Free Blacks to Liberia, 1816–36. *Journal of Negro History* 68(4): 376–89.

Jacoby, Jason. 2006. Minimum Vessel Analysis for Feature 14, Block 8, Lot 2. In *New Philadelphia Archaeology: Race, Community and the Illinois Frontier,* edited by Paul A. Shackel. www.heritage.umd.edu/chrsweb/New%20Philadelphia/2006report/3E.pdf. Accessed March 16, 2010.

Jacoby, Mary. 2004. Madame Cheney's Cultural Revolution: How the Vice President's Powerful Wife Makes Sure That Historians and Other Scholars Follow the Right Path. *Salon.com,* August 26. http://dir.salon.com/story/news/feature/2004/08/26/lynne_cheney/index.html. Accessed June 29, 2007.

Johannsen, Robert W. 1973. *Stephen A. Douglas.* New York: Oxford University Press.

Johnson, Harry. 2005. Interview. June. www.heritage.umd.edu/CHRSWeb/New%20Philadelphia/oralhistories.htm#Harry_Johnson. Accessed March 16, 2010.

Jones, Sian. 1997. *The Archaeology of Ethnicity: Constructing Identities in the Past and Present.* New York: Routledge.

Jordan, Elizabeth. 2005. "Unrelenting Toil": Expanding Archeological Interpretations of the Female Slave Experience. *Slavery and Abolition* 26(2): 217–32.

Jordan, Winthrop. 1978. Unthinking Decision: Enslavement of Negroes in America to 1700. In *Interpreting Colonial America,* edited by Kirby Martin. New York: Harper & Row.

Kauffman, Ned. 2004. Cultural Heritage Needs Assessment: Phase I. National Park Service, Department of the Interior, Washington, DC.

Kelso, William. 1986. Mulberry Row: Slave Life at Thomas Jefferson's Monticello. *Archaeology* 39(5):28–35.

Kern, Susan. 2005. The Material World of Jefferson at Shadwell. *William and Mary Quarterly* 62(2):213–42.

Ketchum, William. 1975. *A Treasury of American Bottles.* Danbury, CT: Rutledge Books.

King, Charlotte. 2006. Census Data for New Philadelphia. www.heritage.umd.edu. Accessed March 16, 2010.

———. 2007. Separated by Death and Color: The African American Cemetery of New Philadelphia, Illinois. Paper presented at the Society for Historical Archeology meetings, Williamsburg, VA.

———. 2008. National Historic Landmark Nomination, New Philadelphia Town Site, 11PK455. U.S. Department of the Interior, National Park Service, Washington, DC.

———. 2010. Separated by Death and Color. In An Archaeology of the Heartland: Race and Memory in New Philadelphia, edited by Christopher Fennel, Terrance Martin, and Paul A. Shackel. Special issue, *Historical Archaeology* 44(1):125–37.

Klingelhofer, Eric. 1985. Afro-American Culture at Garrison Plantation: Initial Project Report. On file, Maryland Historical Trust, Crownsville.

Kulikoff, Allan. 1986. *Tobacco and Slaves: The Development of Southern Culture in the Chesapeake, 1680–1800.* Chapel Hill: University of North Carolina Press.

LaRoche, Cheryl J., and Michael L. Blakey. 1997. Seizing Intellectual Power: The Dialogue at the New York African Burial Ground. *Historical Archaeology* 31(3):84–106.

LaRoche, Cheryl J., and Gary S. McGowan. 2001. "Material Culture": Conservation and Analysis of Textiles Recovered from Five Points. In Becoming New York: The Five Points Neighborhood, edited by Rebecca Yamin. Special issue, *Historical Archaeology* 35(3):65–75.

Laws of Illinois. 1831. Laws of Illinois passed at the Seventh General Assembly, at their Session Held at Vandalia, Commencing on the First Monday in December 1830. Vandalia, IL: Robert Blackwell, Public Printer.

Laws of the State of Illinois. 1837. Laws of the State of Illinois passed by the Tenth General Assembly, at their session, Commencing December 5, 1836, and ending March 6, 1837. Vandalia, IL: William Walters, Public Printer.

Laws of the State of Illinois. 1840. Laws of the State of Illinois, Passed by the Eleventh General Assembly at Their Special Session, began and held at Springfield, on the ninth of December, one thousand eight hundred and thirty nine. Springfield, IL: William Walters, Public Printer.

Layne, Valmont. 2008. The District Six Museum: An Ordinary People's Place. *Public Historian* 30(1):53–62.

Leone, Mark P. 1981. Archaeology's Relationship to the Present and the Past. In *Modern Material Culture: The Archaeology of Us,* edited by Richard A. Gould and Michael B. Schiffer. New York: Academic Press.

Leone, Mark P., Cheryl Janifer LaRoche, and Jennifer Babiarz. 2005. The Archaeology of Black Americans in Recent Times. *Annual Review of Anthropology* 34(1): 575–98.

Levine, Mary Ann, Kelly M. Britt, and James A. Delle. 2005. Heritage Tourism and Community Outreach: Public Archaeology at the Thaddeus Stevens and Lydia Hamilton Smith Site in Lancaster, Pennsylvania, USA. *International Journal of Heritage Studies* 11(5):399–414.

Likes, Pat. 2004. Interview. June 7. www.heritage.umd.edu/CHRSWeb/New %20Philadelphia/oralhistories.htm#Pat_Likes. Accessed March 16, 2010.

Little, Barbara J. 1994. People with History: An Update on Historical Archaeology in the United States. *Journal of Archaeological Method and Theory* 1(1):5–40.

———. 1997. Expressing Ideology without a Voice, or Obfuscation and Enlightenment. *International Journal of Historical Archaeology* 1(3):225–41.

———. 1999. Nominating Archaeological Sites to the National Register of Historic Places: What's the Point? *SAA Bulletin* 17(4):19.

———. 2007. *Historical Archaeology: Why the Past Matters.* Walnut Creek, CA: Left Coast Press.

Little, Barbara J., and Nancy Kassner. 2001. Archaeology in the Alleys of Washington, DC. In *The Archaeology of Urban Landscapes: Explorations in Slumland,* edited by Alan Mayne and Tim Murry. New York: Cambridge University Press.

Little, M. Ruth. 1998. *Sticks and Stones.* Chapel Hill: University of North Carolina Press.

Livingston, Hillary, and Terrance Martin. 2006. Faunal Analysis of Feature 14, Block, Lot 2. In *New Philadelphia Archaeology: Race, Community and the Illinois Frontier,* edited by Paul A. Shackel. www.heritage.umd.edu/chrsweb/ New%20Philadelphia/2006report/3E.pdf. Accessed March 16, 2010.

Loewen, James. 2005. *Sundowner Towns: A Hidden Dimension of American Racism.* New York: New Press.

Loren, Diana DiPaolo. 2001. Social Skins: Orthodoxies and Practices of Dressing in Early Colonial Lower Mississippi Valley. *Journal of Social Archaeology* 1(2):172–89.

Lowenthal, David. 1985. *The Past Is a Foreign Country.* Cambridge, England: Cambridge University Press.

Lucas, Michael T. 1994. A la Russe, à la Pell-Mell, or à la Practical: Ideology and Compromise at the Late Nineteenth-Century Dinner Table. In An Archaeology of Harpers Ferry's Commercial and Residential District, edited by Paul A. Shackel and Susan E. Winter. Special issue, *Historical Archaeology* 28(4):80–93.

Luschan, F. von. 1919. Zusammenhänge und Konvergenz (Connections and Convergence). *Mitteilungen der Anthropologischen Gesellschaft in Wien* (Messages from the Anthropological Community of Vienna) 48:51–58.

Mackenzie, Dana. 2005. Ahead of Its Time? Founded by a Freed Slave, an Illinois Town Was a Rare Example of Biracial Cooperation before the Civil War. *Smithsonian Magazine*. January. www.smithsonianmag.com/issues/2005/january/digs.php?page=2. Accessed February 15, 2007.

Main, Josiah. 1915. *The Agriculture of Pike County, Illinois*. Ithaca, NY: Josiah Main.

Maissie, Capt. William D. 1906. Past and Present of Pike County, Illinois: Together with Biographical Sketches of Many of the Prominent and Leading Citizens and Illustrious Dead. Chicago: S. J. Clarke.

Mansberger, Floyd. 2003. *Archaeological Investigations at the Dyer-Rathbun Farmstead, Will County, Illinois*. Prepared by Fever River Research, Springfield, IL, for Arris Architects + Planners, PC, Plainfield, IL, and Exel, Inc., Westerville, OH.

Mansberger, Floyd, and Christopher Stratton. 1997. *An Archaeological Perspective of Early Town Formation and Abandonment in Marshall County, Illinois: Phase II Archaeological Investigations at the Webster Townsite*. Prepared by Fever River Research, Springfield, IL, for Agrium, U.S. Incorporated and Goodwin and Broms, Incorporated, Springfield, IL.

Maranville, Angela, Terrance Martin, and Shamia Sandels. 2006. New Philadelphia Excavation Unit Summary Form: Block 3, Lot 1. In *New Philadelphia Archaeology: Race, Community and the Illinois Frontier*, edited by Paul A. Shackel. www.heritage.umd.edu/CHRSWeb/New%20Philadelphia/2006report/units/Block_3_Lot_1.pdf. Accessed March 16, 2010.

Martin, Claire, and Terrance Martin. 2010. Agriculture and Regionalism at New Philadelphia. In An Archaeology of the Heartland: Race and Memory in New Philadelphia, edited by Christopher Fennel, Terrance Martin, and Paul A. Shackel. Special issue, *Historical Archaeology* 44(1):72–84.

Martin, Erika K., Mia T. Parsons, and Paul A. Shackel. 1997. Commemorating a Rural African-American Family at a National Battlefield Park. *International Journal of Historical Archaeology* 1(2): 155–75.

Martin, Terrance J., and Erin Brand. 2002. Animal Remains from the Lorain Site (23SL1025), a Mid-19th Century Habitation Site in the Missouri Bottom, St. Louis County, Missouri. Illinois State Museum Landscape History Program, Technical Report No. 2002-000-12, Illinois State Museum, Springfield.

Martin, Terrance, and Clair Fuller Martin. 2010. Courtly, Careful, Thrifty: Subsistence and Regional Origin at New Philadelphia. In An Archaeology of the Heartland: Race and Memory in New Philadelphia, edited by Christopher Fennel, Terrance Martin, and Paul A. Shackel. Special issue, *Historical Archaeology* 44(1):85–101.

Matteson, Grace. 1964. *"Free Frank" McWorter and the "Ghost Town" of New Philadelphia, Pike County, Illinois*. Pike County Historical Society, Pittsfield, IL.

Mausur, Louis P. 2001. *1831: Year of the Eclipse*. New York: Hill and Wang.

Mayer, Henry. 1998. *All on Fire: William Lloyd Garrison and the Abolition of Slavery*. New York: St. Martin's Press.

Mazrim, Robert. 2002. *Now Quite Out of Society: Archaeology and Frontier Illinois. Essays and Excavation Reports*. Illinois Transportation Archaeological Research Program, Transportation Archaeological Bulletins No. 1. Illinois Department of Transportation, Department of Anthropology, University of Illinois at Urbana–Champaign.

——. 2007. *The Sangamo Frontier: History and Archaeology in the Shadow of Lincoln*. Chicago: University of Chicago Press.

McCorvie, M. R. 1987. *The Davis, Baldridge, and Huggins Sites: Three Nineteenth-Century Upland South Farmsteads in Perry County, Illinois*. Carbondale, IL: American Resources Group.

McGuire, Randall H. 1982. The Study of Ethnicity in Historical Archaeology. *Journal of Anthropological Archaeology* 1(2):159–78.

McWorter, Squire. 1915. Appraisement Bill, Pike County, Estate of Squire McWorter. April 14. Record 22, page 135. On file, Pike County Court House, Pike County, IL.

Miller, Daniel. 1987. *Material Culture as Mass Consumption*. New York: Basil Blackwell.

Miller, Daniel, and Christopher Tilley. 1984. Ideology, Power, and Prehistory: An Introduction. In *Ideology and Power in Prehistory*, edited by Daniel Miller and Christopher Tilley. New York: Cambridge University Press.

Miller, Floyd J. 1975. *The Search for Black Nationality: Black Emigration and Colonization, 1787–1863*. Urbana: University of Illinois Press.

Minutes of the Barry Apple Festival Visit. 2004. Transcribed by Carol McCartney. On file, New Philadelphia Association, Pittsfield, IL.

Morgan, Edmund. 1975. *American Slavery: American Freedom*. New York: Norton.

Morgan, Lewis H. 1877. *Ancient Society*. London: Macmillan.

Morrow, Kara Ann. 2002. Bakongo Afterlife and Cosmological Direction: Translation of African Culture into North Florida Cemeteries. *Athanor XX*. Florida State University.

Moss, Shirley McWorter, Allen Kirkpatrick, Sandra McWorter, Gerald McWorter, Patricia McWorter, and Lonie Wilson. 2005. McWorter Family Reunion Press Release, June 24. In possession of the author.

Moyer, Teresa S., and Paul A. Shackel. 2008. *The Making of Harpers Ferry National Historical Park: A Devil, Two Rivers, and a Dream*. Lanham, MD: AltaMira Press.

Mukhopadhyay, Carol C., and Yolanda T. Moses. 1997. Reestablishing "Race" in Anthropological Discourse. *American Anthropologist* 99(3):517–33.

Mullins, Paul R. 1999. *Race and Affluence: An Archaeology of African America and Consumer Culture*. New York: Kluwer Academic/Plenum.

———. 2004. African-American Heritage in a Multicultural Community: An Archaeology of Race, Culture, and Consumption. In *Places in Mind: Public Archaeology as Applied Anthropology*, edited by Paul A. Shackel and Erve J. Chambers. New York: Routledge.

Munsey, Cecil. 1970. *Illustrated Guide to Collecting Bottles*. New York: Hawthorn Books.

Nash, Gary B., Charlotte Crabtree, and Ross E. Dunn. 1997. *History on Trial: Culture Wars and the Teaching of the Past*. New York: Knopf.

National Park Service, U.S. Department of the Interior. 2000. Civic Engagement. www.nps.gov/civic. Accessed April 13, 2005.

———. 2005a. African-American Households from Manassas National Battlefield Park. www.nps.gov.rap/exhibit/mana/text/rhouse.oo.htm. Accessed March 16, 2010.

———. 2005b. The Robinson House. www.cr.nps.gov/aad/robinson/id3.htm. Accessed March 16, 2010.

———. 2006. *Management Policies*. www.nps.gov/policy/MP2006.pdf. Accessed March 16, 2010.

New Philadelphia Association. 2006. New Philadelphia: A Pioneer Town. www.newphiladelphiail.org/index.htm. Accessed March 16, 2010.

Obama, Barack. 2005, Letter of support for the National Register nomination for New Philadelphia. June 1. On file, National Register of Historic Places, National Park Service, Washington, DC.

Old Philadelphia Cemetery Visited by Walkers. 2004. *The Paper (Pike County, IL)*, October 12, 1, 16.

Omi, Michael, and Howard Winant. 1983. By the River of Babylon: Race in the United States. *Socialist Review* 13:31–65.

———. 1994. *Racial Formation in the United States from the 1960s to the 1990s*. New York: Routledge.

Orser, Charles E., Jr. 1998. The Archaeology of the African Diaspora. *Annual Review of Anthropology* 27:63–82.

———. 2004. *Race and Practice in Archaeological Interpretation*. Philadelphia: University of Pennsylvania Press.

———. 2007. *The Archaeology of Race and Racialization in Historic America*. Gainesville: University Press of Florida.

Palus, Matthew, and Paul A. Shackel. 2006. *"They Worked Regular": Craft, Labor, Family and the Archaeology of an Industrial Community*. Knoxville: University of Tennessee Press.

Patten, Drake. 1992. Mankala and Minkisi: Possible Evidence of African American Folk Beliefs and Practices. *African-American Archaeology* 6:5–7.

Pease, William, and Jane Pease. 1962. Organized Negro Communities: A North American Experiment. *Journal of Negro History* 47(1):19–34.

———. 1963. *Black Utopia: Negro Communal Experiments in America*. Madison: Wisconsin State Historical Society.

Phillippe, Joseph. 1990. *The Drake Site: Subsistence and Status at a Rural Illinois Farmstead*. Midwestern Archaeological Research Center, Illinois State University, Normal.

Pike County Deed Book. 1858. On file, Pike County Court House, Pittsfield, IL.

Pike County Illinois Schools, 1823–1995: History and Pictures. 1996. Pike County Historical Society, Pittsfield, IL.

Pike County Railroad Company. 1853. Record of the Pike County Rail Road Company, SC2287. Abraham Lincoln Presidential Library, Springfield, IL.

Pinkowski, Jennifer. 2005. Integrating the Frontier: A Town Founded by a Former Slave Resurfaces in Illinois. *Archaeology*, September/October, 42–47.

Portrait and Biographical Album of Sedgwick County, Kansas, Containing Full Page Portraits and Biographical Sketches of Prominent and Representative Citizens of the County, Together with Portraits and Biographies of all the Governors of Kansas, and of the Presidents of the United States. 1888. Chicago: Chapman Brothers.

Praetzellis, Mary, and Adrian Praetzellis. 1990. *Junk! Archaeology of the Pioneer Junk Store, 1877–1908*. Papers in Northern California Anthropology 4. Anthropological Studies Center, Sonoma State University, Rohnert Park, CA.

Price, Cynthia R. 1985. Patterns of Cultural Behavior and Intra-site Distributions of Faunal Remains at the Widow Harris Site. *Historical Archaeology* 19(2):40–56.

Purple, N. H. 1856. *A Compilation of the Statutes of the State of Illinois of a General Nature in Force January 1, 1856, Collated with Reference to Decisions of the Supreme Court of said State, and to Prior Laws Relating to the Same Subject Matter*. Chicago: Keen & Lee.

Purser, Margaret. 1992. Consumption as Communication in Nineteenth Century Paradise Valley, Nevada. In Meanings and Uses of Material Culture, edited by Barbara J. Little and Paul A. Shackel. Special issue, *Historical Archaeology* 26(3):105–16.

Rabinow, Paul. 1992. For Hire: Resolutely Late Modern. In *Recapturing Anthropology*, edited by Richard Fox. Santa Fe, NM: School of American Research Press.

Race: The Power of Illusion: What Is This Thing Called Race. 2003. Independent Television Service Community Connections Project, San Francisco.

Ranney, Edward, and Emily Harris. 1998. *Prairie Passage: The Illinois and Michigan Canal Corridor*. Urbana: University of Illinois Press.

Rapoport, Amos. 1990. *The Meaning of the Built Environment: A Nonverbal Communication Approach*. Tucson: University of Arizona Press.

Reitz, E. J., and E. S. Wing. 1999. *Zooarchaeology*. New York: Cambridge University Press.

The Revised Code of Laws, of Illinois, Containing Those of a General and Permanent Nature Passed by the Sixth General Assembly, At Their Session held at Vandalia, Commencing on the First Monday Of December 1822; And Those Enacted Previous Thereto, and Ordered by the said General Assembly to Be Republished. 1829. Cincinnati, OH: Alexander F. Grant.

The Revised Laws of Illinois, Containing all Laws of a general and public nature passed by the eighth General Assembly, at their session held at Vandalia, commencing on the third day of December 1832, and ending the second day of March, 1833, together with all Laws required to be re-published by the said General Assembly. 1833. Vandalia, IL: Greiner & Sherman.

Roberts, Margaret. 2005. Interview. July 18. www.heritage.umd.edu/CHRSWeb/ New%20Philadelphia/oralhistories.htm#Margaret_Roberts. Accessed March 16, 2010.

Rodman, M. 1992. Empowering Place: Multilocality and Multivocality. *American Anthropologist* 94:640–56.

Roediger, David R. 1999. *The Wages of Whiteness: Race and the Making of the American Working Class*. London: Verso.

Roseberry, William. 1992. Multiculturalism and the Challenge of Anthropology. *Social Research* 59(4):841–58.

Samford, Patricia. 1994. Searching for West African Cultural Meanings in the Archaeological Record. *African–American Archaeology: Newsletter of the African–American Archaeology Network*, winter (12). www.diaspora.uiuc .edu/A-AAnewsletter/Winter1994.html. Accessed June 6, 2007.

———. 1997. Response to Market: Dating English Underglaze Transfer-Printed Wares. *Historical Archaeology* 31(2):1–30.

Schlereth, Thomas J., editor. 1989. *Material Culture Studies in America*. Nashville, TN: Association for State and Local History.

Schorger, A. W. 1973. *The Passenger Pigeon: Its Natural History and Extinction*. Norman: University of Oklahoma Press.

Schulz, Peter D., and Sherri M. Gust. 1983. Faunal Remains and Social Status in 19th Century Sacramento. *Historical Archaeology* 17(1):44–53.

The Secretary of the Interior's Standards for the Treatment of Historic Properties: With Guidelines for Preserving, Rehabilitating, Restoring and Reconstructing Historic Buildings. n.d. NPS History & Culture, Technical Preservation Services. www.nps.gov/history/hps/tps/standguide/. Accessed March 16, 2010.

Seligman, Samuel. 2007. Hadley Township and New Philadelphia, Illinois: Patterns in Cultural Migration on the Nineteenth Century American Frontier. In partial fulfillment, B.A. Honors in Anthropology, University of Maryland, College Park.

Shackel, Paul A. 1993. *Personal Discipline and Material Culture: An Archaeology of Annapolis, Maryland, 1695–1870*. Knoxville: University of Tennessee Press.

———. 1994. Memorializing Landscapes and the Civil War in Harpers Ferry. In *Look to The Earth: an Archaeology of the Civil War*, edited by Clarence Geier and Susan Winter. Knoxville: University of Tennessee Press.

———. 2001. Public Memory and the Search for Power in American Historical Archaeology. *American Anthropologist* 102(3):655–70.

———. 2003. *Memory in Black and White: Race, Commemoration, and the Post–Bellum Landscape*. Walnut Creek, CA: AltaMira Press.

———. 2005. Local Identity, National Memory and Heritage Tourism: Creating a Sense of Place with Archaeology. *SAA Archaeological Record* 5(3): 33–35.

———. 2010. Social Identity and Collective Action in a Multi-racial Community. In An Archaeology of the Heartland: Race and Memory in New Philadelphia, edited by Christopher Fennel, Terrance Martin, and Paul A. Shackel. Special issue, *Historical Archaeology* 44(1):58–71.

Simeone, James. 2000. *Democracy and Slavery in Frontier Illinois: The Bottomland Republic*. De Kalb: Northern Illinois University Press.

Simpson, Helen McWorter. 1981. *Makers of History*. Evansville, IN: Laddie B. Warren.

Singleton, Theresa. 1995. The Archaeology of Slavery in North America. *Annual Review of Anthropology* 24:119–40.

Smedley, Audrey. 1993. *Race in North America: Origin and Evolution of Worldview*. Boulder, CO: Westview Press.

————. 1998. "Race" and the Construction of Human Identity. *American Anthropologist* 100(3):690–702.

Smith, Charles R., and Shawn K. Bonath. 1982. A Report on Phase I and Phase II Historic Archaeological Investigations on Three Segments of the F.A.P. 408 Highway Corridor, Adams, Pike, and Scott Counties, Illinois (1979–1981). Midwestern Archeological Center, Illinois State University, Normal.

Smith, Erin Susan. 2006. Archaeobotanical Analysis for Features 7, 13, 14, 18, and 19. In *New Philadelphia Archaeology: Race, Community and the Illinois Frontier*, edited by Paul A. Shackel. www.heritage.umd.edu/chrsweb/New%20Philadelphia/2006report/3H.pdf. Accessed, March 16, 2010.

Spivik, Todd. 2004. Revisionist History: "Free Frank" Descendant Takes Aim at New Philadelphia Excavation Project. *Illinois Times* July 15–21, 7,8.

Stine, Linda. 1990. Social Inequality and Turn-of-the-Century Farmsteads: Issues of Class, Status, Ethnicity, and Race. In Historical Archaeology on Southern Plantations and Farms, edited by Charles E. Orser Jr. Special issue, *Historical Archaeology* 24(4):37–49.

Taffee, Edward J., and Howard L. Gauthier Jr. 1973. *Geography of Transportation*. Englewood Cliffs, NJ: Prentice-Hall.

Tanner, Henry. 1881. *The Martyrdom of Lovejoy: An Account of the Life, Trials, and Perils of Rev. Elijah P. Lovejoy Who was Killed by a Pro–Slavery Mob at Alton, Illinois the Night of November 7, 1838*. Chicago: Fergus.

Taylor, Richard S., and Mark Johnson. 2004a. A Fragile Illusion: The Reconstruction of Lincoln's New Salem. *Journal of Illinois History* 7(4):254–80.

————. 2004b. The Spirit of the Place: Origins of the Movement to Reconstruct Lincoln's New Salem. *Journal of Illinois History* 7(3):174–200.

Temperley, Howard. 2000. African-American Aspirations and the Settlement of Liberia. *Slavery & Abolition* 21(2):67–92

Thomas, David Hurst. 2000. *Skull Wars: Kennewick Man, Archaeology, and the Battle for Native American Identity*. New York: Basic Books.

Thompson, Jess M. 1967. *Pike County History: As Printed in Installments in the Pike County Republican, Pittsfield, Illinois, 1935–1939*. Racine, WI: Preston Miller.

Tillson, Christian Holmes. 1995. *A Woman's Story of Pioneer Illinois*. Edited by Milo Milton Quaife. Carbondale: Southern Illinois University Press.

Torvinen, Andrea, and Terrance Martin. 2006. Faunal Analysis of Feature 1, Block 9, Lot 5. In *New Philadelphia Archaeology: Race, Community and the Illinois Frontier*, edited by Paul A. Shackel. www.heritage.umd.edu/chrsweb/New%20Philadelphia/2006report/3F.pdf. Accessed March 16, 2010.

Trigger, Bruce G. 2006. *A History of Archaeological Thought*. New York: Cambridge University Press.

Triplett, Margaret. 1929. Jim Washington, a Slave at Age of Ten, Now Enjoys Life on Own Farm at Age 83; Remembers Civil War and Considers it the Greatest Event in Human History; Was well treated in Missouri Plantation. *Barry (IL) Adage*. Photocopy in the possession of Carol McCartney, New Philadelphia Association.

Tylor, Edward B. 1874. *Primitive Culture*. New York: Henry Holt.

Upton, Dell. 1988. White and Black Landscapes in Eighteenth-Century Virginia. In *Material Life in America, 1600–1800*, edited by Robert Blair St. George. Boston: Northeastern University Press.

———. 1996. Ethnicity, Authenticity, and Invented Traditions. *Historical Archaeology* 30(2):1–7.

Vermeersch, Peter. 2004. Archaeology and Identity Politics: A Cross-Disciplinary Perspective. *Archaeological Dialogues* 11(1):22–27.

Visweswaran, Kamala. 1998. Race and the Culture of Anthropology. *American Anthropologist* 100(1):70–83.

Vlach, John M. 1990. *Afro-American Tradition in Decorative Arts*. Athens: University of Georgia Press.

———. 1993. *Back of the Big House: The Architecture of Plantation Slavery*. Chapel Hill: University of North Carolina Press.

Voss, Barbara L. 2005. The Archaeology of Overseas Chinese Communities. *World Archaeology* 37(3):424–39.

Waggoner, Walter S. 1999. *Copperheads, Black Republicans and Bushwackers: Pike County, Illinois and the Civil War*. Independence, MO: Blue and Grey Book Shoppe.

Walker, Juliet E. K. 1983a. *Free Frank: A Black Pioneer on the Antebellum Frontier*. Lexington: University Press of Kentucky.

———. 1983b. Legal Processes and Judicial Challenges: Black Land Ownership in Western Illinois. *Western Illinois Regional Studies* 6(2):23–48.

———. 1983c. Pioneer Slave Entrepreneurship: Patterns, Processes, and Perspectives. The Case of the Slave Free Frank on the Kentucky Pennyroyal, 1795–1819. *Journal of Negro History* 68(3):289–308.

———. 1985. Entrepreneurial Ventures in the Origin of Nineteenth-Century Agricultural Towns: Pike County, 1823–1880. *Illinois Historical Journal* 78(1):45–64.

Wall, Diana Di Zerga. 1991. Sacred Dinners and Secular Teas: Constructing Domesticity in Mid-19th–Century New York. *Historical Archaeology* 25(4):69–80.

Warren, Robert E., and John A. Walthall. 1998. Illini Indians and the Illinois Country 1673–1832. *Living Museum* 60(11):4–8.

White, Vibert. 2001. *Inside the Nation of Islam: A Historical and Personal Testimony by a Black Muslim*. Gainesville: University Press of Florida.

Whittaker, William E. 1999. Production of Animal Commodities at Plum Grove, Iowa City. *Historical Archaeology* 33(4):44–57.

Wilke, Laurie. 2000. *Creating Freedom: Material Culture and African American Identity at Oakley Plantation, Louisiana, 1840–1950*. Baton Rouge: Louisiana State University Press.

Williams, Brackette. 1992. Of Straightening Combs, Sodium Hydroxide, and Potassium Hydroxide in Archaeological and Cultural-Anthropological Analyses of Ethnogenesis. *American Antiquity* 57(4):608–12.

Williams, Petra. 1978. *Staffordshire—Romantic Transfer Patterns: Cups Plates and Early Victorian China*. Vol. 1. Jeffersontown, KY: Fountain House East.

Woodson, Carter G. 1930. The Negro Washerwoman, a Vanishing Figure. *Journal of Negro History* 15(3):269–77.

Zinn, Howard. 2003. *A People's History of the United States: 1492–Present*. New York: HarperCollins.

Index

TEXT
10/13 Sabon Open Type

DISPLAY
Sabon Open Type

COMPOSITOR
Westchester Book Group

PRINTER AND BINDER
Maple-Vail Book Manufacturing Group